Studies in Neuroscience, Psychology and Behavioral Economics

This interdisciplinary book series addresses research findings and methods in the intersection of the fields of neuroscience, psychology and behavioral economics. At the core of the series is the biological basis of human decision making, including aspects of an economic, cognitive, affective and motivational nature. Contributions from fundamental and applied sciences are equally represented and cover a broad range of scientific work, reaching from mathematical modeling to scholarly introductions into new research disciplines and related methodologies and technologies (e.g. genetics, psychophysiology, brain imaging, computational neuroscience, animal modeling). The book series presents empirical and methodological scientific innovations bridging the gap from brain to behavior. It includes research works in neuroeconomics and neuro-information systems (e.g. human-machine interaction) as well as social, cognitive and affective neuroscience, which aim at enhancing the understanding of human decision making.

Christian Montag · Raian Ali
Editors

The Impact of Artificial Intelligence on Societies

Understanding Attitude Formation Towards AI

Springer

Editors
Christian Montag
Department of Molecular Psychology
Institute of Psychology and Education
Ulm University
Ulm, Germany

Raian Ali
College of Science and Engineering
Hamad Bin Khalifa University
Doha, Qatar

ISSN 2196-6605 ISSN 2196-6613 (electronic)
Studies in Neuroscience, Psychology and Behavioral Economics
ISBN 978-3-031-70354-6 ISBN 978-3-031-70355-3 (eBook)
https://doi.org/10.1007/978-3-031-70355-3

This Springer imprint is published by the registered company Springer Nature Switzerland AG
The registered company address is: Gewerbestrasse 11, 6330 Cham, Switzerland

Preface

The present book is an early attempt to grasp how artificial intelligence (AI) will impact in diverse ways on our societies. To find a nuanced and balanced view regarding the coming AI wave will for sure not be easy, as many variables around AI must be considered. As discussed in this book, aside from the modality of AI, for sure psychological factors need to be considered, but also political regulation, cultural specifics and of course also the area, where AI will be used in the future. We hope that the present book with contributions by scholars from around the world helps to structure the complexities arising from the AI revolution.

Certainly, we are just at the beginning of forming an understanding of what it will be like to live in societies where AI will be everywhere. As Andrew Ng and Kai Fu-Lee mentioned: "AI is the new electricity".[1] This means that AI represents an omni-use-technology to be found in many products and services, we will use daily. Our understanding is not passive; it goes beyond interpreting the current state of AI. It is meant to support emerging efforts in formulating AI policies and regulations, as well as in methods for designing and testing AI, particularly concerning human factors.

We believe that it is time to face what's coming. Instead of responding with fear or over-enthusiasm to AI, we believe it to be much better to respond with curiosity towards the AI revolution, and at the same time, societies must prepare for the rapid progress likely being made and the challenges coming for all of us, including what the coming AI wave will mean for economies and the job market around the world. In this realm, we find the response of Singapore's government very thoughtful. They aim to uplift their people by providing their citizens being 40 years or older to visit university again to prepare for the uncertainties going along with the AI revolution.[2] What remains largely unexplored is the content of AI literacy and the methods for

[1] https://www.gsb.stanford.edu/insights/andrew-ng-why-ai-new-electricity.
https://mbzuai.ac.ae/news/mbzuai-talks-ai-is-the-new-electricity-dr-kai-fu-lee-explores-the-evolution-of-artificial-intelligence/.

[2] https://www.hindustantimes.com/education/ai-singapore-budget-subsidy-for-diploma-40-years-old-and-above-going-back-to-university-artificial-intelligence-101711353713925.html.

delivering that education. For example, should psychological literacy and ethical decision-making be prioritized, and to what extent do policymakers and the general public need them? What should be the content of this literacy, and is it suitable to deliver it via traditional lecturing methods, or are more innovative approaches required?

In the end, we are convinced that this is what's needed: lifelong learning to profit as best as possible from the new possibilities arising from AI technology. The education sector will be crucial in this regard.

Ulm, Germany Christian Montag
Doha, Qatar Raian Ali

Contents

Chapter 1
Starting the Journey to Understand Attitudes Towards Artificial Intelligence in Global Societies

Christian Montag and Raian Ali

Abstract The introductory chapter to this book on AI attitudes explains why the study of AI attitudes is of high international relevance. In this context, the prominent Technology Acceptance Model and the Theory of Planned Behavior will be shortly revisited in the context of AI underlining that research on attitudes towards AI represents a cornerstone variable to understand if people will ultimately master the coming AI wave in societies around the globe. Beyond this, the introductory chapter reflects on the recently proposed IMPACT framework. IMPACT stands for Interplay of Modality, Person, Area, Country/Culture and Transparency categories helping laypersons and scientists alike to better understand what factors influence AI attitudes, its impact on wellbeing and also if AI might be a benevolent or a dangerous technology within certain context, governance protocol and modality of operation. Further, the IMPACT framework serves as structure of the present book, whereas the individual contributions of the book are shortly previewed.

Keywords Attitudes · Artificial intelligence · Theory of planned behavior · Technology acceptance model · IMPACT framework

1.1 Background

Milestones in AI research such as the Alpha Go moment in 2015 or the launch of the generative AI ChatGPT in November 2022 demonstrate the current capabilities of artificial intelligence. Without doubt artificial intelligence (AI) will be in-built into a growing number of systems and products, people are interacting with on a daily

---

C. Montag (✉)
Department of Molecular Psychology, Institute of Psychology and Education, Ulm University, Ulm, Germany
e-mail: mail@christianmontag.de

R. Ali
College of Science and Engineering, Hamad Bin Khalifa University, Doha, Qatar

C. Montag and R. Ali (eds.), *The Impact of Artificial Intelligence on Societies*, Studies in Neuroscience, Psychology and Behavioral Economics,
https://doi.org/10.1007/978-3-031-70355-3_1

level. Therefore, we find ourselves in a transit zone from a pre-AI society towards an AI society, where much of what we experience as humans will be influenced by AI systems (Suleyman and Bhaskar 2023). Already today we interact with AI systems such as when asking Siri about the weather or when we are "firing up" our social media apps and see content, which has been pre-selected by an AI system (giving way to topics such as the filter-bubble; Pariser 2011; Sindermann et al. 2020). Therefore, the large question is looming about how AI exactly will impact upon global societies?

One way to answer this pressing question, is to ask people directly about their views on AI and also collect data unobtrusively, representing their interaction with it in terms of frequency, style, and purpose. From our view, user study research represents an important cornerstone of understanding AI's impact upon society, because ultimately, it is the people who embrace technology and use it—either for good or bad. Also, from an entrepreneur's or policymaker's perspective it is important to know what people think about AI (Furman and Seamans 2019; Girasa 2020). Such knowledge will not only help us to understand if people are willing to use AI, but also if their skepticism is so large that AI technology might need to be regulated. Another outcome of AI attitude (and AI-literacy) research could be that people will need to update their education to master the coming AI wave. Life-long-learning of citizens (Laal and Salamati 2012) could get an even more important prerequisite for successful nations in the age of AI. In this regard the Singaporean government launched a highly interesting initiative, hence providing every Singaporean from 40 years on the means to visit university again to get the needed education in the context of AI.[1]

1.2 On the Importance of AI-Attitude Research from a Theoretical Perspective

Both the psychological and computer sciences have been interested since many years in the research question on why people embrace and use technologies. Going back to the uses and gratification theory (UGT) the idea was put forward that humans only then start to sustainably use a new technology, when it satisfies (or gratifies) inner needs (Katz et al. 1973). Such needs could be that a technology is fun to use (hedonic need), provides people with means to socially interact (social need) or can be used as a tool (utilitarian need). For instance, these needs are fulfilled for many when they are using social media—as mentioned a product which is strongly relying on AI technology (Schivinski et al. 2020). Other well established theories explaining technology use directly mention attitudes as a relevant factor to predict if people use a new technology or abstain from using it. Among these theories are the *Technology Acceptance Model* (short TAM; Venkatesh and Davis 2000) or the *Theory of Planned Behavior* (Ajzen 1991), having a bit broader scope, but can also be

[1] https://www.smartnation.gov.sg/nais/.

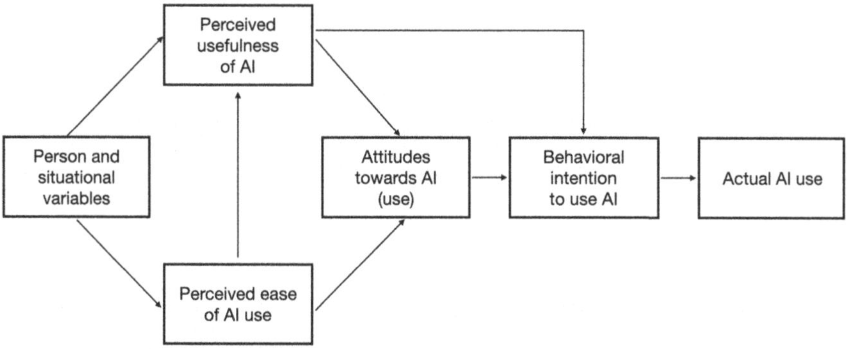

Fig. 1.1 The technology acceptance model (modified and adjusted to the topic of AI; original by Davis et al. 1989—exemplary citation)

applied to technology use.[2] TAM comes up with the idea that perceiving a technology both as *useful* (perhaps to satisfy an inner need, see above the UGT) and *easy to use* results in a positive attitude towards the technology, which might be a necessary prerequisite to form an intention to use the technology and then also *behavioral use* of it. In Fig. 1.1, we depict the TAM being adapted to the context of the AI technology. As one can see there are further arrows (going beyond the made explanations) such as one suggesting that perceived ease of use of the AI technology also positively influences the perceived usefulness of this technology.

Attitude relates to the persuasion stage of the process of adopting new ideas or technologies, according to the Diffusion of Innovation Theory (DOI) (Rogers 2003). The theory also identifies factors influencing adoption, such as perceived advantage, compatibility, complexity, trialability, and observability. These factors may shape attitudes towards AI and should be incorporated into attitude measures. They are also aligned with the Theory of Planned Behavior and the Technology Acceptance Model (TAM). The DOI theory emphasizes the importance of communication channels, timing, and social systems, all of which are incorporated into our IMPACT framework.

The related Theory of Planned Behavior (TPB) comes to comparable ideas than the TAM and is depicted for the context of AI in Fig. 1.2. Here the interplay of attitudes towards AI (e.g. positive/negative) with subjective norms (such as "My closest friends all use AI technology") and perceived control over the AI technology (e.g. "I can handle AI") should result in a higher intention to use an AI-system and then also the behavioral use of the AI. Of particular interest is clearly here also the reference to the perceived control over technology, which indeed has been already shown—in form of technology self-efficacy—to be linked to more positive AI attitudes (Montag et al. 2023).

[2] Please note that the Theory of Planned Action was developed on the foundations of Theory of Reasoned Action (Ajzen and Fishbein 1980), which also inspired the TAM.

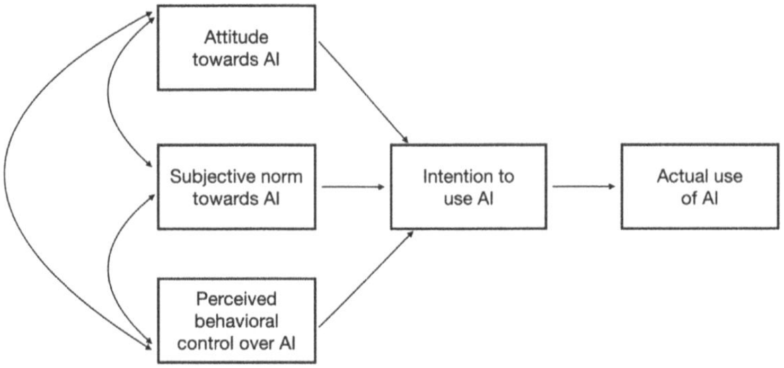

Fig. 1.2 The theory of planned behavior (adjusted to the topic of AI, original by Ajzen, 1991)

In sum, both TAM and TPB and DOI stress the importance of AI attitudes to understand if people and societies will embrace this new technology or not. This also makes a strong case for the overarching focus of the book.

1.3 The IMPACT Framework: Why the General-Purpose Character of AI-Technologies Makes It Difficult to Predict Its Consequences

Doing social science research in the field of AI—where the study of AI attitudes belongs to—is not trivial, because AI is a general-purpose-technology which will be used in very different settings. Therefore, the question already arises if it is meaningful to run studies using a general term such as AI, or should we better directly ask people about their views on applying AI for instance in the field of medicine? Without doubt specific and nuanced measures are important to understand how AI impacts on societies (Montag et al. 2024b), but asking about AI in general in attitude research still has its merits. Recent observations have been made showing that for instance a more positive view on AI indeed translates into higher willingness to use or trust distinct products where AI is in-built ranging from self-driving cars to language assistants on smartphones (Sindermann et al. 2021). Same observations have been made linking general AI attitude measures to trusting ChatGPT (Montag and Ali 2023). Moreover, most representative surveys will not allow to include many measures assessing AI attitudes, hence we cannot ask thousands of people around the global about the specific views on AI in hundreds of fields. Hence, applying general AI attitude measures have their place in research, but it is also true that nuanced measures will provide additional important insights about what people feel, think and know about this key technology.

So how are AI attitudes formed? We believe that a lot of variables play a role here, which all need to be considered to come to a nuanced view towards the AI technology.

In two recent papers, we proposed the IMPACT framework, providing interested readers with an easy acronym to consider highly relevant variables to understand AI and its consequences on societies (Montag et al. 2024a, b). The acronym IMPACT stands for Interplay of Modality, Person, Area, Country/Culture and Transparency variables. We shortly explain in the following what this means.

With the Modality category, we want to make the point that the way the AI is designed makes a strong difference for user's view on the AI system. Modality could confront users with the questions: How reliable is the AI? Is the AI interactive (such as ChatGPT) or just an output system? Is the AI-system operating autonomously or semi-autonomously? These are just few examples illustrating the Modality category to be further explained in this book. The Person variable takes a closer look at the individuum coming to an AI attitude. How old is this person? Is the person educated and what looks the personality structure of a person like? People of course differ in terms of many variables likely impacting upon AI attitude formation.

The Area variable of the IMPACT framework stresses the fact that AI is operating in very different products ranging from medicine to military. In other words, the area where an AI system operates (and there also for what reason) will shape our views on AI.

The Country/Culture variable focuses on cultural specifics which might shape our views towards AI and also on political environments with differences in their attempts to regulate AI. Finally, we come to another modality variable, which is presented separately in the IMPACT-framework due to its large importance: Transparency. Here, we believe that the degree of transparency of an AI system—both in ways of explaining the user what the AI is doing and being transparent regarding its code, etc.—shapes our views. How opaque is the AI system?

The variables put forward in the IMPACT-framework should not be seen as exhaustive, but as a start to systematically investigate how the different categories/variables of the IMPACT framework shape our views towards AI systems and promote our well-being when interacting with such AI-systems.

A further note: The acronym IMPACT begins with the letter I representing the word "Interplay". Ultimately, this means that each single category alone will not be sufficient to understand how our views on AI are shaped, but that the interplay between the categories of the IMPACT-framework must be considered. For instance: Some people might like to have more explanations on how an AI-system comes to a certain result, hence they ask for different degrees of explainable AI (XAI). But the need to get an explanation for the outcome of an AI system might also rely on the gravity of the AI's result for a person's life. A medical diagnosis is for sure of more importance for most of us then getting explained how the feed of social media is endowed with news by an AI system.

While understanding and calculating how the Interplay of Modality, Person, Area, Country/Culture and Transparency categories forms or influences attitudes towards AI might be challenging, asking about general attitudes towards AI, perhaps as a single item, is justified (see also recent work correlating single item AI attitude measures with other and more elaborate survey tools, Montag and Ali 2023). For sure, we are just at the beginning of the journey understanding AI attitude formation and this book should be seen as a start to get an overview on the complexities arising in this vivid research field.

1.4 How to Read This Book

This book is structured in line with the IMPACT framework. Hence, after this introductory Chap. 1 and the following overview on available general AI attitude measures (Chap. 2), a closer look will be taken at the Modality category (Chaps. 3 and 4). This is followed by an investigation of Person-factors with reflections on the role of personality (Chap. 5) and the uniqueness of patients in the age of AI (Chap. 6). A section consisting of three chapters then is reflecting on the importance to consider the Area-variable, hence making the point that the area matters, in which AI operates, to understand its consequences. The Areas of medicine (Chap. 7: focus on autism), education (Chap. 8) and autonomous cars (Chap. 9) are discussed in this book. Chapters 10 and 11 focus on the cultural aspects in the context of AI attitude formation (Country/Culture category), whereas the book ends with reflections on ethics and transparent AI with Chaps. 12 and 13 (Transparency category). The book must not necessarily be read from this chapter to Chap. 13, but of course with having the IMPACT framework in mind, it helps to find yourself through the book.

References

Ajzen I (1991) The theory of planned behavior. Organ Behav Hum Decis Process 50(2):179–211. https://doi.org/10.1016/0749-5978(91)90020-T

Ajzen I, Fishbein M (1980) Understanding attitudes and predicting social behavior. Prentice-Hall

Davis FD, Bagozzi RP, Warshaw PR (1989) User acceptance of computer technology: a comparison of two theoretical models. Manage Sci 35(8):982–1003. http://www.jstor.org/stable/2632151

Furman J, Seamans R (2019) AI and the economy. Innov Policy Econ 19:161–191. https://doi.org/10.1086/699936

Girasa R (2020) International initiatives in AI. In Girasa R (ed) Artificial intelligence as a disruptive technology: economic transformation and government regulation. Springer International Publishing, pp 255–298. https://doi.org/10.1007/978-3-030-35975-1_8

Katz E, Blumler JG, Gurevitch M (1973) Uses and gratifications research. Public Opin Quar 37(4):509–523. https://www.jstor.org/stable/2747854

Laal M, Salamati P (2012) Lifelong learning; why do we need it? Procedia Soc Behav Sci 31:399–403. https://doi.org/10.1016/j.sbspro.2011.12.073

Montag C, Ali R (2023) Can we assess attitudes toward AI with single items? Associations with existing attitudes toward AI measures and trust in ChatGPT in two German speaking samples. Research Square. https://doi.org/10.21203/rs.3.rs-3325511/v1

Montag C, Kraus J, Baumann M, Rozgonjuk D (2023) The propensity to trust in automated technology mediates the links between technology self-efficacy and fear and acceptance of artificial intelligence. Comput Hum Behav Rep:100315. https://doi.org/10.1016/j.chbr.2023.100315

Montag C, Nakov P, Ali R (2024a) Considering the IMPACT framework to understand the AI-well-being-complex from an interdisciplinary perspective. Tele Inform Rep 13:100112. https://doi.org/10.1016/j.teler.2023.100112

Montag C, Nakov P, Ali R (2024b) On the need to develop nuanced measures assessing attitudes towards AI and AI literacy in representative large-scale samples. AI & Society. https://doi.org/10.1007/s00146-024-01888-1

Pariser E (2011) The filter bubble: what the internet is hiding from you. Penguin UK

Rogers EM (2003) Diffusion of innovations, 5th ed. Free Press

Schivinski B, Brzozowska-Woś M, Stansbury E, Satel J, Montag C, Pontes HM (2020) Exploring the role of social media use motives, psychological well-being, self-esteem, and affect in problematic social media use. Front Psychol 11:617140. https://doi.org/10.3389/fpsyg.2020.617140

Sindermann C, Elhai JD, Moshagen M, Montag C (2020) Age, gender, personality, ideological attitudes and individual differences in a person's news spectrum: How many and who might be prone to "filter bubbles" and "echo chambers" online? Heliyon 6(1):e03214. https://doi.org/10.1016/j.heliyon.2020.e03214

Sindermann C, Sha P, Zhou M, Wernicke J, Schmitt HS, Li M, Sariyska R, Stavrou M, Becker B, Montag C (2021) Assessing the attitude towards artificial intelligence: introduction of a short measure in German, Chinese, and English language. KI—Künstliche Intelligenz 35(1):109–118. https://doi.org/10.1007/s13218-020-00689-0

Suleyman M, Bhaskar M (2023) The coming wave: technology, power, and the twenty-first century's greatest dilemma. Crown

Venkatesh V, Davis F (2000) A theoretical extension of the technology acceptance model: four longitudinal field studies. Manage Sci 46:186–204. https://doi.org/10.1287/mnsc.46.2.186.11926

Chapter 2
The Measurement of Attitudes Towards Artificial Intelligence: An Overview and Recommendations

Astrid Schepman and Paul Rodway

Abstract The growth in use of Artificial Intelligence is having a major impact on society, with further impacts anticipated in the coming years and decades. There are individual differences in attitudes towards Artificial Intelligence and it is important for scientists and others to be able to measure these. Individual differences in attitudes towards Artificial Intelligence may be associated with other major psychological or circumstantial factors, and understanding these associations is beneficial. In addition, it is important to be able to track attitudes towards Artificial Intelligence over time. For this purpose, scientists have developed psychometric measurement tools to measure attitudes towards Artificial Intelligence. This Chapter provides an overview and evaluation of these tools, with a focus on tools that measure general attitudes towards Artificial Intelligence, and that are quantitative measurements, which can be analysed statistically. Semantic, methodological, and psychometric factors that the user should consider when choosing a suitable tool are discussed. The choice of measurement tool may depend on many researcher-driven considerations, including time, cost, and practical factors, but the quality and validity of the measurement tool should be a major factor in this choice. A scale's ability to capture important dimensions in the data should also be a key consideration. We recommend that observed ambivalence about AI is best captured with a bi-dimensional AI attitudes scale.

Keywords Psychometric scale · Artificial Intelligence · Attitude · Measurement · Validation · Validity · Internal consistency · Reliability · Factor · Dimension

---

There are no conflicts of interest to declare.

A. Schepman (✉) · P. Rodway
Division of Psychology, University of Chester, Parkgate Road, Chester, Cheshire CH1 4BJ, UK
e-mail: a.schepman@chester.ac.uk

P. Rodway
e-mail: p.rodway@chester.ac.uk

C. Montag and R. Ali (eds.), *The Impact of Artificial Intelligence on Societies*, Studies in Neuroscience, Psychology and Behavioral Economics,
https://doi.org/10.1007/978-3-031-70355-3_2

2.1 Introduction

Measuring attitudes towards Artificial Intelligence (AI) is a key component to understanding the role of influences Montag and Ali theorised about in Chap. 1 (this volume). The current Chapter provides a discussion and evaluation of different ways of measuring AI attitudes.

Attitudes have been measured for a long time (e.g. Thurstone 1928). Albarracín et al. (2005, p. 4, quoting Eagly and Chaiken 1993, p. 1, their italics) adopt a consensus definition: "*attitude is a psychological tendency that is expressed by evaluating a particular entity with some degree of favor or disfavor*". Albarracín, et al. set out key characteristics of attitudes as being evaluative, and showing inter-judge variation, unlike beliefs. For example, a set of raters would tend to show high inter-rater agreement on water freezing at zero degrees Celsius, but would not necessarily agree to the same extent on their evaluations of consumer preferences, political stances, or social attitudes. Albarracín, et al. also set out that attitudes are not necessarily stable over time, and that attitudes are linked to cognition, affect, and behaviour, but that these elements are not necessarily the "component parts" of attitudes, which are, instead, evaluations held towards an entity.

Before we move to technical details, let us consider a member of the general public, with general mass media exposure, average information technology skills, and no specialist knowledge about AI. This person may encounter news reports about AI or robots taking over job roles, thus displacing workers and impacting livelihoods. They may also encounter discussions about ethical issues surrounding AI such as the use of copyrighted data, (see e.g. Guadamuz 2024) or high energy consumption by AI (e.g. van Wynsberghe 2021). This same person may also read media stories about AI being used in beneficial medical applications such as in cancer screening (e.g. Hunter et al. 2022), or may have heard of AI facilitating efficiencies in managing complex processes or scarce resources (e.g. Helo and Hao 2022). In light of this kind of exposure, this person may develop a neutral general attitude towards AI reflecting the balance of gains and drawbacks that AI may bring. Alternatively, the person may simultaneous hold positive and negative attitudes that are independent of each other. A further outcome may be that the person holds an overall positive (or negative) attitude towards AI. It is important for a measurement tool aimed at measuring general attitudes towards AI to capture this range of possibilities.

This Chapter is organised as follows. First, we briefly describe key processes of scale development. We then evaluate scales that measure general attitudes towards AI in relation to these key attributes. We end with recommendations.

2.2 Scale Development and Psychometrics: A Brief Primer

Psychometric tools that measure AI attitudes must be fit for purpose. Psychometricians have developed key criteria that psychological measurement scales should meet, and prospective users should satisfy themselves that the measurement tool that they choose satisfies as many of these criteria as is practicable.

2.2.1 Latent Constructs and Dimensionality

A psychometric scale measures a hidden or latent construct using surface manifestations of this latent construct. These surface manifestations are mostly phrased as verbal statements, also known as items, to which the participants typically respond using a Likert-style rating scale, which may include verbal anchors (e.g. "Strongly disagree", "Strongly agree"), which map onto numbers e.g. 1–5, or 1–7, or 1–10, depending on the developers' choices. Formulation and selection of the items is often informed by prior research, either conducted by the developers of the scale, or sourced via previously published research, or both. The meanings of the items should collectively represent the meaning of the latent construct to demonstrate construct validity. Scales can be unidimensional (all items belong to one construct) or multidimensional (items belong to a subconstruct or subscale), or both (there are subconstructs, but also an overarching general construct). The item meanings are evaluated by human scale developers and/or experts, and then further validated against quantitative data that are provided by participants who complete the scale.

Typically, single items or questions do not constitute a scale, and many researchers would find it risky to use single items when measuring important research constructs, because responses to single items tend to be less reliable and less stable than combined responses to multiple items. There has been some discussion on this notion, with some researchers claiming that single items can be as valid as multi-item scales (Allen et al. 2022; Bergkvist and Rossiter 2007), but with other researchers demonstrating empirically and via simulations that such claims would only be valid in limited circumstances, e.g. in exploratory research with small samples, and when the construct is relatively easy to capture in a single item statement, e.g. to express a simple attitude, rather than a more psychologically complex one (Diamantopoulos et al. 2012). Of course, single items may be more cost-effective in large samples (Montag et al. 2024c) and may be necessary in circumstances that limit the number of questions. On balance, many researchers feel that the use of single items can be inadequate or risky in some circumstances, because validity cannot always be demonstrated, and because it could adversely impact the conclusion validity of the research.

2.2.2 Psychometrics During Validation

Initial validation of a psychometric scale typically involves acquiring data from human participants and then subjecting these data to Exploratory Factor Analysis (EFA). The aim of this analysis is to identify the dimensionality and factor structure of the scale, and to ascertain which items fit well in the scale, and which items need to be dropped.

Confirmatory validation typically follows. This involves collecting new data using the scale items identified during EFA, and subjecting those data to Confirmatory Factor Analysis (CFA). In this, the factors or dimensions are pre-specified by the data analyst, often based on the factor(s) discovered during EFA, and the aim is to determine whether the data show a satisfactory fit with the structure. A useful brief overview of EFA and CFA is provided in Tavakol and Wetzel (2020).

Each factor analysis provides metrics to allow the developer to assess the quality of the scale statistically. These include fit measures which indicate whether the data form a good overall fit with the structure. The most commonly reported fit indices are the Tucker-Lewis Index (TLI) and the Comparative Fit Index (CFI), which should be 0.95 or above, and the root mean square error of approximation (RMSEA), which should be 0.06 or below (Hu and Bentler 1999). Other researchers have proposed different cut-offs, and additional fit measures are used.

Individual items also have metrics, known as factor loadings, which show the correlation of each item to the overall construct. There is no fixed cut-off for these loadings, but a minimum of 0.3 should be observed (e.g. Tavakol and Wetzel 2020), with some researchers setting this cut-off higher.

In addition, the internal consistency of the items is quantified by Cronbach's alpha, a measure that captures the overall inter-item correlation of a scale or subscale. This is an important measure, because surface manifestations of latent constructs should be statistically associated with these latent constructs. Cronbach's alpha for the relevant scale or subscale should be 0.7 or above to show that the items are associated to a satisfactory level, though scores over 0.9 may indicate that the items are simply the same question in a different guise, or that there may be redundancy due to high intercorrelations among items (Tavakol and Dennick 2011). Cronbach's alpha is sensitive to the number of items on a scale or subscale. Scales with few items often undershoot the cut-off of 0.7.

To ensure that a new scale measures the intended construct, developers often use a previously validated scale that measures a similar but somewhat different construct against which to calibrate the new construct (criterion validity). The new scale should correlate with these comparator instruments (convergent validity) but it should not correlate so strongly that it is essentially measuring the same construct as the previous scale (divergent validity).

It is possible for psychometric measures such as fit indices or internal consistency measures to be high, providing seeming reassurance on the quality of the scale, yet for the scale to have other problems. For example, a scale in which the same statements with minor rephrasing are presented multiple times (e.g. "I take pleasure in using

AI" and "I get joy from using AI") will have high fit and internal consistency metrics, but may have limitations in the breadth of coverage of the construct. Therefore, it is important for all scale requirements to be balanced.

2.2.3 Psychometrics for Post-validation Use

Once the scale is validated and published, other users can use it (sometimes with author/publisher permission, sometimes without further permission, depending on the authors/publishers). In recent years, many researchers have adopted Open Science practices and Creative Commons licenses, making research information and scales more readily available to other researchers than had been the case in the past.

Because Cronbach's alpha applies specifically to the data for which it was calculated, it is recommended that all users of a published scale calculate Cronbach's alpha for their sample to demonstrate internal consistency in their own data. In addition, some researchers repeat the Confirmatory Factor Analysis with their new data and report the fit measures, though this is less common. The validation of attitude scales across different ages and cultures enables generalizability. Some attitude scales can be more generic than others and could be used in any domain. Users can also use theoretical arguments to justify their choice of scale. Researchers should always satisfy themselves that the scale they intend to use fits the context.

2.3 Considerations in AI Attitude Measurement

When choosing a scale, it is important to select one that suits the goal of the researcher. One key dimension is whether the attitudes that people hold towards Artificial Intelligence are attitudes towards AI in general, or to specific domains or aspects. This Chapter focuses on domain-general AI attitude scales that capture broad attitudes, not on scales that have been developed for more specific domains such as work (Park et al. 2024), defence (Hadlington et al. 2023), or teaching (Galindo-Domínguez et al. in press), nor for scales that focus solely on specific feelings towards AI, such as anxiety (Wang and Wang 2022). Similarly, we do not evaluate in detail scales that measure AI Literacy (for this, see e.g. Carolus et al. 2023; Laupichler et al. 2023; Wang et al. 2023) other than to note that these mostly rely on self-reported AI Literacy, which can be somewhat subjective or inaccurate. We also do not focus on surveys which use multiple questions that gauge attitudes towards AI, but do not attempt to form a scale construct (e.g. Dos Santos et al. 2019 for medical students' attitudes towards the use of AI in radiology and medicine; Centre for Data Ethics and Innovation, 2024, for a survey of the UK general public's attitudes towards AI, tracked over time in multiple waves). Finally, we do not focus on attitude measurement whereby participants rate their attitudes to a set of specific AI use cases (e.g. specific robots, specific chatbots, specific AI applications, etc.), because attitudes towards these use cases can change rapidly over time, as applications fade in and out of fashion, and may lose relevance too quickly to be of optimal value in AI attitude research that spans more than a brief timeframe. In addition, such views are specific to the selected use cases, and do not measure general AI attitudes. Instead, we focus on attitudes towards AI in general.

A key consideration in scale choice is the breadth of coverage of the latent construct. If a construct is measured too narrowly, its validity may be limited. Relatedly, some researchers, particularly those involved in studies that measure a large number of constructs, value an instrument's speed and simplicity of administration, which favours short scales, or even single items. However, there can be a speed–accuracy trade-off, and researchers should consider carefully whether saving a modest amount of participant time is worth the potential reduction in validity, or the loss of being able to demonstrate internal consistency.

2.4 Specific Measurement Tools

We now describe and evaluate four specific scales that measure general attitudes towards Artificial Intelligence, in chronological order by publication date.

2.4.1 General Attitudes Towards Artificial Intelligence Scale: GAAIS

The General Attitudes towards Artificial Intelligence Scale (GAAIS; Schepman and Rodway 2020, 2023) consists of 20 statements across two subscales, the Positive GAAIS, and the Negative GAAIS. The authors pronounce the abbreviation GAAIS as a homophone of "guys", and other users are invited to do the same.

For the initial validation (Schepman and Rodway 2020, data from May 2019), the authors generated 32 items, collectively representing cognitive, affective, and behavioural domains. Of these, 16 initial items expressed positive elements, such as opportunities, benefits, positive emotions, and potential own use, and 16 initial items expressed negative elements, such as concerns and negative emotions. These items were presented to 100 non-student UK participants, balanced for sex. A Likert scale (1–5) captured the responses. Negative items were reverse-scored so that all items had the same polarity to facilitate factor analysis. If this is not done, the factors can artefactually arise from the opposite polarity of the positive and negative items, though note that a disadvantage is that additional explanations are needed to aid the interpretation (i.e. high scores on negative items means that participants are forgiving about AI drawbacks). Screening for low correlations was performed, and items that correlated weakly with multiple others were pruned.

Subsequently, Exploratory Factor Analysis was performed using parallel analysis, in which the number of factors is determined algorithmically using simulated data (see Hayton et al. 2004). Parallel analysis identified two factors. The EFA led to further pruning of items that did not load onto either factor, or that cross-loaded onto both factors approximately evenly. The two factors were subsequently labelled the Positive GAAIS (12 items) and the Negative GAAIS (8 items), with item loadings onto these factors matching the initial conceptualisation. The solution showed an acceptable fit and good internal consistency (Positive GAAIS $\alpha = 0.88$; Negative GAAIS $\alpha = 0.83$). A model using bifactor analysis to test whether an overall scale score could be constructed showed that this was disfavoured because a general overarching factor showed a poor fit. This was further reinforced by a moderate correlation ($r = 0.509$) between the two subscales. The scale scores showed approximately normal distributions, with relatively modest negative skews ($M = 3.60$ out of 5, $SD = 0.67$, $Skew = -0.509$ for the Positive GAAIS; $M = 2.93$, $SD = 0.75$, $Skew = -0.173$).

Criterion validation was performed against the Technology Readiness Index (TRI, Lam et al. 2008), an instrument that measures attitudes towards non-AI technologies, and both the Positive GAAIS and Negative GAAIS showed good convergent validity (correlating significantly) and divergent validity (not correlating so strongly as to be identical measures). In addition, Schepman and Rodway (2020) used a list of use cases of AI sourced from UK newspapers, and participants rated how comfortable they would be with these AI applications, and to what extent they felt these applications would perform better than humans on the tasks for which they were created. Scores for these ratings were also subjected to EFA, and two factors were identified and means calculated across the relevant use cases. Particularly for comfortableness, both of these factors correlated well with the Positive and Negative GAAIS, showing additional semantic validation, demonstrating that the general attitudes captured by the GAAIS showed significant associations with attitudes towards coherent clusters of specific use cases.

In Schepman and Rodway (2023, data from March, June, and July, 2021) two new samples of 304 (Study 1) and 300 (Study 2) UK participants were used to perform Confirmatory Factor Analysis on the GAAIS with its 20 items. In both samples, the fit measures were excellent, and Cronbach alpha values were good. In Study 1 Positive: $\alpha = 0.88$; Negative GAAIS $\alpha = 0.82$, in Study 2: Positive: $\alpha = 0.85$, Negative: $\alpha = 0.82$. As established via the bifactor analysis in Schepman and Rodway (2020), here the Expected Cross-Validation Index (ECVI) for a tentative overall scale score showed that two separate subscales were a better fit with the data than a single scale, once again reinforced by moderate correlations between the two subscales (Study 1: $r = 0.397$; Study 2: $r = 0.48$). In Study 1, there were significant, but not overly strong, correlations with the TRI, replicating the convergent validity and divergent validity shown in the initial validation.

A subsequent study (Rodway and Schepman 2023, data from July and August, 2022) also validated the scale in a UK-wide student sample ($N = 302$), again showing a strong fit, and high internal consistency, as measured through Cronbach's alpha, $\alpha = 0.87$ for the Positive GAAIS, and $\alpha = 0.83$ for the Negative GAAIS. In this sample, the bi-dimensionality of the scale was replicated once more via the ECVI and moderate correlations between the subscales ($r = 0.39$). The stability across the four studies shows that the scale is stable over time, with different samples, and in an ever-changing AI landscape.

Subscales scores for the GAAIS are computed by taking the mean across the relevant items (score range: 1–5). A person who scores high on the Positive GAAIS tends to see the benefits of AI, may want to use AI, and has positive emotions regarding AI. A person who scores high on the Negative GAAIS, which is reverse-scored, tends to be forgiving about the drawbacks of AI, and tends not to have strong negative emotions regarding AI. An individual can be high on both subscales, showing an overall positive and forgiving attitude towards AI and its drawbacks, but they can also simultaneously have high scores for the Positive GAAIS, while showing strong concerns, as indicated by low scores on the Negative GAAIS. This is relatively common, leading to the consistently replicated moderate positive correlations between the two GAAIS subscales. This pattern has been demonstrated elsewhere, e.g. in recent national UK survey ($N = 4010$, representative sample) in which the subtle and nuanced mixed views (positive views blended with concerns) were documented based on use cases (Ada Lovelace Institute and The Alan Turing Institute 2023). Similarly, the same pattern was observed in Hadlington et al. (2023). Because this ambivalence towards AI is so common, it is important for AI attitude scales to be able to capture this. Unidimensional scales can be at risk of missing this.

The GAAIS has been widely used across the world. The GAAIS has been validated in translated forms in Korean (Seo and Ahn 2022), Turkish (Kaya et al. 2024), and has been translated into German (Montag and Ali, forthcoming), with further validated translations in the pipeline. The GAAIS has been used across a variety of disciplines, including health (e.g. Lukić et al. 2023), psychology (Bergdahl et al. 2023), aesthetics (Bellaiche et al. 2023), AI text evaluation (Darda et al. 2023; Lim and Schmälzle 2024), and leadership studies (Fousiani et al. 2024). The GAAIS has been found to be associated with personality traits (Kaya et al. 2024; Schepman and Rodway 2023) trust, and corporate distrust (Schepman and Rodway 2023), aspects of AI Anxiety (Kaya et al. 2024), and Higher Education students' attitudes towards AI in Education, or AIEd (Rodway and Schepman 2023). It has also been found to be a moderator in measures of the digital divide (Bentley et al. 2024), and it was found to be a predictor of behavioural intentions to use automated text generation (Lermann-Henestrosa and Kimmerle, forthcoming). In examining emotions and a sense of threat experienced in response to ChatGPT, the GAAIS was a significant correlate (Alessandro et al. 2024). In a study examining the influence of AI recommendations on mental health diagnoses, the GAAIS was an important covariate (Bashkirova and Krpan 2024). It must be noted that some authors made minor changes to the recommended use of the GAAIS, including expanding the response scale from 1–5 to 1–7, or removing items. While this is not always the ideal way of working with validated scales, the measure seemed robust under such modifications. The GAAIS has also been used as a comparator scale in new AI scales measuring specific aspects such as attitudes towards AI in defence (Hadlington et al. 2023), in workplace settings (Park et al. 2024), or in measuring AI use motives (Yurt and Kasarci 2024). These are some examples, but the list is not exhaustive. In all, the GAAIS has shown a high level of utility and use in AI attitude research.

Time and again, it has been demonstrated that the two-factor structure of the GAAIS is valuable, because the two subscales are differentially predictive of other measures. Each time, the two-factor structure of the GAAIS has been shown to replicate across a wide range of samples, locations, and settings. This, alongside the consistently high fit and internal consistency measures, makes the GAAIS a valuable tool with which to measure general attitudes towards Artificial Intelligence.

Readers interested in using the GAAIS can download it from the Appendix of Schepman and Rodway (2023), an open access journal article, where it appears with instructions for participants and scoring instructions (note that the items are in the Table in the Appendix, and scoring instructions are in the Table caption below). Readers are recommended to change the attention check item to "To show that you are reading this, please select Strongly agree", which some readers find easier to process than the attention check listed. This does not change the scale in any way, but leads to reduced data loss. The scale is free to use and the article is open access.

2.4.2 Attitude Towards Artificial Intelligence Scale: ATAI

The Attitude Towards Artificial Intelligence Scale (Sindermann et al. 2021) is a bi-dimensional, five-item scale that measures Acceptance of AI (two items) and Fear of AI (three items), using an 11-point Likert rating scale (0–10). The scale was validated using Principal Components Analysis (PCA), a slightly different statistical technique from EFA, typically aimed at reducing data dimensionality rather than the discovery of latent factors. The authors used a factor identification method based on eigenvalues, a less accurate method than parallel analysis. There was no reverse-scoring for negative items. In general, this can risk the creation of artefactual factors. This is because participants respond in opposite directions to the positive and negative items, and without reverse-scoring, the PCA would identify these opposite responses as statistical patterns, without those patterns necessarily being meaningful. For that reason, it could be valuable to determine whether the structure would persist following reverse-scoring of the negative items. Note that not reverse scoring does come with easier administration and more straightforward interpretation. The ATAI was validated in three languages, using samples that were not sex-balanced. There is no report of back-translation for accurate semantic alignment across the languages. The Acceptance and Fear subscales in the German sample ($N = 461$; 75% female) showed Cronbach alpha values that were somewhat low $\alpha = 0.65$ and $\alpha = 0.66$, respectively. In the Chinese sample ($N = 413$; 65% male) the Acceptance subscale reached > 0.7, namely $\alpha = 0.73$, but the Fear subscale did not, $\alpha = 0.61$. In the UK sample ($N = 84$; 77% female), both were lower, $\alpha = 0.64$ and $\alpha = 0.65$, respectively. It is known that a low number of items can lead to low Cronbach's alpha values and it may be tempting to therefore class these lower Cronbach's alpha values as acceptable, but this is not a valid interpretation. It is not possible to assess the internal consistency of a scale with a low number of items if Cronbach's alpha is low, because it cannot be known in principle whether this is due to the low number of items, or due to the actual low internal consistency. For this reason, using more items is advantageous, as it allows scale users to interpret the Cronbach's alpha unambiguously, and potentially demonstrate internal consistency more securely. In subsequent uses of the ATAI, higher Cronbach alpha values of 0.77 (accepting) and 0.76 (fear) were observed for both subscales in a German sample (Montag et al. 2024b), suggesting some sample variations.

Following PCA, CFA was conducted on the data from the same participants. This practice is not optimal, because there is an inherent risk that the structure found during factor discovery may be specific to the initial sample(s), which is why using a new data set is typically recommended. Using the same sample reduces the validity of the scale. Fit measures for the CFA were mostly acceptable, although some undershot the standard cut-offs. The ATAI scores predicted attitudes towards specific use cases, such as Alexa, Siri, and specific humanoid robots. It was not validated against a similar, previously validated instrument, so that convergent and divergent validity could not be demonstrated at validation. However, predictive power of related constructs such as willingness to use AI can be an acceptable substitute, and this was demonstrated. The ATAI has been used in subsequent research. For example, it has shown correlations with Sadness and Fear, as measured by the Affective Neuroscience Personality Scales (Montag et al. 2024a, b, c), and it has been used to explore mediation pathways between trust in technology, technology self-efficacy, and AI attitudes (Montag et al. 2023). In all, the ATAI is a brief, easy-to-administer, and bi-dimensional AI attitudes measurement tool, but, because of the limitations in the psychometric validation, prospective users should exercise caution when considering utilising this tool. Readers who would like to inspect the ATAI scale can find it in Sindermann et al. (2021, Table 1 therein).

2.4.3 AI Attitude Scale: AIAS-4

The AI Attitude Scale (AIAS-4; Grassini 2023) is a brief, four-item instrument, with responses expressed on a ten-point Likert scale (1–10). In its initial round of validation using a sex-balanced UK sample ($N = 230$) the scale had five items, one of which was negative and reverse-scored ("think AI technology is a threat to humans"), and the remainder positive (e.g. "I believe that AI will improve my life"). The author provides good justification for the choice of items. Upon initial EFA, the negative item led to a poor fit, so it was eliminated from the scale, leaving four positive items. Cronbach's alpha for this four-item scale was high, $\alpha = 0.902$. CFA was performed on data from a new, sex-balanced US sample ($N = 300$). The CFA showed a strong fit on all measures. The AIAS-4 was validated against the attitude dimension of the Media and Technology Usage and Attitudes Scale (MTUAS, Rosen et al. 2013), showing significant correlations that were not overly strong, demonstrating convergent and divergent validity. This is a strongly validated scale, which has the advantage of being brief, and quick and simple to administer. A significant drawback is that there are no reverse-scored items, which can make the scale subject to "straight-lining" (participants responding to each question with the same answer), or acquiescence bias (participants agreeing uniformly with all questions, because agreeing feels better than disagreeing). In addition, as indicated by the very high Cronbach's alpha, the items are somewhat similar to each other and may therefore not represent a broad construct. Furthermore, because all the items have a positive meaning, the scale can only measure positive attitudes (or the lack of a positive attitudes, if the participant has a low score), but it cannot capture the types of concerns that e.g. the Negative GAAIS can capture. In light of prior research, which shows that many participants are ambivalent about AI, holding positive and negative attitudes simultaneously, this is also a significant drawback of this scale. Indeed, this makes the AIAS-4 a measure of positive attitudes to AI rather than a balanced measure of general attitudes to AI. It is most closely aligned to positive subscales of other AI attitude scales such as the GAAIS, and low scores should not be regarded as negative attitudes to AI, but lower agreement with statements that capture positive aspects of AI attitudes, which, data have shown, is different semantically. Despite the scale having only been published recently, it has been used in research on student attitudes towards AI (Hajam and Gahir 2024). Readers who would like to see the full set of items can find these in the open-access journal article by Grassini (2023, Sect. 2.1 therein), and should note that item 4 was dropped in the final version.

2.4.4 Attitudes Towards Artificial Intelligence Scale: ATTARI-12

The ATTARI-12 (Stein et al. 2024) was designed to address the perceived drawbacks of prior scales, among which were that for the ATAI, "the low number of items resulted in a notable lack of reliability" (Stein et al. 2024, p. 2), and the perceived inconvenience of the bi-dimensionality of the GAAIS. Stein et al. (2024) argue that negative attitudes are simply the polar opposite of positive attitudes, and that therefore a unidimensional scale is preferable, as it simplifies handling and is more economic during data acquisition. The authors generated 24 items and self-eliminated 12 of these prior to data collection for Study 1 in the US ($N = 490$ members of the general public; 56% male; scale in English,) and Study 2 in Germany ($N = 163$ at Time 1, $N = 160$ at Time 2, 26–36 days after Time 1, and $N = 150$ for participants at both times, of which 75% female; scale presented in German to a student sample).

Following Study 1, a number of CFA models were fitted on the positive and reverse-scored negative items, and the authors observed bi-dimensionality, and an initial poor fit for unidimensionality. However, they argued that the scale should nevertheless be seen as essentially unidimensional in line with the authors' intentions, basing this on a bifactor model with "item wording" as a factor and a general factor both contributing to the fit. It is noteworthy that all the items that loaded onto an additional factor labelled "item wording" were negative items (2, 4, 7, 8, 10, and 12). The authors argued that the "item wording" was a minor factor, and that there was an overarching general factor which was essentially unidimensional. The overall scale showed very strong internal consistency, Cronbach's $\alpha = 0.93$, a value that is potentially somewhat high, suggestive of a narrow construct. There were correlations with attitudes towards electronic personal assistants ($r = 0.60$) and with attitudes towards robots ($r = 0.68$), which were somewhat high for divergent validity, but which showed good convergent validity. The scale responses showed no evidence of being driven by social desirability bias.

In Study 2, the authors assessed test-re-test reliability between Time 1 and Time 2, and this was strong, $r = 0.804$. The scale once more showed strong internal consistency via Cronbach's alpha, T1: $\alpha = 0.91$; T2: $\alpha = 0.89$. The factor structure was not assessed in this sample. In Study 3, the authors replicated (Schepman and Rodway 2023; Kaya et al. 2024) findings that demonstrated associations between personality traits and AI attitudes, and extended these with additional psychological trait measures. Due to its recency, the scale has not yet been used in other published research.

Overall, the scale provides a quick and efficient way of testing AI attitudes, but users may encounter some issues. Because there was no EFA stage, the factor structure was imposed a priori, with the intention of finding a unidimensional scale, motivated by economy and convenience. However, at CFA, the single factor structure did not show a strong fit (e.g. $RMSEA = 0.15$), and there was evidence that all the negative items formed a separate factor, labelled as "item wording". Future users who perform CFA on their scale in their own samples may encounter manifestations of an underlying bi-dimensional construct, with positive and negative factors, as observed in the GAAIS, notwithstanding Stein et al.'s (2024) desire and drive to produce a unidimensional construct. If the data tell us that there is a level of independence between positive and negative attitudes towards AI, then it seems preferable for a measurement instrument to capture this, instead of attempting to eliminate it for the sake of simplicity or perceived economy. Readers who would like to inspect the scale items can find the ATTARI-12 in the Appendix of Stein et al. (2024), an open-access journal article.

2.5 Summary and Recommendations

Over recent years, several general AI attitude measurement scales (alongside more specific scales) have been developed. Each have their own balance of strengths and weaknesses, and prospective users should appraise themselves of these with regard to their own measurement requirements to choose the best scale for their purpose.

It is conceivable that additional scales will be developed. We would recommend that researchers investigate prior literature thoroughly before developing their measurement tools, because many lessons have been learnt since the development of the scales reported here, and it is useful to build on this learning to enhance the field, rather than to start de novo.

Further, because of the well-documented rapidly changing AI landscape, it is valuable if authors reporting scale development and validation report the time point of their data collection at the granularity of month(s) and year. That way other researchers can assess the state of AI development and spread through society at that timepoint and calibrate the data against other data collected in the same time period. This will aid the interpretation of the data, and it will be indispensable information for future meta-analyses or systematic reviews.

We have reviewed two bi-dimensional scales (GAAIS, ATAI) and two unidimensional scales (AIAS-4, ATTARI-12), and have pointed out the advantages of bi-dimensional scales in capturing the ambivalent attitudes that people hold towards AI. We recommend that researchers do not reduce underlying bi-dimensional AI attitudes to single constructs, on the assumption that negative and positive attitudes are simply the same thing with its polarity reversed. While it may save a few seconds of participants' time, and some researcher time in computing statistics, this saving may be a false economy. If attitudes towards AI are ambivalent, with people holding both positive and negative attitudes towards AI simultaneously, then a unidimensional scale cannot capture this. Shoehorning AI attitudes into a unidimensional measurement model for the sake of convenience or economy would seem contrary to the purpose of accurate measurement. Accurate measurement should be a priority for all scientists, including the many scientists who are currently fascinated by the rapid societal changes that AI is likely to bring. We recommend that they consider their choice of measurement instruments carefully. When selecting a measurement tool, factoring in cultural dimensions can be important. In some cultures, job losses or perceived existential threats may be less concerning than in other cultures. Similarly, thinking through the nature of the AI under investigation and its context is of growing importance. The IMPACT (Interaction of Modality-Person-Area-Culture-Transparency) framework (Chap. 1, this volume) aim to capture these other dimensions that are of key importance in AI attitudes, and due consideration to these factors when measuring AI attitudes can have a positive impact on our collective understanding.

We close this Chapter advising AI attitude researchers to use rigorous methods and meticulous documentation, alongside thorough reviews of the prior literature before embarking on new research in the burgeoning and exciting field of research of attitudes towards Artificial Intelligence.

References

Ada Lovelace Institute and The Alan Turing Institute (2023) How do people feel about AI? A nationally representative survey of public attitudes to artificial intelligence in Britain. https://adalovelaceinstitute.org/report/public-attitudes-ai

Albarracín D, Zanna MP, Johnson BT, Kumkale GT (2005) Attitudes: introduction and scope. In: Albarracín D, Johnson BT, Zanna MP (eds) The handbook of attitudes. Lawrence Erlbaum Associates Publishers, pp 3–19

Alessandro G, Dimitri O, Cristina B, Anna M (2024) The emotional impact of generative AI: negative emotions and perception of threat. Behav Inf Technol:1–18. https://doi.org/10.1080/0144929X.2024.2333933

Allen MS, Iliescu D, Greiff S (2022) Single item measures in psychological science. Eur J Psychol Assess. https://doi.org/10.1027/1015-5759/a000699

Bashkirova A, Krpan D (2024) Confirmation bias in AI-assisted decision-making: AI triage recommendations congruent with expert judgments increase psychologist trust and recommendation acceptance. Comput Hum Behav: Artif Hum:100066. https://doi.org/10.1016/j.chbah.2024.100066

Bellaiche L, Shahi R, Turpin MH, Ragnhildstveit A, Sprockett S, Barr N, Seli P (2023) Humans versus AI: whether and why we prefer human-created compared to AI-created artwork. Cogn Res: Principles Implications 8(1):42. https://doi.org/10.1186/s41235-023-00499-6

Bentley SV, Naughtin CK, McGrath MJ, Irons JL, Cooper PS (2024) The digital divide in action: how experiences of digital technology shape future relationships with artificial intelligence. AI and Ethics:1–15. https://doi.org/10.1007/s43681-024-00452-3

Bergdahl J, Latikka R, Celuch M, Savolainen I, Mantere ES, Savela N, Oksanen A (2023) Self-determination and attitudes toward artificial intelligence: cross-national and longitudinal perspectives. Telematics Inform 82:102013. https://doi.org/10.1016/j.tele.2023.102013

Bergkvist L, Rossiter JR (2007) The predictive validity of multiple-item versus single-item measures of the same constructs. J Mark Res 44(2):175–184. https://doi.org/10.1509/jmkr.44.2.175

Carolus A, Koch MJ, Straka S, Latoschik ME, Wienrich C (2023) MAILS-Meta AI literacy scale: development and testing of an AI literacy questionnaire based on well-founded competency models and psychological change-and meta-competencies. Comput Hum Behav: Artif Hum 1(2):100014. https://doi.org/10.1016/j.chbah.2023.100014

Centre for Ethics and Innovation (2024) Public attitudes to data and AI: tracker survey (Wave 3). https://www.gov.uk/government/publications/public-attitudes-to-data-and-ai-tracker-survey-wave-3/public-attitudes-to-data-and-ai-tracker-survey-wave-3

Darda K, Carre M, Cross E (2023) Value attributed to text-based archives generated by artificial intelligence. R Soc Open Sci 10(2):220915. https://doi.org/10.1098/rsos.220915

Diamantopoulos A, Sarstedt M, Fuchs C, Wilczynski P, Kaiser S (2012) Guidelines for choosing between multi-item and single-item scales for construct measurement: a predictive validity perspective. J Acad Mark Sci 40:434–449. https://doi.org/10.1007/s11747-011-0300-3

Dos Santos DP, Giese D, Brodehl S, Chon SH, Staab W, Kleinert R, Maintz D, Baeßler B (2019) Medical students' attitude toward artificial intelligence: a multicentre survey. Eur Radiol 29(4):1640–1646. https://doi.org/10.1007/s00330-018-5601-1

Eagly AH, Chaiken S (1993) The psychology of attitudes. Harcourt Brace Jovanovich

Fousiani K, Michelakis G, Minnigh PA, De Jonge KM (2024) Competitive organizational climate and artificial intelligence (AI) acceptance: the moderating role of leaders' power construal. Front Psychol 15:1359164. https://doi.org/10.3389/fpsyg.2024.1359164

Galindo-Domínguez H, Sainz De La Maza M, Campo L, Losada D (in press) Design and validation of a multidimensional scale for assessing teachers' perceptions towards artificial intelligence in education. Int J Learn Technol. https://doi.org/10.1504/IJLT.2023.10062094 [via https://www.researchgate.net/publication/377935914_Design_and_Validation_of_a_Multidimensional_Scale_for_Assessing_Teachers'_Perceptions_Towards_Artificial_Intelligence_in_Education]

Grassini S (2023) Development and validation of the AI attitude scale (AIAS-4): a brief measure of general attitude toward artificial intelligence. Front Psychol 14:1191628. https://doi.org/10.3389/fpsyg.2023.1191628

Guadamuz A (2024) A scanner darkly: copyright liability and exceptions in artificial intelligence inputs and outputs. GRUR Int 73(2):111–127. https://doi.org/10.1093/grurint/ikad140

Hadlington L, Binder J, Gardner S, Karanika-Murray M, Knight S (2023) The use of artificial intelligence in a military context: development of the attitudes toward AI in defense (AAID) scale. Front Psychol 14:1164810. https://doi.org/10.3389/fpsyg.2023.1164810

Hajam KB, Gahir S (2024) Unveiling the attitudes of university students toward artificial intelligence. J Educ Technol Syst 52(3):335–345. https://doi.org/10.1177/00472395231225920
Hayton JC, Allen DG, Scarpello V (2004) Factor retention decisions in exploratory factor analysis: a tutorial on parallel analysis. Organ Res Methods 7(2):191–205. https://doi.org/10.1177/1094428104263675
Helo P, Hao Y (2022) Artificial intelligence in operations management and supply chain management: an exploratory case study. Prod Plann Control 33(16):1573–1590. https://doi.org/10.1080/09537287.2021.1882690
Hu L, Bentler PM (1999) Cutoff criteria for fit indexes in covariance structure analysis: conventional criteria versus new alternatives. Struct Equ Modeling 6(1):1–55. https://doi.org/10.1080/10705519909540118
Hunter B, Hindocha S, Lee RW (2022) The role of artificial intelligence in early cancer diagnosis. Cancers 14(6):1524. https://doi.org/10.3390/cancers14061524
Kaya F, Aydin F, Schepman A, Rodway P, Yetişensoy O, Demir Kaya M (2024) The roles of personality traits, AI anxiety, and demographic factors in attitudes toward artificial intelligence. Int J Human-Computer Interact 40(2):497–514. https://doi.org/10.1080/10447318.2022.2151730
Lam SY, Chiang J, Parasuraman A (2008) The effects of the dimensions of technology readiness on technology acceptance: an empirical analysis. J Interact Mark 22(4):19–39. https://doi.org/10.1002/dir.20119
Laupichler MC, Aster A, Haverkamp N, Raupach T (2023) Development of the "scale for the assessment of non-experts' AI literacy"–an exploratory factor analysis. Comput Hum Behav Reports 12:100338. https://doi.org/10.1016/j.chbr.2023.100338
Lermann-Henestrosa A, Kimmerle J (forthcoming) Understanding and perception of automated text generation among the public: two surveys with representative samples in Germany. https://doi.org/10.21203/rs.3.rs-3614540/v1
Lim S, Schmälzle R (2024) The effect of source disclosure on evaluation of AI-generated messages: a two-part study. Comput Hum Behav: Artif Hum:100058. https://doi.org/10.1016/j.chbah.2024.100058
Lukić A, Kudelić N, Antičević V, Lazić-Mosler E, Glunčić V, Hren D, Lukić IK (2023) First-year nursing students' attitudes towards artificial intelligence: Cross-sectional multi-center study. Nurse Educ Pract 71:103735. https://doi.org/10.1016/j.nepr.2023.103735
Montag C, Ali R (forthcoming) Can we assess attitudes toward AI with single items? Associations with existing attitudes toward AI measures and trust in ChatGPT in two German speaking samples. https://doi.org/10.21203/rs.3.rs-3325511/v1
Montag C, Kraus J, Baumann M, Rozgonjuk D (2023) The propensity to trust in (automated) technology mediates the links between technology self-efficacy and fear and acceptance of artificial intelligence. Comput Hum Behav Reports 11:100315. https://doi.org/10.1016/j.chbr.2023.100315
Montag C, Ali R, Davis KL (2024c) Affective neuroscience theory and attitudes towards artificial intelligence. AI & Soc:1–8. https://doi.org/10.1007/s00146-023-01841-8
Montag C, Becker B, Li BJ (2024b) On trust in humans and trust in artificial intelligence: a study with samples from Singapore and Germany extending recent research. Comput Human Behav Artif Hum:100070. https://doi.org/10.1016/j.chbah.2024.100070
Montag C, Nakov P, Ali R (2024c) On the need to develop nuanced measures assessing attitudes towards AI and AI literacy in representative large-scale samples. AI & Society. https://doi.org/10.1007/s00146-024-01888-1
Park J, Woo SE, Kim J (2024) Attitudes towards artificial intelligence at work: Scale development and validation. J Occup Org Psychol. https://doi.org/10.1111/joop.12502
Rodway P, Schepman A (2023) The impact of adopting AI educational technologies on projected course satisfaction in university students. Comput Educ: Artificial Intelligence 5:100150. https://doi.org/10.1016/j.caeai.2023.100150

Rosen LD, Whaling K, Carrier LM, Cheever NA, Rokkum J (2013) The media and technology usage and attitudes scale: an empirical investigation. Comput Hum Behav 29:2501–2511. https://doi.org/10.1016/j.chb.2013.06.006
Schepman A, Rodway P (2020) Initial validation of the general attitudes towards Artificial Intelligence Scale. Comp Human Behav Reports 1:100014. https://doi.org/10.1016/j.chbr.2020.100014
Schepman A, Rodway P (2023) The General Attitudes towards Artificial Intelligence Scale (GAAIS): confirmatory validation and associations with personality, corporate distrust, and general trust. Int J Human-Comp Interact 39(13):2724–2741. https://doi.org/10.1080/10447318.2022.2085400
Sindermann C, Sha P, Zhou M, Wernicke J, Schmitt HS, Li M, Montag C (2021) Assessing the attitude towards artificial intelligence: introduction of a short measure in German, Chinese, and English language. KI-Künstliche Intelligenz 35(1):109–118. https://doi.org/10.1007/s13218-020-00689-0
Seo YH, Ahn JW (2022) The validity and reliability of the Korean version of the general attitudes towards artificial intelligence scale for nursing students. J Korean Acad Soc Nurs Educ 28(4):357–367. https://doi.org/10.5977/jkasne.2022.28.4.357
Stein JP, Messingschlager T, Gnambs T, Hutmacher F, Appel M (2024) Attitudes towards AI: measurement and associations with personality. Sci Rep 14(1):2909. https://doi.org/10.1038/s41598-024-53335-2
Tavakol M, Dennick R (2011) Making sense of Cronbach's alpha. Int J Med Educ 2:53–55. https://doi.org/10.5116/ijme.4dfb.8dfd
Tavakol M, Wetzel A (2020) Factor Analysis: a means for theory and instrument development in support of construct validity. Int J Med Educ 11:245–247. https://doi.org/10.5116/ijme.5f96.0f4a
Thurstone LL (1928) Attitudes can be measured. Am J Sociol 33:529–544. https://doi.org/10.1086/214483
van Wynsberghe A (2021) Sustainable AI: AI for sustainability and the sustainability of AI. AI Ethics 1:213–218. https://doi.org/10.1007/s43681-021-00043-6
Wang YY, Wang YS (2022) Development and validation of an artificial intelligence anxiety scale: an initial application in predicting motivated learning behavior. Interact Learn Environ 30(4):619–634. https://doi.org/10.1080/10494820.2019.1674887
Wang B, Rau PLP, Yuan T (2023) Measuring user competence in using artificial intelligence: validity and reliability of artificial intelligence literacy scale. Behav Inform Technol 42(9):1324–1337. https://doi.org/10.1080/0144929X.2022.2072768
Yurt E, Kasarci I (2024) A questionnaire of artificial intelligence use motives: a contribution to investigating the connection between AI and motivation. Int J Technol Educ (IJTE) 7(2):308–325. https://doi.org/10.46328/ijte.725

Chapter 3
Modalities of AI Operations and Their Impact on Users' Attitude Towards AI

Magnus Liebherr

Abstract Understanding modality in artificial intelligence is essential for grasping its varied applications and implications for human interaction. Modality encompasses dimensions like interactivity, adaptiveness, and explainability, each influencing user attitudes and adoption of AI systems. This chapter delves into how these facets shape attitudes towards AI, drawing from psychology frameworks to highlight the affective and cognitive components of user perceptions. Trust and acceptance emerge as critical factors intertwined with attitude, affecting intentions to use AI technologies. The chapter navigates through diverse modalities—from interactive versus non-interactive to personalized versus generalized—illuminating their nuanced impacts on user attitudes and societal acceptance of AI. Through this lens, it underscores the multidimensional nature of AI modality and its profound implications for fostering responsible AI deployment and enhancing user engagement.

Keywords User-centric AI · Modality · Attitude · Trust · Acceptance

Modality in the context of artificial intelligence (AI) refers to the diverse ways in which the technology is applied and how it intersects with human agency. This includes considering various facets such as interactivity, adaptiveness, and explainability. Understanding these dimensions is crucial for comprehending AI's role in shaping human interactions with technology. Each dimension uniquely contributes to the overall user experience and perception of AI systems, influencing attitudes, behaviors, and adoption patterns. By exploring these dimensions, we gain deeper insights into the complexities of human-AI interactions and the broader societal implications of AI deployment. Within the IMPACT model (see Chap. 1), modality emerges as a pivotal variable shaping attitudes toward AI and, consequently, the overall well-being of individuals within the context of AI (Montag et al. 2024b). In the present chapter, I embark on an exploration of the various facets of AI modality,

M. Liebherr (✉)
University Duisburg-Essen, Duisburg, Germany
e-mail: magnus.liebherr@uni-due.de

C. Montag and R. Ali (eds.), *The Impact of Artificial Intelligence on Societies*, Studies in Neuroscience, Psychology and Behavioral Economics,
https://doi.org/10.1007/978-3-031-70355-3_3

from interactive versus non-interactive to reactive versus proactive, unravelling their significance and interplay in shaping users' attitude towards AI.

Attitude towards AI is a person's general evaluation or feeling towards the technology. According to social psychology literature, attitude consists of both affective and cognitive components. The affective component relates to the emotional response or the extent to which a person likes the object of thought (McGuire 1985). Conversely, the cognitive component encompasses an individual's specific beliefs and thoughts about the object (Bagozzi and Burnkrant 1979, 1985). Attitude towards AI is deeply intertwined with related constructs such as trust (Montag et al. 2023), acceptance (Yang and Yoo 2004), and intention to use (Sindermann et al. 2021). Beyond the connection between trust and attitude (Montag et al. 2023), path analyses have revealed that trust is a significant predictor of the intention to use AI, operating through perceived usefulness and participants' attitudes toward the technology (Choung et al. 2023). Furthermore, within the framework of the Technology Acceptance Model (Davis 1985), user attitude is identified as a key variable mediating the relationship between perceived ease of use/perceived usefulness and the intention to use/accept a technology (Zhu et al. 2012). However, when distinguishing between the two components of attitude, cognitive attitude has emerged as a significant mediator, whereas the affective component appears to play a more subordinate role (Yang and Yoo 2004). Research across different samples demonstrates that a more positive attitude towards AI is linked to an increased willingness to utilize AI products. In contrast, a more negative attitude corresponds with a reduced willingness to adopt these technologies (Sindermann et al. 2021).

As mentioned, attitude towards AI is shaped by different factors, such as person-centered variables, area specific attributes, modalities, cultural aspects, and the levels of transparency (Montag et al. 2024b). The concept of modality encompasses multiple sub-facets that are closely interlinked (e.g., personalized/generalized and static/dynamic) and will be explored in the following (see Fig. 3.1). Notably, these sub-facets should not be viewed as binary opposites. Rather, the focus should be on the characteristics and their impact on attitudes towards AI technologies, which is the focus of interest within this chapter.

3.1 Interactive Versus Non-interactive

Interactive AI systems engage users in dynamic and responsive interactions, adapting to user inputs and providing real-time feedback. These systems are prevalent in various applications, including healthcare (Lai et al. 2021; Montag et al. 2024a), shipping (Veitch and Alsos 2022), and organizations (Raftopoulos and Hamari 2023). By facilitating more meaningful, adaptable, and personalized interactions, interactive AI systems significantly enhance user satisfaction and adoption. Examples of interactive AI include virtual assistants, chatbots, healthcare AI applications, and gaming AI.

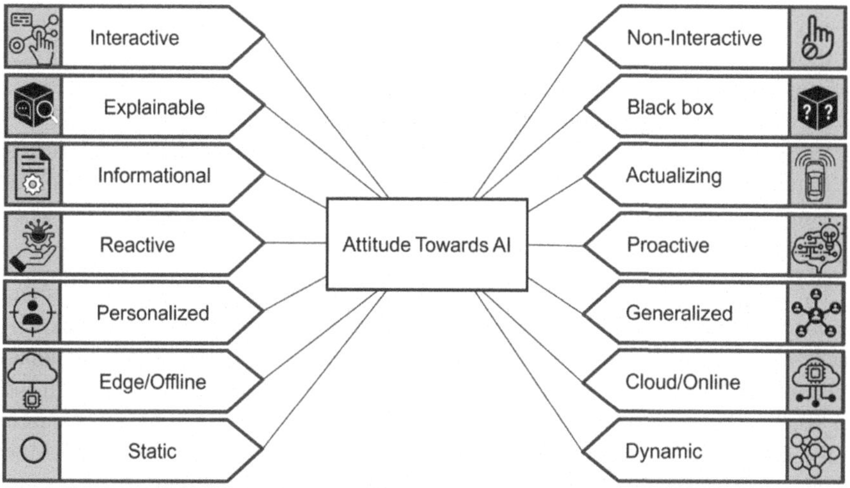

Fig. 3.1 Different modalities of AI Operations and their impact on users' attitude towards AI

- Virtual Assistants: AI-powered virtual assistants like Apple's Siri, Amazon's Alexa, and Google Assistant engage in conversational interactions, responding to voice commands and controlling smart home devices.
- Chatbots: Customer service chatbots used by companies provide real-time assistance, answering queries, helping with product searches, and resolving issues through text-based conversations.
- Healthcare AI: Systems like IBM Watson Health interact with medical professionals by analyzing patient data and offering diagnostic and treatment recommendations.
- Gaming AI: AI in video games, such as NPCs (non-player characters) in "The Elder Scrolls V: Skyrim" or "Red Dead Redemption 2," respond to player actions, creating immersive gaming experiences.

Non-interactive AI systems, on the other hand, operate based on pre-defined rules or algorithms without user interaction. These systems are less flexible and provide limited user engagement, often resulting in reduced user satisfaction and lower adoption rates. Examples of non-interactive AI include predictive analytics, automated fraud detection, recommendation engines, and image/speech recognition.

- Predictive Analytics: AI systems used in predictive analytics, like those for stock market forecasting or weather prediction, analyze data and provide predictions without user interaction. These systems run algorithms on historical data to generate forecasts.
- Automated Fraud Detection: Many financial institutions use AI systems to detect fraudulent transactions. These systems analyze transaction patterns and flag anomalies without interacting with users, operating in the background to ensure security.

- Recommendation Engines: Non-interactive recommendation engines, such as those used by Netflix or Amazon, analyze user data and browsing history to suggest movies, TV shows, or products. While they personalize recommendations, they do not engage in real-time conversations with users.
- Image and Speech Recognition: AI systems used for image and speech recognition, like those in security surveillance systems or voice-to-text applications, process inputs and provide outputs without interactive engagement. They recognize patterns and convert them into usable data.

By responding to user input in real-time and adapting to user preferences and behavior, interactive AI systems can create more immersive and engaging experiences. In this context, the discussion surrounding anthropomorphism and the human likeness of AI agents has been a prominent topic of exploration (Fink 2012; Kim and Im 2023). The most well-known hypothesis that has garnered significant attention in the field is the concept of the uncanny valley, first proposed in the 1970s (Mori 1970). The uncanny valley posits that as humanoid robots or animated characters become increasingly lifelike, there is a point at which their resemblance to humans becomes unsettling rather than endearing. This unsettling feeling arises when artificial entities closely mimic human appearance and behavior but still exhibit subtle flaws or deviations from natural human attributes. In other words, as the realism of artificial entities approaches that of humans, there is a dip in the emotional response from observers, creating a "valley" of discomfort before acceptance is regained at a higher level of similarity (Kätsyri et al. 2015) (see also Fig. 3.2).

Recent empirical studies have shed light on the significance of imbuing AI chatbots with human-like competencies, particularly in relation to user trust and engagement (Chandra et al. 2022). The findings underscore the importance of conversational skills, emotional intelligence, and cognitive abilities akin to those of humans. By exhibiting traits such as empathy, adaptability, and responsiveness, interactive

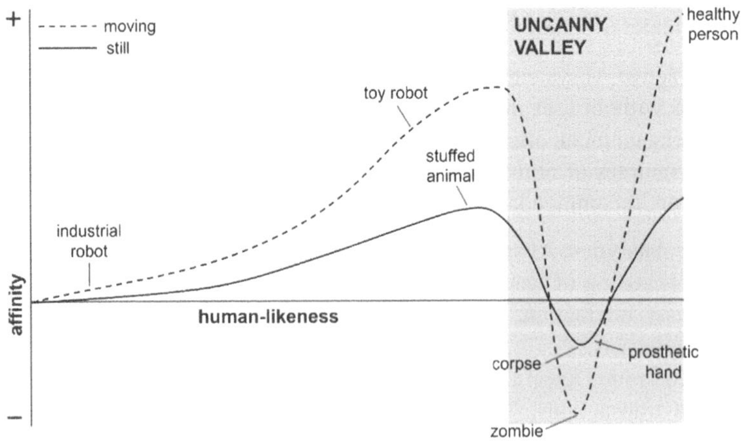

Fig. 3.2 Mori's uncanny valley, adapted from Kätsyri et al. (2015)

AI systems can foster deeper connections with users, leading to increased trust, satisfaction, and overall engagement with the technology (Huang and Rust 2018).

3.2 Explainable Versus Black Box

Explainable refers to the ability of AI systems to elucidate their reasoning processes in a manner understandable to humans (Gunning et al. 2019). In recent years, the pursuit of explainability within the realm of AI has emerged as a promising endeavor, aiming to demystify the often-opaque nature of AI algorithms. By shedding light on the inner workings of AI models, explainability endeavors to transcend the 'black box' paradigm, thereby enhancing levels of accountability and transparency in AI-driven decision-making (see Fig. 3.3).

However, in the realm of AI, there exists a spectrum of modalities between purely Explainable AI and Black box models. These include global versus local explanations as well as various explanation classes. Global explanations provide an overarching understanding of the entire model's behavior, while local explanations focus on elucidating specific predictions or decisions made by the AI. Additionally, different explanation classes, such as example-based explanations, feature importance, and surrogate models, offer diverse ways to design and operate AI systems to enhance their interpretability and usability (Guidotti et al. 2018).

Explanations have been shown to be crucial in fostering trust among users and stakeholders, as it allows for a deeper understanding of how AI arrives at its conclusions, potentially uncovering biases, errors, or unintended consequences (Adadi and Berrada 2018). Thus, explainability serves not only as a technical imperative but also as an ethical imperative, facilitating responsible and trustworthy deployment of AI systems across various domains. Highlighting the importance of providing accessible and easily understandable explanations to users has been demonstrated to be critical in fostering reliability, trust, and human control while mitigating fear, and influencing the intention to use AI (Das and Rad 2020; Shin 2021). For instance, within the realm of healthcare, prior studies underscore the potential of explainable modelling to enhance the trustworthiness of artificial intelligence. However, it is argued that the

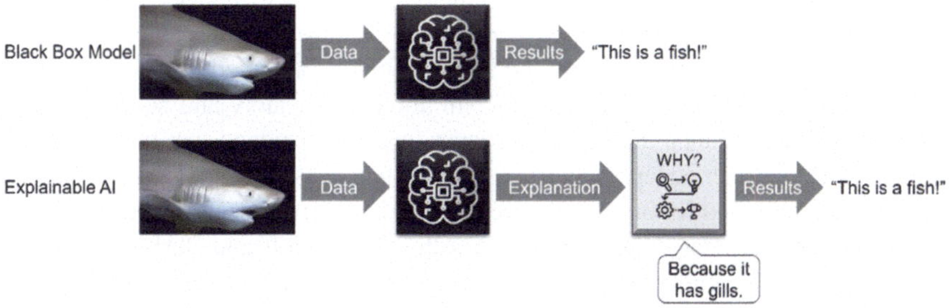

Fig. 3.3 Black box versus explainable AI

rationale behind the demand for explainability determines what aspects should be elucidated, thereby influencing the relative importance of interpretability and fidelity (Markus et al. 2021). Taking this aspect further, previous critiques have consistently focused on the complexity and clarity of explanations, often indicating that the information might be exclusive to experts. This presents substantial obstacles for lay users, underscoring the imperative for forthcoming endeavors to tackle this concern and improve accessibility for all (Mittelstadt et al. 2019).

3.3 Informational Versus Actualizing

Informational AI systems provide users with data, insights, and recommendations without taking direct actions. These systems, such as recommendation engines and data analysis tools, assist users in making informed decisions based on the information provided. The key aspect of informational AI is its role as an advisor rather than an actor. For example, a recommendation engine on an e-commerce website suggests products based on user preferences, but it does not purchase items on behalf of the user. Users appreciate the support provided by recommender systems without feeling that they are losing control over important decisions (Sinha and Swearingen 2001). Together with the transparency and passive nature of the systems, informational AI can positively influence user attitudes, trust, and acceptance (Beldad et al. 2010; Benbasat and Wang 2005). Users generally perceive these systems as improving their decision-making processes while allowing them to retain control over the outcomes (Tintarev and Masthoff 2010). Based on the Self-Determination Theory, I suggest that the perceived autonomy in informational AI is a key aspect leading to higher levels of trust and acceptance, as users feel they retain ultimate control over their actions (Deci and Ryan 1985).

Actualizing AI systems, in contrast, go beyond providing information and take direct actions based on their analysis. Examples include autonomous vehicles, robotic process automation, and AI-driven healthcare interventions. These systems not only analyze data but also make decisions and execute tasks autonomously. According to Affordance Actualization Theory, users develop mental models that shape their expectations and interactions with these systems (Leonardi 2013). In the context of AI, users may anticipate an autonomous vehicle's capability to interpret and navigate traffic conditions, aligning with their perceived affordances of efficiency and reliability (Keller et al. 2019). Based on the theory it can be assumed that control to AI systems can provoke anxiety and scepticism about their safety and accountability, affecting user acceptance and trust. However, previous evidence on the impact of actualizing AI on user acceptance, trust, and attitudes has shown mixed results. On one hand, the potential for increased efficiency and effectiveness in various tasks can lead to higher acceptance (Glikson and Woolley 2020; Hoff and Bashir 2015). On the other hand, the relinquishing of control to an AI system can provoke fear and anxiety among users, particularly regarding the reliability and safety of these systems (Zhan et al. 2023). Studies have shown that users are more likely to accept and trust

AI systems that offer transparency and explainability, regardless of whether they are informational or actualizing (Shin 2021). However, the initial stages of interaction with actualizing AI systems can be fraught with uncertainty and scepticism. Moreover, the adaptive capabilities of actualizing AI can either mitigate or exacerbate these fears. Systems that can adapt to user feedback and demonstrate reliability over time are more likely to be trusted (Schneider and Kummert 2021), which I will discuss later on under the paragraph "static versus dynamic/adaptive". Having examined the impact of informational and actualizing AI on user attitudes, fear, and acceptance, it is essential to delve deeper into how AI systems can be tailored to individual users.

3.4 Personalized Versus Generalized

Personalized AI systems tailor their responses, recommendations, and actions based on individual user preferences, behaviors, and needs. Their adaptive nature allows them to actively solicit and incorporate user feedback to iteratively adjust their algorithms, features, and functionalities. By analyzing user interactions, mental states, preferences, and satisfaction levels, these systems fine-tune their recommendations, predictions, and decision-making processes, thereby better aligning with user expectations and goals. Furthermore, personalized AI systems enhance user experience by providing customized interactions, such as personalized marketing, individualized learning, and adaptive healthcare. Generalized AI systems, on the other hand, offer standardized responses and solutions that apply broadly to all users. These systems are less flexible and may not meet the specific needs of individual users, resulting in lower user satisfaction and engagement. Prominent examples include voice assistants (e.g., amazon alexa, google assistant) or search engines (e.g., google). To deliver effective personalization and meet users' needs and requirements, it is essential to gather sufficient information about their preferences (Ahmad et al. 2018; Maroto-Gómez et al. 2023; Tapus et al. 2008).

The relationship between technology personalization and user responses, such as trust, attitude, and adoption, has been extensively studied across various domains (Adomavicius and Tuzhilin 2005; Pataranutaporn et al. 2021; Sundar 2020). Research has consistently shown that when users perceive technology as personalized to their needs and preferences, their trust in the technology increases, leading to more positive attitudes and a higher likelihood of adoption. For instance, personalized web services and e-commerce platforms have demonstrated that users who receive tailored recommendations are more likely to trust the platform, exhibit positive attitudes towards it, and continue using it (Tam and Ho 2006). Similarly, personalized marketing strategies have been shown to enhance user engagement and satisfaction, thereby fostering a sense of loyalty and trust towards the service provider (Bleier and Eisenbeiss 2015). In the context of personalized AI applications, educational platforms that adapt content and teaching methods to individual students' learning styles have been shown to improve learning outcomes and user satisfaction (Khan et al. 2017). In healthcare, AI systems that provide personalized treatment recommendations based on patient data have also demonstrated increased patient trust and adherence to treatment plans (Shortliffe and Sepúlveda 2018).

The impact of personalization in AI applications can be explained by various theories. For instance, the Technology Acceptance Model posits that perceived usefulness and perceived ease of use are the primary factors influencing technology acceptance (Davis et al. 1989). In the context of AI technologies, studies describe a significant impact of tailored recommendations and responses that more effectively meet individual needs on perceived usefulness (Liu and Tao 2022). Furthermore, the Unified Theory of Acceptance and Use of Technology integrates several models to explain intentions to use technology and subsequent usage behavior, focusing on performance expectancy, effort expectancy, social influence, and facilitating conditions (Venkatesh et al. 2003). Based on the theory, it can be argued that performance expectancy and effort expectancy in AI applications can be enhanced by delivering more relevant and efficient user experiences. In addition, social influence can also be affected when users perceive personalized AI systems as being endorsed or used by their peers (Venkatesh et al. 2012). From a more fundamental standpoint, the cognitive dissonance theory provides further explanations for the impact of personalized information. The theory posits that individuals strive for internal consistency and will change their attitudes or beliefs to reduce cognitive dissonance (Festinger 1957). Based on the theory, we can assume that personalized information can reduce cognitive dissonance by aligning content with the user's existing beliefs and preferences, thereby increasing trust and acceptance. Furthermore, the Self-Determination Theory emphasizes the role of intrinsic motivation in driving human behavior, focusing on autonomy, competence, and relatedness (Deci and Ryan 2000). Personalized information can enhance feelings of autonomy and competence by providing content that is relevant and empowering, leading to higher trust and acceptance (Fink et al. 2024; Sankaran and Markopoulos 2021).

While personalization offers clear benefits, it also raises concerns regarding the information used by the system, privacy issues, and potential misuse of data (Meurisch and Mühlhäuser 2021). This becomes particularly critical when considering vulnerable groups such as children or individuals with disabilities, as they may be more susceptible to the risks associated with data privacy and security. For a more comprehensive assessment, it is crucial to evaluate the types of data required for effective personalisation, which in turn depend on the specific context in which the AI is used. For example, a distinction can be made between personalised AI applications that are tailored to individual preferences (e.g. preferred music genres), specific needs (e.g. dietary restrictions), cognitive abilities (e.g. intellect), and the user's current emotional state. By understanding and delineating these dimensions, we can better navigate the balance between the benefits of personalized AI and the protection of user privacy and security.

Generalized AI applications frequently prioritize popular trends or majority opinions over individualized information. This prioritization is evident in various platforms, such as social media, where algorithms often highlight and promote content that is already popular or trending. For example, on social media feeds, posts with higher engagement metrics like likes, shares, and comments are algorithmically boosted to maximize visibility. While this approach can enhance user engagement and interaction with content, it also raises significant concerns regarding its impact on individual behaviors and attitudes. By emphasizing popular content, AI-driven systems may inadvertently steer users towards conforming to prevailing societal norms and dominant viewpoints. This phenomenon occurs because users are more likely to encounter and engage with content that aligns with popular trends, potentially reinforcing existing beliefs and attitudes.

The influence on individual behaviors and mindsets is multifaceted. Firstly, repeated exposure to popular content can create a perception of consensus or majority opinion, leading users to adopt or reinforce their views in line with what is presented as widely accepted (Bond et al. 2012; Centola 2010). This subtle influence can shape perceptions of social norms and expectations, affecting how individuals perceive their own beliefs and behaviors relative to those of others. Moreover, the prioritization of popular content can impact user trust and acceptance of the information presented (Bakshy et al. 2015). Users may perceive the AI algorithms as steering content in ways that prioritize popularity over accuracy or diversity of viewpoints. This perception can undermine trust in the platform and reduce acceptance of the information being disseminated, especially if users feel that their individual preferences or diverse perspectives are not adequately represented.

3.5 Reactive Versus Proactive

Reactive AI systems respond to specific inputs or stimuli from users or the environment, providing appropriate responses or actions. These systems are designed to react to situations as they occur, such as virtual assistants responding to voice commands or customer service chatbots addressing user queries. In recent years, proactive AI systems have been on the rise and promise to anticipate requires and take pre-emptive actions without explicit user input (Pejovic and Musolesi 2015). These systems, like predictive maintenance in industrial settings or personalized content delivery, enhance user experience by addressing needs before they arise. This shift from reactive to proactive AI systems entails higher levels of intelligence, adaptability, and user engagement (Bickmore et al. 2013; De Visser et al. 2017; DeLone and McLean 2003; Hui et al. 2023) leading to lower user acceptance and lower adoption of the technology (Michalco et al. 2015). Notably, the degree of acceptance is significantly influenced by the level of proactive support, with increased openness observed at lower levels of support. Participants' preferences for the level of proactive support depend on various factors, including personality, socio-demographic characteristics, and the specific use case (Meurisch et al. 2020). Based on these findings, I suggest that future developments in proactive AI systems should focus on being intelligible and adaptable to different support areas, user characteristics, and varying levels of privacy affinity. This consideration on adaptive systems will be further explored in the next subchapter.

3.6 Static Versus Dynamic/Adaptive

Static AI systems operate based on fixed rules and algorithms, providing consistent and predictable outputs. These systems are less flexible and may struggle to adapt to changing conditions or user needs. Dynamic AI systems, however, adapt their behavior, strategies, and decision-making processes in real-time, responding to changing circumstances, user feedback, and evolving data landscapes. They enhance user experience by offering more relevant, timely, and accurate responses, fostering higher levels of trust and acceptance (de Visser and Parasuraman 2011; Hajek et al. 2013; Schneider and Kummert 2021). For instance, in autonomous vehicles, adaptive AI algorithms can adjust driving behaviors based on varying factors such as road conditions, traffic patterns, and weather changes, ensuring safe and efficient navigation. Similarly, in healthcare, adaptive AI models modify treatment recommendations in response to patients' evolving health statuses and medical histories, improving the dynamic character of care interventions. Adaptive AI technologies actively solicit and incorporate user feedback to iteratively adjust their algorithms, features, and functionalities. Analyzing various external and internal factors allows these systems to fine-tune their recommendations, predictions, and decision-making processes, thereby better aligning with user expectations and goals. Adaptive AI systems demonstrate the capacity to assimilate and leverage new data effectively as the volume and variety of data sources expand. Employing techniques such as incremental learning and transfer learning, these systems can incorporate fresh data streams and update their models accordingly. By staying abreast of emerging trends, patterns, and insights, adaptive AI technologies deliver more accurate predictions, insights, and recommendations, enhancing decision-making and problem-solving capabilities across various domains. The adaptiveness of AI systems fosters a collaborative and dynamic interaction between humans and machines, rendering it the preferred mode of interaction with AI systems. This preference finds validation in prior empirical research, which demonstrates a heightened level of trust (Schneider and Kummert 2021) and acceptance (Hajek et al. 2013) in adaptive systems compared to those with fixed autonomy levels. Participants in these studies consistently valued the AI assistant's ability to anticipate and actively engage in supportive actions, particularly in contexts where such adaptability was deemed appropriate. Moreover, operating within an adaptive framework is associated with increased self-assurance and a notable reduction in users' workload, underscoring the tangible benefits of embracing adaptivity in human-AI collaboration (de Visser and Parasuraman 2011). In the realm Adaptive Cruise Control systems, AI technologies enhance system's ability to process sensor data make predictive decisions, and dynamically adjust to varying driving environments. In this context previous studies highlighted the relevance of mental models as adaptive systems evolve over time (Beggiato and Krems 2013). Furthermore, mental models—internal representations that individuals form about how systems work—play a significant role in how users interact with and trust adaptive technologies (Johnson-Laird 2004). When users' mental models align well with the actual functioning of an adaptive system, they are more likely to use the system effectively and trust its decisions, which has been shown in different contexts such as virtual assistant systems (Tenhundfeld et al. 2021). In the context of adaptive systems, this alignment is dynamic and must be continuously managed. As the system changes and improves through learning from new data, users need to update their mental models to reflect these changes. This ongoing adaptation can be challenging but is essential for maintaining user trust and ensuring optimal use of the technology. Moreover, discrepancies between users' mental models and the system's behavior can lead to misunderstandings, misuse, and reduced trust (Beggiato and Krems 2013). For example, if an adaptive cruise control system makes unexpected adjustments that the driver does not understand, the driver may become wary of using the system, potentially disengaging it or overriding its decisions.

Within the present section I focused increasingly on the influence of the level of adaptation with regard to changing circumstances, and evolving data landscapes. Adaptation to user feedback—as further component of adaptation—involves aspects that have already been discussed in the context of personalisation.

3.7 Edge/Offline Versus Cloud/Online

Edge AI systems process data locally on devices, reducing latency and improving real-time performance. These systems are particularly useful for applications that require immediate response, such as autonomous vehicles, industrial automation and smart home devices that operate primarily offline. Cloud AI systems, however, rely on centralized online servers for data processing and storage, enabling more complex computations and large-scale data analysis. These systems are beneficial for applications requiring extensive computational power and data integration, such as big data analytics and AI-as-a-service.

The extent to which data are collected, stored, and utilized online/in cloud systems is directly correlated with privacy concerns, encompassing individuals' apprehensions about their personal information. This concept, studied for decades by scholars across diverse fields, significantly impacts users' trust in technology and plays a pivotal role in shaping their willingness to engage with it (Dhagarra et al. 2020; Harborth and Pape 2020; Keszey 2020; Lutz et al. 2018; Maseeh et al. 2021). Alongside classic technology acceptance antecedents (e.g., perceived ease of use, perceived usefulness), customers' privacy concerns are described as influencing their attitudes towards and usage of applications (Faqih 2016; Luna Cortés and Royo Vela 2013). Additional support comes from the privacy calculus theory, a framework used to explain how individuals decide whether to disclose personal information (Culnan and Armstrong 1999; Laufer and Wolfe 1977). The theory is often utilized to examine online privacy practices, such as users' decisions regarding sharing data on social media or e-commerce platforms (Jozani et al. 2020; Ozturk et al. 2017). In light of these considerations, the integration of cloud systems amplifies these dynamics, underscoring the need for robust privacy protections, transparency, and user control over data (Dinev and Hart 2005; Tang et al. 2008). This holistic approach is crucial for fostering trust and promoting the responsible use of AI technologies, a significance that becomes even more pronounced when considering personalized AI applications.

3.8 Summary

In my exploration of AI modality, I have traversed a landscape rich with diversity, spanning from the foundational aspects of availability to the perceptible tangibility of AI systems. Each facet of modality contributes uniquely to the intricate dynamics of human-AI interactions, shaping user experiences and perceptions in profound ways across various domains, including robotics, embedded systems, chatbots, virtual assistants, and more. Throughout this chapter, it has become evident how intricately interconnected these modalities are. For example, the influence of edge versus cloud-based systems largely hinges on the amount of personal information being processed, which is intricately linked to the degree of AI personalization. The broad variance of AI-based systems, ranging from the physical presence of robots to the virtual interactions facilitated by chatbots and virtual assistants, highlights the pivotal role that modality plays in navigating the complexities of AI deployment across different applications. Within the IMPACT model, modality emerges as a pivotal factor in shaping attitudes toward artificial intelligence and, consequently, the overall well-being of individuals within the context of AI or broader human well-being (Montag et al. 2024b). By understanding and embracing the nuances of AI modality in diverse domains, we can foster responsible AI deployment, enhance user trust, and promote equitable access to AI technologies tailored to specific needs and contexts. As we conclude our exploration, we recognize the ongoing evolution of AI systems and the ever-changing dynamics of human-AI interactions across different applications. This chapter has shed light on the intricate interplay of AI modality and its significance in shaping the future of technology and society at large. Through continued research, dialogue, and collaboration, we can harness the transformative potential of AI while safeguarding against potential risks and pitfalls, ultimately creating a more inclusive, transparent, and ethically grounded AI system for all.

References

Adadi A, Berrada M (2018) Peeking inside the black-box: a survey on explainable artificial intelligence (XAI). IEEE Access 6:52138–52160

Adomavicius G, Tuzhilin A (2005) Toward the next generation of recommender systems: a survey of the state-of-the-art and possible extensions. IEEE Trans Knowl Data Eng 17(6):734–749

Ahmad BI, Hare C, Singh H, Shabani A, Lindsay B, Skrypchuk L, Langdon P, Godsill S (2018) Selection facilitation schemes for predictive touch with mid-air pointing gestures in automotive displays. In: Proceedings of the 10th international conference on automotive user interfaces and interactive vehicular applications

Bagozzi RP, Burnkrant RE (1979) Attitude organization and the attitude–behavior relationship. J Pers Soc Psychol 37(6):913
Bagozzi RP, Burnkrant RE (1985) Attitude organization and the attitude-behavior relation: a reply to Dillon and Kumar. J Pers Soc Psychol 49:47–57
Bakshy E, Messing S, Adamic LA (2015) Exposure to ideologically diverse news and opinion on Facebook. Science 348(6239):1130–1132
Beggiato M, Krems JF (2013) The evolution of mental model, trust and acceptance of adaptive cruise control in relation to initial information. Transport Res F: Traffic Psychol Behav 18:47–57
Beldad A, De Jong M, Steehouder M (2010) How shall I trust the faceless and the intangible? A literature review on the antecedents of online trust. Comput Hum Behav 26(5):857–869
Benbasat I, Wang W (2005) Trust in and adoption of online recommendation agents. J Assoc Inf Syst 6(3):4
Bickmore TW, Vardoulakis LMP, Schulman D (2013) Tinker: a relational agent museum guide. Auton Agent Multi-Agent Syst 27:254–276
Bleier A, Eisenbeiss M (2015) The importance of trust for personalized online advertising. J Retail 91(3):390–409
Bond RM, Fariss CJ, Jones JJ, Kramer AD, Marlow C, Settle JE, Fowler JH (2012) A 61-million-person experiment in social influence and political mobilization. Nature 489(7415):295–298
Centola D (2010) The spread of behavior in an online social network experiment. Science 329(5996):1194–1197
Chandra S, Shirish A, Srivastava SC (2022) To be or not to be... human? Theorizing the role of human-like competencies in conversational artificial intelligence agents. J Manag Inf Syst 39(4):969–1005
Choung H, David P, Ross A (2023) Trust in AI and its role in the acceptance of AI technologies. Int J Human-Comp Interact 39(9):1727–1739
Culnan MJ, Armstrong PK (1999) Information privacy concerns, procedural fairness, and impersonal trust: an empirical investigation. Organ Sci 10(1):104–115
Das A, Rad P (2020) Opportunities and challenges in explainable artificial intelligence (xai): a survey. arXiv preprint arXiv:2006.11371
Davis FD (1985) A technology acceptance model for empirically testing new end-user information systems: theory and results. Ph.D. Thesis, Massachusetts Institute of Technology
Davis FD, Bagozzi RP, Warshaw PR (1989) User acceptance of computer technology: a comparison of two theoretical models. Manage Sci 35(8):982–1003
de Visser E, Parasuraman R (2011) Adaptive aiding of human-robot teaming: effects of imperfect automation on performance, trust, and workload. J Cogn Eng Decis Making 5(2):209–231
De Visser EJ, Monfort SS, Goodyear K, Lu L, O'Hara M, Lee MR, Parasuraman R, Krueger F (2017) A little anthropomorphism goes a long way: Effects of oxytocin on trust, compliance, and team performance with automated agents. Hum Factors 59(1):116–133
Deci EL, Ryan RM (1985) The general causality orientations scale: self-determination in personality. J Res Pers 19(2):109–134
Deci EL, Ryan RM (2000) The" what" and" why" of goal pursuits: human needs and the self-determination of behavior. Psychol Inq 11(4):227–268
DeLone WH, McLean ER (2003) The DeLone and McLean model of information systems success: a ten-year update. J Manag Inf Syst 19(4):9–30
Dhagarra D, Goswami M, Kumar G (2020) Impact of trust and privacy concerns on technology acceptance in healthcare: an Indian perspective. Int J Med Informatics 141:104164
Dinev T, Hart P (2005) Internet privacy concerns and social awareness as determinants of intention to transact. Int J Electron Commer 10(2):7–29
Faqih KM (2016) An empirical analysis of factors predicting the behavioral intention to adopt Internet shopping technology among non-shoppers in a developing country context: does gender matter? J Retail Consum Serv 30:140–164
Festinger L (1957) 17. A theory of cognitive dissonance. Evanston, IL: Row, Peterson

Fink J (2012) Anthropomorphism and human likeness in the design of robots and human-robot interaction. In: Proceedings, Social robotics: 4th international conference, ICSR 2012, Chengdu, China, October 29–31, 2012
Fink L, Newman L, Haran U (2024) Let me decide: Increasing user autonomy increases recommendation acceptance. Comput Hum Behav 156:108244
Glikson E, Woolley AW (2020) Human trust in artificial intelligence: review of empirical research. Acad Manag Ann 14(2):627–660
Guidotti R, Monreale A, Ruggieri S, Turini F, Giannotti F, Pedreschi D (2018) A survey of methods for explaining black box models. ACM Comp Surv (CSUR) 51(5):1–42
Gunning D, Stefik M, Choi J, Miller T, Stumpf S, Yang G-Z (2019) XAI—Explainable artificial intelligence. Sci Robot 4(37):eaay7120
Hajek W, Gaponova I, Fleischer K, Krems J (2013) Workload-adaptive cruise control–a new generation of advanced driver assistance systems. Transport Res F: Traffic Psychol Behav 20:108–120
Harborth D, Pape S (2020) How privacy concerns, trust and risk beliefs, and privacy literacy influence users' intentions to use privacy-enhancing technologies: the case of Tor. ACM SIGMIS Database 51(1):51–69
Hoff KA, Bashir M (2015) Trust in automation: Integrating empirical evidence on factors that influence trust. Hum Factors 57(3):407–434
Huang M-H, Rust RT (2018) Artificial intelligence in service. J Serv Res 21(2):155–172
Hui Z, Khan AN, Chenglong Z, Khan NA (2023) When service quality is enhanced by human–artificial intelligence interaction: an examination of anthropomorphism, responsiveness from the perspectives of employees and customers. Int J Human–Comput Interact:1–16
Johnson-Laird PN (2004) The history of mental models. In: Psychology of reasoning. Psychology Press, pp 189–222
Jozani M, Ayaburi E, Ko M, Choo K-KR (2020) Privacy concerns and benefits of engagement with social media-enabled apps: a privacy calculus perspective. Comput Hum Behav 107:106260
Kätsyri J, Förger K, Mäkäräinen M, Takala T (2015) A review of empirical evidence on different uncanny valley hypotheses: support for perceptual mismatch as one road to the valley of eeriness. Front Psychol 6:113465
Keller R, Stohr A, Fridgen G, Lockl J, Rieger A (2019) Affordance-experimentation-actualization theory in artificial intelligence research: a predictive maintenance story. In: 40th International conference on information systems
Keszey T (2020) Behavioural intention to use autonomous vehicles: systematic review and empirical extension. Transp Res Part C: Emerg Technol 119:102732
Khan A, Egbue O, Palkie B, Madden J (2017) Active learning: engaging students to maximize learning in an online course. Electron J e-learning 15(2):107–115
Kim J, Im I (2023) Anthropomorphic response: understanding interactions between humans and artificial intelligence agents. Comput Hum Behav 139:107512
Lai Y, Kankanhalli A, Ong D (2021) Human-AI collaboration in healthcare: a review and research agenda. Proc. 54th Hawaii Int Conf Syst Sci
Laufer RS, Wolfe M (1977) Privacy as a concept and a social issue: a multidimensional developmental theory. J Soc Issues 33(3):22–42
Leonardi PM (2013) When does technology use enable network change in organizations? A comparative study of feature use and shared affordances. MIS Q:749–775
Liu K, Tao D (2022) The roles of trust, personalization, loss of privacy, and anthropomorphism in public acceptance of smart healthcare services. Comput Hum Behav 127:107026
Luna Cortés G, Royo Vela M (2013) The antecedents of consumers' negative attitudes toward SMS advertising: a theoretical framework and empirical study. J Interact Advert 13(2):109–117
Lutz C, Hoffmann CP, Bucher E, Fieseler C (2018) The role of privacy concerns in the sharing economy. Inf Commun Soc 21(10):1472–1492

Markus AF, Kors JA, Rijnbeek PR (2021) The role of explainability in creating trustworthy artificial intelligence for health care: a comprehensive survey of the terminology, design choices, and evaluation strategies. J Biomed Inform 113:103655

Maroto-Gómez M, Castro-González Á, Castillo JC, Malfaz M, Salichs MÁ (2023) An adaptive decision-making system supported on user preference predictions for human–robot interactive communication. User Model User-Adap Inter 33(2):359–403

Maseeh HI, Jebarajakirthy C, Pentecost R, Arli D, Weaven S, Ashaduzzaman M (2021) Privacy concerns in e-commerce: a multilevel meta-analysis. Psychol Mark 38(10):1779–1798

McGuire WJ (1985) Chapter attitudes and attitude change. In: Handbook of social psychology, pp 233–346

Meurisch C, Mihale-Wilson CA, Hawlitschek A, Giger F, Müller F, Hinz O, Mühlhäuser M (2020) Exploring user expectations of proactive AI systems. Proc ACM Interact Mob Wearable Ubiquitous Technol 4(4):1–22

Meurisch C, Mühlhäuser M (2021) Data protection in AI services: a survey. ACM Comp Surv (CSUR) 54(2):1–38

Michalco J, Simonsen JG, Hornbæk K (2015) An exploration of the relation between expectations and user experience. Int J Human-Comput Interact 31(9):603–617

Mittelstadt B, Russell C, Wachter S (2019) Explaining explanations in AI. In: Proceedings of the conference on fairness, accountability, and transparency

Montag C, Kraus J, Baumann M, Rozgonjuk D (2023) The propensity to trust in (automated) technology mediates the links between technology self-efficacy and fear and acceptance of artificial intelligence. Comput Hum Behav Reports 11:100315

Montag C, Ali R, Al-Thani D, Hall BJ (2024a) On artificial intelligence and global mental health. Asian J Psychiatr 91:103855

Montag C, Nakov P, Ali R (2024b) Considering the IMPACT framework to understand the AI-well-being-complex from an interdisciplinary perspective. Tele Inform Reports 13:100112

Mori M (1970) Bukimi no tani [The uncanny valley]. Energy 7:33

Ozturk AB, Nusair K, Okumus F, Singh D (2017) Understanding mobile hotel booking loyalty: an integration of privacy calculus theory and trust-risk framework. Inf Syst Front 19:753–767

Pataranutaporn P, Danry V, Leong J, Punpongsanon P, Novy D, Maes P, Sra M (2021) AI-generated characters for supporting personalized learning and well-being. Nat Mach Intell 3(12):1013–1022

Pejovic V, Musolesi M (2015) Anticipatory mobile computing: a survey of the state of the art and research challenges. ACM Comp Surv (CSUR) 47(3):1–29

Raftopoulos M, Hamari J (2023) Human-AI collaboration in organisations: a literature review on enabling value creation. ECIS 2023 Research Papers. 381

Sankaran S, Markopoulos P (2021) It's like a puppet master: user perceptions of personal autonomy when interacting with intelligent technologies. In: Proceedings of the 29th ACM conference on user modeling, adaptation and personalization

Schneider S, Kummert F (2021) Comparing robot and human guided personalization: adaptive exercise robots are perceived as more competent and trustworthy. Int J Soc Robot 13(2):169–185

Shin D (2021) The effects of explainability and causability on perception, trust, and acceptance: implications for explainable AI. Int J Hum Comput Stud 146:102551

Shortliffe EH, Sepúlveda MJ (2018) Clinical decision support in the era of artificial intelligence. JAMA 320(21):2199–2200

Sindermann C, Sha P, Zhou M, Wernicke J, Schmitt HS, Li M, Sariyska R, Stavrou M, Becker B, Montag C (2021) Assessing the attitude towards artificial intelligence: introduction of a short measure in German, Chinese, and English language. KI-Künstliche Intelligenz 35:109–118

Sinha RR, Swearingen K (2001) Comparing recommendations made by online systems and friends. DELOS 106(1):1–6

Sundar SS (2020) Rise of machine agency: a framework for studying the psychology of human–AI interaction (HAII). J Comput-Mediat Commun 25(1):74–88

Tam KY, Ho SY (2006) Understanding the impact of web personalization on user information processing and decision outcomes. MIS Quar:865–890

Tang Z, Hu Y, Smith MD (2008) Gaining trust through online privacy protection: self-regulation, mandatory standards, or caveat emptor. J Manag Inf Syst 24(4):153–173

Tapus A, Ţăpuş C, Matarić MJ (2008) User—robot personality matching and assistive robot behavior adaptation for post-stroke rehabilitation therapy. Intel Serv Robot 1:169–183

Tenhundfeld NL, Barr HM, Emily H, Weger K (2021) Is my Siri the same as your Siri? An exploration of users' mental model of virtual personal assistants, implications for trust. IEEE Trans Human-Machine Syst 52(3):512–521

Tintarev N, Masthoff J (2010) Designing and evaluating explanations for recommender systems. In: Recommender systems handbook. Springer, pp 479–510

Veitch E, Alsos OA (2022) A systematic review of human-AI interaction in autonomous ship systems. Saf Sci 152:105778

Venkatesh V, Morris MG, Davis GB, Davis FD (2003) User acceptance of information technology: toward a unified view. MIS Quar:425–478

Venkatesh V, Thong JY, Xu X (2012) Consumer acceptance and use of information technology: extending the unified theory of acceptance and use of technology. MIS Quar:157–178

Yang H-D, Yoo Y (2004) It's all about attitude: revisiting the technology acceptance model. Decis Support Syst 38(1):19–31

Zhan ES, Molina MD, Rheu M, Peng W (2023) What is there to fear? Understanding multi-dimensional fear of AI from a technological affordance perspective. Int J Human–Comput Interact:1–18

Zhu D-S, Lin TC-T, Hsu Y-C (2012) Using the technology acceptance model to evaluate user attitude and intention of use for online games. Total Qual Manag Bus Excell 23(7–8):965–980

Chapter 4
Exploring AI Interaction Modalities in Virtual Environments and Its Impact on Users' Attitudes

Yinshu Zhao and Nilufar Baghaei

Abstract Individuals have a tendency to treat computers as social entities and exhibit social behaviours towards a computer system, according to the Social Response Theory. AI powered computer systems such as chatbot and virtual assistant have been widely used in various fields such as e-commerce, social media, healthcare, education, entertainment etc. With the advent of Head Mounted Devices (HMDs), the integration of AI into immersive virtual environment (VEs) has gained significant attention by both industry and academia. It also provides another opportunity to enable intelligent interaction through AI avatars or characters in VEs in order to enhance user experience and further impact on human well-being. In this chapter, we introduce the AI adoption in VEs especially with a focus on virtual avatars and characters, and we shed light on their interaction modalities design. We also provide insights about users' attitude towards AI and the impact of AI interactions in VEs on human well-being. The limitations and future directions of this research fields are discussed.

Keywords Artificial Intelligence · Virtual reality · Augmented reality · Virtual avatar · Interaction · Well-being · Attitude

The theory of social response states that individuals tend to treat computers as social entities, even though the machines do not express human feelings, intentions, or motivations (Reeves and Nass 1996). With the integration of Artificial Intelligence (AI) into computer systems such as chatbots and voice assistants, AI is changing the way individuals interact with technology. In recent years, the integration of AI into immersive Virtual Environments (VEs) such as Virtual Reality (VR) and Augmented

---

Y. Zhao · N. Baghaei (✉)
School of Electrical Engineering and Computer Science, The University of Queensland, St. Lucia, Australia
e-mail: n.baghaei@uq.edu.au

Y. Zhao
e-mail: yinshu.zhao@uq.edu.au

C. Montag and R. Ali (eds.), *The Impact of Artificial Intelligence on Societies*, Studies in Neuroscience, Psychology and Behavioral Economics,
https://doi.org/10.1007/978-3-031-70355-3_4

Reality (AR) has gained significant attention, offering opportunities for enhancing user experiences and engagement (Baghaei et al. 2021; Zhao et al. 2022). These immersive technologies create compelling environments where users can engage with virtual content and experiences in unprecedented ways. In VR, users are fully immersed in a computer-generated environment, while AR overlays digital information onto the physical world, seamlessly blending virtual and real-world elements. Within these immersive settings, virtual avatars and characters serve as intermediaries between users and AI systems, facilitating interactions and delivering personalized assistance. Thus, understanding the dynamics of AI interaction and its impact on attitudes towards AI becomes increasingly crucial.

Research also suggests that attitudes towards AI are influenced by various factors, including user experience, perception of AI capabilities, and the nature of interactions with AI systems (see Chap. 1 of this book). As users engage with assistant avatars in XR environments, their perception of AI is shaped not only by the functionality and effectiveness of these avatars, but also the modality of how AI is applied in VEs, the characteristics and transparency of the AI, the person who use the system, the context and cultural background of the VEs (Montag et al. 2024). Moreover, users' attitude towards these immersive interaction technologies could also further influence human well-being both positive and negatively (Kitson et al. 2018).

This chapter aims to explore the AI powered interaction design in VEs, specifically through virtual characters such as assistant avatars, as well as people's attitudes towards AI and how it further impacts on well-beings. By examining the role of modality of interaction in shaping user perceptions and attitudes, we seek to provide valuable insights into the evolving human-AI interaction in immersive environments.

4.1 AI Powered Virtual Entities in VEs

Individuals tend to treat computers as social entities, as mentioned earlier. Moreover, when a set of human characteristics were presented by the computer, including but not limited to appearance, emotion, language and interaction, individuals could exhibit social behaviours as a response (Nass and Moon 2000). With the integration of AI into computer systems, chatbots and virtual assistants are widely adopted in various platforms and fields such as e-commerce (See Fig. 4.1 in Zhao 2023), social media, healthcare, entertainment and education (Baghaei et al. 2021; Curtis et al. 2021; Halim et al. 2023; Kamoonpuri and Sengar 2023; Labadze et al. 2023; Schnack et al. 2023). In 2017, the size of the global chatbot market reached almost 370 million U.S. dollars and it will continue to grow 5 times till 2024 (Statista 2024). The common form of AI powered interaction has been evolved from text-based interaction, providing users with live text response according to input queries or commands, to voice-based interaction such as Apple's Siri, Google Assistant, and Amazon's Alexa. By integrating speech recognition (SR), the concept of AI interaction extended to voice-activated commands, allowing users to perform tasks and access information using spoken languages.

Fig. 4.1 Virtual shopper avatars in a VR Store in Zhao (2023)

While the virtual assistant could incorporate elements of personalization and context awareness, their interaction modalities are primarily confined to the limitations of the visual components and the input and output devices such as mouse, keyboard and 2D screen (Mendes et al. 2019). Nowadays, Extended Reality (XR) technology such as Augmented Reality (AR), Mixed Reality (MR) and Virtual Reality (VR) are becoming more prevalent and widely adopted in both industry and academia. With the advent of the accessible head-mounted devices (HMDs) such as Meta Quest, HP, Apple Vision Pro and HTC VIVE, a great range of realistic images, sounds and surroundings can be generated in virtual environments (VEs), creating a more immersive virtual experience compared to the simplistic visualizations on the 2D screen (Marto and Gonçalves 2022; Shu et al. 2019). Compared to traditional online platforms, such as websites and smart devices, XR technologies offer new possibilities for enhancing virtual interactions by introducing avatars as representatives of virtual entities. The avatars could be generated in VEs with anthropomorphic appearance, realistic texture, taking various forms to engage users to interact with virtual worlds, objects, and other entities. It has been shown that the presence of avatars played a crucial role in enhancing user experience and shaping participants' interaction within VEs. This type of avatars can also be called as non-player character (NPC), who is not controlled by the user but is designed to enhance the user experience. Different roles of the avatars range from storyteller in game and entertainment (Pyjas et al. 2022), and training instructor in VR education system (Yasin et al. 2012), to human representation in virtual collaboration (Wu et al. 2021), therapeutics companions in mental health care (Davis and Alexanian 2024; Zhao et al. 2021), and virtual assistant in retail and marketing (Bigne et al. 2024).

More researchers have begun to explore the use of AI including natural language processing (NLP), speech synthesis (SS), gesture and facial recognition methods to mimic human behaviour within avatars when they interact with users in VEs.

These AI enabled avatars can recognize user gestures, facial expressions and voice commands and respond with providing information, answering queries and performing tasks to create more immersive and interactive virtual experiences.

The earliest AR interface to include AI and VEs was the ALIVE system proposed by Maes et al. (1995), which enabled the full body interaction between users and the graphical world inhabited by autonomous agents. In early 2000s, smart agents gradually evolved from entities with limited visual feedback to avatars with anthropomorphic appearance and the ability to interact with users. In Cassell et al. (2000), a virtual playmate 'sam' was introduced as a companion incorporated with a 'story-listening model' to tell imaginative stories and give live responsive audio feedback. Similarly, Balcisoy et al. (2002) developed a virtual human avatar in an AR checker game with AI imitating the human thinking process to enrich the game experience by raising the hand and taking a piece of the chess instead of producing instant move. Moreover, some responsive behavioural features such as speech, facial expression and body animation were also integrated in the virtual human avatar in a more natural way. Later in 2004, Cavazza et al. (2004) proposed the first AI controlled virtual characters in 2004 with the ability to detect users' gestures input through computer vision and allowed users to interact through speech and 15 semiotic gestures.

Chatbot-based non-player characters (NPCs) were firstly deployed within non-immersive 3D worlds, Second Life, as virtual receptionists, that had the ability to greet visitors and answer basic questions. Since then, creating useful or believable virtual characters has been a goal for AI simulation for applications such as simulating military forces (Stytz and Banks 2003), or crowds (Hamagami and Hirata 2003) in virtual scenes. Johnsen et al. (2005) proposed a projector-based life-sized virtual character as a patient to train medical students using gestures and speech interaction. In immersive VR with HMD, the use of virtual humans was described in Rickel and Johnson (2002), where the virtual humans represented instructors or missing team members when some or all human instructors and teammates are unavailable, allowing students to practice team tasks and to work together.

By the late 2010s, most of the AR and VR studies still focused on scripted animations and speech with virtual characters that provided only static interaction rather than being dynamically interactive and reactive to the user's input (Sharma et al. 2013; Wagner et al. 2006; Zhao et al. 2019). In 2019, a series of experiments about NPCs were conducted by Kim et al. (2018, 2019) to test the effect of social presence using Microsoft HoloLens. The scenarios ranged from an intelligent virtual human asking for help on a wheelchair to the integration of Amazon's Alexa with an AI assistant. Similarly, Amazon's Alexa was integrated with a virtual assistant in a VR fashion store to facilitate real time vocal dialogues with users (Morotti et al. 2022). Same year in 2022, intelligent virtual avatars were adopted in VR by Hassan et al. (Hassan et al. 2022) by utilising advanced dialogue models on virtual child avatar in VR to achieve intelligent interaction with users. In 2024, an embodied virtual avatar powered by ChatGPT (OpenAI) were adopted by Chheang et al. (2024) as a training assistant to support participants through verbal communication in medical anatomy education. In this case, the assistant avatar could respond to anatomy questions with varying complexity stemming from user's audio input. Moreover, an AI-based library

(Avatar SDK, Itseez3D Inc., USA) was used to generate a realistic model of the virtual assistant. To enable a more natural interaction, the Microsoft Azure Speech service was leveraged to use conversion of text responses from ChatGPT into the virtual avatar's voice and facial expressions.

Thus, it can be expected that the AI powered Virtual Entities in XR are evolving continuously alongside the rapidly developing generative AI to better shape an immersive experience with natural interaction.

4.2 AI Character Interaction Modalities Design in VEs

In XR environments, AI powered interaction plays a critical role in enhancing user experience and enabling natural interactions. One of the goals to integrate AI into virtual avatars or characters in VEs is to meet users' expectations in different virtual scenarios. Thus, the design of the interaction modalities is highly dependent on the roles of the virtual avatars, which means that the virtual character should exist for certain reasons (Bichlmeier 2023). For instance, considering a virtual game where a virtual enemy's job is to attack the user. Then the enemy of the user in the VR setting should have the ability to move seamlessly and be able to recognise and identify the user's location. Contrastingly, in a virtual training simulation, an assisting AI nurse is expected to respond to the user's requests, such as handing over surgical instruments to the player who is put in the role of a surgeon. In this case, the AI nurse requires more responsive intelligence to follow a predetermined script of the surgical procedure accurately (perhaps compared to another skill such the ability to move through the virtual room). When considering the potential behaviours of this kind of AI avatars, the nurse could be designed to remain stationed at a designated spot next to the patient, eliminating the need for extensive movement. Similarly, in another context, a virtual training partner for practicing sales conversations may not need to physically move in the VEs. Instead, the virtual character must exhibit proficient verbal and non-verbal communication skills to effectively simulate sales scenarios.

Imagine a Mixed Reality Museum app featuring an AI tour guide that can assist users in navigating through exhibits and provide information about artworks or artifacts. The design of this AI tour guide should focus more on utilizing natural language processing to interpret user queries and deliver relevant explanations. In this case, a text-based interaction or verbal interaction is crucial to enhance the users' educational experience in exploring the museum virtually. However, it is more valuable when a virtual assistant is integrated into the virtual task procedure, providing enough sensory feedback to guide users while staying unobtrusive to reduce any unnecessary mental effort. In this case, it may not be necessary to put effort in providing real intelligence that closely mimics human intelligence in every aspect. Instead, it is crucial to ensure that these virtual characters possess sufficient intelligence to fulfill user expectations and steer clear of actions or responses perceived as blatantly illogical. In other words, while it's important for agents to demonstrate intelligence, the priority lies in their ability to effectively engage users and deliver experiences that align with their expectations, based on specific roles and virtual context, and to better enhance user satisfaction and the overall effectiveness of the interaction.

4.2.1 Verbal Interaction

Verbal interaction refers to the language communication between users and AI characters in VEs. NLP and speech recognition are fundamental in facilitating verbal interaction in XR because they enable users to communicate with virtual worlds through spoken language. In this case, speech recognition refers to the act of converting spoken words into text, whereas NLP focuses on understanding and interpreting natural language text to extract its meaning (Natural Language Understanding) and generating response (Natural Language Generation) (Kamoonpuri and Sengar 2023). Moreover, speech synthesis also known as text-to-speech (TTS) is usually adopted to converting text into spoken words. Apart from the speech interaction, text-based interaction is also considered as a form of verbal interaction. Although it does not involve any spoken words, text-based communication still relies on language understanding and generation, two areas representing key components of verbal interaction. In the context of AI avatars in XR environments, text-based interactions usually involve the avatar responding with written text based on user's input. This form of interaction requires similar considerations to spoken dialogue such as NLP.

Voice interaction in virtual environments can sometimes benefit from additional visual feedback, such as the appearance of interaction entities in the form of avatars and the display of the text of the speech dialogue. Moreover, the avatar's lip movements synchronized with speech can also improve clarity and understanding during verbal communication. Kim et al. (2018) investigated whether having visual body appearance and performing actions in VE could enhance user's perception of the virtual avatar. Three forms of the virtual assistant were thus introduced, one with no visual body appearance, one with full body visualization and gestures such as pretend to switch the lamp on in the environment, and one with not only the gesturing but also the ability to walk around in the experimental room. The study found that having visual feedback (i.e. gesturing and locomotion) in an AI assistant improved the perceived social presence and positively impacted on users' sense of engagement in the VEs.

Similarly, in Morotti et al. (2022), a smiling emoticon were used as a visual representation of the virtual voice assistant powered by Amazon Alexa in an iVR fashion store. Participants were required to hold the button on the controller to activate the voice assistance and speak the preset command out loud. Based on the user's verbal command, the assistant was able to provide information on how to use this iVR shopping platform and also about product information which were selected by the user before. The information was not only spoken out by Alexa but also shown as text next to the virtual assistant (See Fig. 4.2 in Morotti et al. 2022).

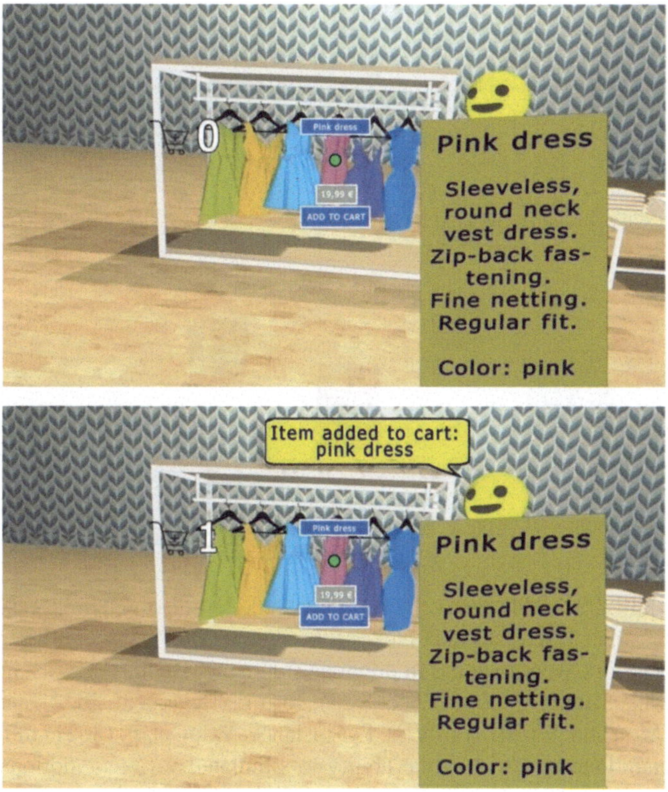

Fig. 4.2 The design of virtual AI assistant in Morotti et al. (2022)

4.2.2 Non-verbal Interaction

Non-verbal interaction refers to any form of information transmission that is apart from spoken or written words. It could involve any non-linguistic cues such as facial expressions, gestures, body language, eye contact, and spatial distance. The 7-38-55 rules indicate that in human–human communication, verbal messages account for 7%, paraverbal (i.e. accent, volume, and pitch) 38% and non-verbal account for 55%. Fabri et al. (2002) also emphasized that in virtual environments, nonverbal communication is considered to be equal or more powerful than verbal communication as a means of expression and judging emotional states. Thus, non-verbal interaction became an essential part when designing interaction with an AI-system especially in situations when verbal interactions may be limited in VEs.

Gesture and facial recognition refer to the process of classifying and identifying user's hand motions and facial expression. In this case, computer vision is a typical AI technique employed in the recognition process. A wide variety of user gestures and facial expression can be recognised by the AI avatar (Chakraborty et al. 2018;

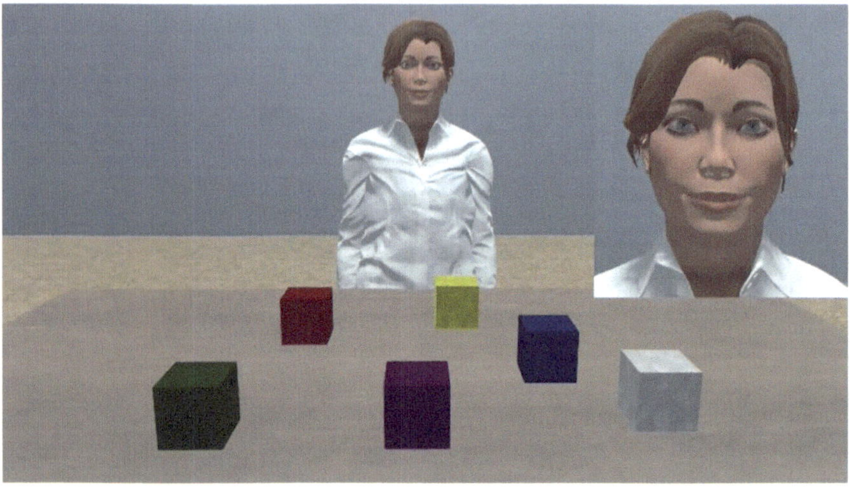

Fig. 4.3 The appearance of Diana's 'Joy' facial expression in Wang et al. (2021)

Lakhani et al. 2022). Alternatively, AI characters can also generate gestures and facial expressions based on the context of the interaction (Wang et al. 2021). Non-verbal interactions were adopted in previous studies where the AI assistant had the ability to walk (Kim et al. 2018; Zhao 2023), gesture (Pyjas et al. 2022), and express emotions (Mou and Xu 2017) in VEs. For instance, Wang et al. (2021) introduced a virtual avatar 'Diana' who had the ability to simulated various emotions through facial expression. 'Diana' were designed to have either static facial expression, mimic users' facial expression, or provide 5 responsive facial expressions based on user's emotional state (i.e. Fig. 4.3). Results indicated that participants tent to spend longer time with the mimicry 'Diana' and expressed more positive responses towards emotionally responsive 'Diana'.

By studying how people engage in various interactions with AI virtual characters in immersive VEs, we can better understand people's reactions and attitudes towards AI. This is something we want to explore with the next section in more detail.

4.3 Attitude Towards AI Character in VEs

While the fact that how AI technology could potentially impact on user's attitude and further impact people's digital well-being still remains an open question, user's acceptance has been considered as a primary factor in any AI interaction design. Following the IMPACT framework as discussed in Montag et al. (2024), we will discuss the user's attitude and acceptance towards virtual AI characters with a focus on the MODALITY of how AI character is applied in VEs, the PERSON who interact with AI characters and the TRANSPARENCY of the AI character in different AREA and CULTURE. Moreover, this section also covers how human attitude towards AI characters in VEs impact on digital social well-being.

The social response theory, as discussed in the first section, offers insights into how individuals establish the psychological boundaries when interacting with AI characters. Evidence indicates that these boundaries are influenced by the physical and behavioural characteristics of the computing device, which is in line with the MODALITY of the IMPACT framework (Montag et al. 2024). In studies involving text-based computer interfaces, researchers have observed that users tend to mentally attribute social significance to the physical platform of the computer, even treating two identical computers as distinct social entities, despite knowing that the same person is operating both (Nass et al. 1997). Similarly, investigations into computers equipped with voice output have shown that users psychologically align themselves with the voice, considering different voices from the same computer as separate social entities, while regarding a single voice emanating from two identical computers as a singular social entity (Edwards et al. 2014; Nass et al. 1994). For instance, considering two smartphone devices with Siri the voice assistant, one uses a female voice and the other uses a male voice. Users would psychologically align themselves with each voice separately, considering the female-voiced Siri and the male-voiced Siri as distinct social entities, even though both voices are coming from Siri on two different iPhones. Conversely, if both devices use the same female-voiced Siri, users will perceive it as the same singular entity, despite the voice emanating from two different devices. In essence, it appears that the most prominent social cue—whether it be the physical platform, the voice, or the agent—is also the primary target of the relational response.

Speaking of the PERSON category in the IMPACT framework (Montag et al. 2024) in VEs, it is necessary to focus not only on the characteristics of the users, but also on the characteristics of the virtual avatars. Mou and Xu (2017) compared participant's personality traits and communicative attributes between human–human and human-AI interactions. After being evaluated by additional viewers of their interaction transcripts, results showed that users demonstrated different communicative attributes towards AI compared to their self-reported personality traits. Specifically, users themselves tended to be less open, less agreeable and less conscientious and self-disclosing when facing AI than facing real human. One possible explanation was, if users were not aware that they were interacting with an AI that acted like a real human, users could show more openness and extraversion. Previous research reported similar findings that people who thought they were interacting with robots had lower level of attractiveness perceived to robots than those who thought they were interacting with real people (Duffy and Zawieska 2012). Moreover, Mou and Xu (2017) also found that the sensed personalities of the AI (i.e. naughty AI girl that tells joke) and other social functions might be the reason to let users feel insecure. Duffy and Zawieska's (2012) investigated how AI chatbot disclosure would impact on customer purchase during sales calls. Results showed that users perceived the AI chatbot to be less knowledgeable and less empathetic when they knew that they were talking with AI chatbot (instead of thinking talking to a human). Moreover, they presented disbelief toward social robots and the degree of perceived strangeness and naturalness between the interaction of users and AI could lead to change of the trustfulness. Thus, it is likely that if the AI's responses were not perceived as natural as compared to a real human, users also less tended to believe they were interacting with a real person, and reacted negatively and less open in the conversations (Gupta et al. 2020).

The psychological boundaries associated with AI interactions could also refer to the mental and emotional limits that individuals establish in their interactions with AI characters. It is essential to reduce the psychological boundaries as these can potentially influence a user's social well-being during the interaction in VEs regarding positive emotions, engagement, relationships with the AI character, meaning, and achievement (Seligman's PERMA theory (Seligman 2018)). The psychological boundaries could be impacted by the degree of sense of presence and the need to feel with others (AI characters) within the interaction environment. Users may experience a sense of immersion and engagement when interacting with AI that feels natural and responsive, while interactions that are too detached or difficult to use may lead to feelings of disconnection or detachment. For instance, Morotti et al. (2022) designed a VR fashion store with Amazon Alexa integrated with a virtual assistant to support vocal dialogues. While participants exhibited a satisfactory shopping experience, the voice commands increased the complexity of the interactions, and led to a negative attitude towards AI assistant. Some participants stated that the limited number of vocal commands was restrictive and using the Alexa AI assistant would make the virtual shopping process slower as they had to reactivate the verbal interaction session after every 10 s. This emphasizes the importance of user autonomy in VEs, i.e., whether AI characters allow users the freedom to make choices and personalize their experience in XR. Similarly, in Chheang et al. (2024), users stated that they required more explanation when having verbal communication with the AI assistant. On the contrary, when the AI assistant performed natural and showed an intuitive form of behaviour such as walking between different spatial locations, a high sense of confidence in the agent's awareness would be elicited by users. In Kim et al. (2018), authors found that the user's confidence and trust towards the AI character increased, when the agent was fully animated. Moreover, when a richer and smooth interaction of the virtual assistant was generated through speech, gesture, and locomotion, the users felt more comfortable with the virtual assistant, and it resulted in a higher trust level towards the technology.

With regards to the TRANSPARENCY, Gupta et al. (2020) collected physiological signals through EEG headset when participants were interacting with the voice assistant in VR. They found that the virtual agent who was able to provide 100% accuracy in the VR shape-selection task reduced participants cognitive load when facing tasks and led to positive comments towards the AI assistant. For the virtual agent who was only able to provide 50% accuracy, participants still preferred to follow the suggested direction by the agent even if they realized that the information provided may not be accurate. This finding is also in line with Maes et al. (1995), in that users could be more tolerant of imperfections when interacting with AI compared to non-intelligent objects. Users believed AIs may think and behave in their own ways even when they should follow up on a task as expected. However, some participants showed negative attitude towards the virtual agent after a few trials. They started to not follow what the agent suggested, and they got frustrated by the inaccurate information. Similarly, in the field of retail marketing, the quality and conversational ability of the voice interaction with a virtual AI assistant could have an impact on customer's perceived satisfaction and purchase intention. Some studies also indicated that users tend to treat AI characters as social entities and keep physical distance between the AI and themselves. In Balcisoy et al. (2002) study, participants stated that they felt uncomfortable when AI Welbo got too close to them. They appreciated that the intelligent avatar respected their privacy by leaving the shared virtual space, when required. These behaviours enhanced users' sense of engagement, social richness, and social presence (Kim et al. 2018).

4.4 Conclusion and Future Directions

This chapter addressed the adoption of AI powered entities in VEs in the form of virtual avatars and characters. We focused on the non-verbal and verbal AI interaction modalities design in VEs by reviewing the literature. We then discussed user's positive and negative attitudes towards AIs during their interaction in VEs.

Although AI-powered virtual characters have been adopted in various VEs, only a limited amount of research on the integration of AI avatars and characters in XR environments has been published so far. Advanced AI techniques such as NLP, SS, gesture, and facial recognition have been mostly neglected. Most of the avatars used in VR settings only show very little AI design, and the interaction modalities are limited to a set of pre-scripted animations. In the future, more studies should focus on the integration of AI in generating dynamic reactions to the user's input, as well as creating more natural and appealing interactions between user and virtual avatars. Researchers will also need to pay attention to the factors that can foster a positive attitude associated with the interaction between users and AI, as well as making the interaction more effective to facilitate a better user experience in VEs.

References

Baghaei N, Chitale V, Hlasnik A, Stemmet L, Liang H-N, Porter R (2021) Virtual reality for supporting the treatment of depression and anxiety: scoping review. JMIR Ment. Health 8:e29681. https://doi.org/10.2196/29681

Balcisoy S, Kallmann M, Torre R, Fua P, Thalmann D (2002) Interaction techniques with virtual humans in mixed environments. In: 5th IEEE EMBS international summer school on biomedical imaging. Presented at the 5th IEEE EMBS international summer school on biomedical imaging, IEEE, Berder Island, France, p VI_2_1–VI_2_6. https://doi.org/10.1109/SSBI.2002.1233993

Bichlmeier C (2023) Interaction with AI-controlled characters in AR worlds. In: Nee AYC, Ong SK (eds) Springer handbook of augmented reality, Springer handbooks. Springer International Publishing, Cham, pp 131–155. https://doi.org/10.1007/978-3-030-67822-7_6

Bigne E, Ruiz C, Curras-Perez R (2024) Furnishing your home? The impact of voice assistant avatars in virtual reality shopping: A neurophysiological study. Comput Hum Behav 153:108104. https://doi.org/10.1016/j.chb.2023.108104

Cassell J, Ananny M, Basu A, Bickmore T, Chong P, Mellis D, Ryokai K, Smith J, Vilhjálmsson H, Yan H (2000) Shared reality: physical collaboration with a virtual peer. In: CHI '00 extended abstracts on human factors in computing systems. Presented at the CHI' 00: human factors in computing systems, ACM, The Hague The Netherlands, pp 259–260. https://doi.org/10.1145/633292.633443

Cavazza M, Charles F, Mead SJ, Martin O, Marichal X, Nandi A (2004) Multimodal acting in mixed reality interactive storytelling. IEEE Multimed 11:30–39. https://doi.org/10.1109/MMUL.2004.11

Chakraborty BK, Sarma D, Bhuyan MK, MacDorman KF (2018) Review of constraints on vision-based gesture recognition for human–computer interaction. IET Comput vis 12:3–15. https://doi.org/10.1049/iet-cvi.2017.0052

Chheang V, Sharmin S, Márquez-Hernández R, Patel M, Rajasekaran D, Caulfield G, Kiafar B, Li J, Kullu P, Barmaki RL (2024) Towards anatomy education with generative AI-based virtual assistants in immersive virtual reality environments. In: 2024 IEEE international conference on artificial intelligence and eXtended and virtual reality (AIxVR). Presented at the 2024 IEEE international conference on artificial intelligence and eXtended and virtual reality (AIxVR), IEEE, Los Angeles, CA, USA, pp 21–30. https://doi.org/10.1109/AIxVR59861.2024.00011

Curtis RG, Bartel B, Ferguson T, Blake HT, Northcott C, Virgara R, Maher CA (2021) Improving user experience of virtual health assistants: scoping review. J Med Internet Res 23:e31737. https://doi.org/10.2196/31737

Davis D, Alexanian S (2024) Role-playing recovery in social virtual worlds: adult use of child avatars as PTSD therapy. Comput Methods Programs Biomed Update 5:100129. https://doi.org/10.1016/j.cmpbup.2023.100129

Duffy BR, Zawieska K (2012) Suspension of disbelief in social robotics, in: 2012 IEEE RO-MAN: the 21st IEEE international symposium on robot and human interactive communication. Presented at the 2012 RO-MAN: The 21st IEEE international symposium on robot and human interactive communication, IEEE, Paris, France, pp 484–489. https://doi.org/10.1109/ROMAN.2012.6343798

Edwards C, Edwards A, Spence PR, Shelton AK (2014) Is that a bot running the social media feed? Testing the differences in perceptions of communication quality for a human agent and a bot agent on Twitter. Comput Hum Behav 33:372–376. https://doi.org/10.1016/j.chb.2013.08.013

Fabri M, Moore D, Hobbs D (2002) Expressive agents: Non-verbal communication in collaborative virtual environments. In: Proceedings of autonomous agents and multi-agent systems (embodied conversational agents)

Gupta K, Hajika R, Pai YS, Duenser A, Lochner M, Billinghurst M (2020) Measuring human trust in a virtual assistant using physiological sensing in virtual reality. In: 2020 IEEE conference on virtual reality and 3d user interfaces (VR). Presented at the 2020 IEEE conference on virtual reality and 3d user interfaces (VR), IEEE, Atlanta, GA, USA, pp 756–765. https://doi.org/10.1109/VR46266.2020.00099

Halim I, Stemmet L, Hach S, Porter R, Liang H-N, Vaezipour A, Henry JD, Baghaei N (2023) Individualized virtual reality for increasing self-compassion: evaluation study. JMIR Ment Health 10:e47617. https://doi.org/10.2196/47617

Hamagami T, Hirata H (2003) Method of crowd simulation by using multiagent on cellular automata. In: IEEE/WIC International conference on intelligent agent technology, 2003. IAT 2003. Presented at the 2003 IEEE/WIC international conference on intelligent agent technology, IEEE Computer Society, Halifax, NS, Canada, pp 46–52. https://doi.org/10.1109/IAT.2003.1241047

Hassan SZ, Salehi P, Røed RK, Halvorsen P, Baugerud GA, Johnson MS, Lison P, Riegler M, Lamb ME, Griwodz C, Sabet SS (2022) Towards an AI-driven talking avatar in virtual reality for investigative interviews of children. In: Proceedings of the 2nd workshop on games systems.

Presented at the MMSys '22: 13th ACM multimedia systems conference, ACM, Athlone Ireland, pp 9–15. https://doi.org/10.1145/3534085.3534340

Johnsen K, Dickerson R, Jackson J, Shin M, Hernandez J, Stevens A, Raij A, Lok B, Lind DS (2005) Experiences in using immersive virtual characters to educate medical communication skills. In: IEEE Proceedings. VR 2005. Virtual Reality, 2005. Presented at the IEEE Proceedings. VR 2005. Virtual Reality, 2005, IEEE, Bonn, Germany, pp 179–324. https://doi.org/10.1109/VR.2005.1492772

Kamoonpuri SZ, Sengar A (2023) Hi, May AI help you? An analysis of the barriers impeding the implementation and use of artificial intelligence-enabled virtual assistants in retail. J Retail Consum Serv 72:103258. https://doi.org/10.1016/j.jretconser.2023.103258

Kim K, Boelling L, Haesler S, Bailenson J, Bruder G, Welch GF (2018) Does a digital assistant need a body? The influence of visual embodiment and social behavior on the perception of intelligent virtual agents in AR. In: 2018 IEEE international symposium on mixed and augmented reality (ISMAR). Presented at the 2018 IEEE international symposium on mixed and augmented reality (ISMAR), IEEE, Munich, Germany, pp 105–114. https://doi.org/10.1109/ISMAR.2018.00039

Kim K, Schubert R, Hochreiter J, Bruder G, Welch G (2019) Blowing in the wind: Increasing social presence with a virtual human via environmental airflow interaction in mixed reality. Comput Graph 83:23–32. https://doi.org/10.1016/j.cag.2019.06.006

Kitson A, Prpa M, Riecke BE (2018) Immersive interactive technologies for positive change: a scoping review and design considerations. Front Psychol 9:1354. https://doi.org/10.3389/fpsyg.2018.01354

Labadze L, Grigolia M, Machaidze L (2023) Role of AI chatbots in education: systematic literature review. Int J Educ Technol High Educ 20:56. https://doi.org/10.1186/s41239-023-00426-1

Lakhani MI, McDermott J, Glavin FG, Nagarajan SP (2022) Facial expression recognition of animated characters using deep learning. In: 2022 International joint conference on neural networks (IJCNN). Presented at the 2022 international joint conference on neural networks (IJCNN), IEEE, Padua, Italy, pp 1–9. https://doi.org/10.1109/IJCNN55064.2022.9892186

Maes P, Darrell T, Blumberg B, Pentland A (1995) The ALIVE system: full-body interaction with autonomous agents. In: Proceedings computer animation'95. Presented at the computer animation'95, IEEE Computer Society Press, Geneva, Switzerland, pp 11–18. https://doi.org/10.1109/CA.1995.393553

Marto A, Gonçalves A (2022) Augmented reality games and presence: a systematic review. J Imaging 8:91. https://doi.org/10.3390/jimaging8040091

Mendes D, Caputo FM, Giachetti A, Ferreira A, Jorge J (2019) A Survey on 3D virtual object manipulation: from the desktop to immersive virtual environments. Comput Graph Forum 38:21–45. https://doi.org/10.1111/cgf.13390

Montag C, Nakov P, Ali R (2024) Considering the IMPACT framework to understand the AI-well-being-complex from an interdisciplinary perspective. Telemat Inform Rep 13:100112. https://doi.org/10.1016/j.teler.2023.100112

Morotti E, Stacchio L, Donatiello L, Roccetti M, Tarabelli J, Marfia G (2022) Exploiting fashion x-commerce through the empowerment of voice in the fashion virtual reality arena: integrating voice assistant and virtual reality technologies for fashion communication. Virtual Real 26:871–884. https://doi.org/10.1007/s10055-021-00602-6

Mou Y, Xu K (2017) The media inequality: comparing the initial human-human and human-AI social interactions. Comput Hum Behav 72:432–440. https://doi.org/10.1016/j.chb.2017.02.067

Nass C, Moon Y (2000) Machines and mindlessness: social responses to computers. J Soc Issues 56:81–103. https://doi.org/10.1111/0022-4537.00153

Nass C, Steuer J, Tauber ER (1994) Computers are social actors. In: Proceedings of the SIGCHI conference on human factors in computing systems celebrating interdependence—CHI '94. Presented at the SIGCHI conference, ACM Press, Boston, Massachusetts, United States, pp 72–78. https://doi.org/10.1145/191666.191703

Nass C, Moon Y, Green N (1997) Are machines gender neutral? Gender-stereotypic responses to computers with voices. J Appl Soc Psychol 27:864–876. https://doi.org/10.1111/j.1559-1816.1997.tb00275.x

Pyjas GM, Weinel J, Broadhead M (2022) Storytelling and VR: Inducing emotions through AI characters. Presented at the proceedings of EVA London 2022. https://doi.org/10.14236/ewic/EVA2022.37

Reeves B, Nass C (1996) The media equation: how people treat computers, television, and new media like real people. Camb. UK 10

Rickel J, Johnson WL (2002) Extending virtual humans to support team training in virtual reality. Explor Artif Intell New Millenium 217–238

Schnack A, Zhao Y, Baghaei N (2023) Introducing shopper avatars in a virtual reality store. In: 2023 IEEE conference on virtual reality and 3d user interfaces abstracts and workshops (VRW). Presented at the 2023 IEEE conference on virtual reality and 3d user interfaces abstracts and workshops (VRW), IEEE, Shanghai, China, pp 863–864. https://doi.org/10.1109/VRW58643.2023.00274

Seligman M (2018) PERMA and the building blocks of well-being. J Posit Psychol 13:333–335. https://doi.org/10.1080/17439760.2018.1437466

Sharma S, Agada R, Ruffin J (2013) Virtual reality classroom as an constructivist approach. In: 2013 Proceedings of IEEE Southeastcon. Presented at the IEEE SOUTHEASTCON 2013, IEEE, Jacksonville, FL, USA, pp 1–5. https://doi.org/10.1109/SECON.2013.6567441

Shu Y, Huang Y-Z, Chang S-H, Chen M-Y (2019) Do virtual reality head-mounted displays make a difference? A comparison of presence and self-efficacy between head-mounted displays and desktop computer-facilitated virtual environments. Virtual Real 23:437–446. https://doi.org/10.1007/s10055-018-0376-x

Statista (2018) Size of the chatbot market worldwide in 2017 and 2024 (in million U.S. dollars) [Chart]. Statista. https://www.statista.com/statistics/966893/worldwide-chatbot-market-value/

Stytz MR, Banks SB (2003) An architecture to address uncertain requirements and composability for intelligent agents in distributed simulations. In: Design and application of hybrid intelligent systems, pp 749–758

Wagner D, Billinghurst M, Schmalstieg D (2006) How real should virtual characters be? In: Proceedings of the 2006 ACM SIGCHI international conference on advances in computer entertainment technology. Presented at the ACE2006: International conference in advances in computer entertainment technology, ACM, Hollywood California USA, p 57. https://doi.org/10.1145/1178823.1178891

Wang H, Gaddy V, Beveridge JR, Ortega FR (2021) Building an emotionally responsive avatar with dynamic facial expressions in human—computer interactions. Multimodal Technol Interact 5:13. https://doi.org/10.3390/mti5030013

Wu Y, Wang Y, Jung S, Hoermann S, Lindeman RW (2021) Using a fully expressive avatar to collaborate in virtual reality: evaluation of task performance, presence, and attraction. Front Virtual Real 2:641296. https://doi.org/10.3389/frvir.2021.641296

Yasin AM, Darleena Z, Isa MAM (2012) Avatar implementation in virtual reality environment using situated learning for "Tawaf." Procedia—Soc Behav Sci 67:73–80. https://doi.org/10.1016/j.sbspro.2012.11.308

Zhao Y (2023) Investigating avatars' impact on shopper's perception and behaviour in an immersive virtual store. In: 2023 IEEE international symposium on mixed and augmented reality adjunct (ISMAR-Adjunct). Presented at the 2023 IEEE international symposium on mixed and augmented reality adjunct (ISMAR-Adjunct), IEEE, Sydney, Australia, pp 777–780. https://doi.org/10.1109/ISMAR-Adjunct60411.2023.00171

Zhao Z, Han F, Ma X (2019) A live storytelling virtual reality system with programmable cartoon-style emotion embodiment. In: 2019 IEEE international conference on artificial intelligence and virtual reality (AIVR). Presented at the 2019 IEEE international conference on artificial intelligence and virtual reality (AIVR), IEEE, San Diego, CA, USA, pp 102–1027. https://doi.org/10.1109/AIVR46125.2019.00024

Zhao Y, Baghaei N, Schnack A, Stemmet L (2021) Assessing telepresence, social presence and stress response in a virtual reality store. In: 2021 IEEE international symposium on mixed and augmented reality adjunct (ISMAR-adjunct). Presented at the 2021 IEEE international symposium on mixed and augmented reality adjunct (ISMAR-Adjunct), IEEE, Bari, Italy, pp 52–56. https://doi.org/10.1109/ISMAR-Adjunct54149.2021.00020

Zhao Y, Schnack A, Mathrani A, Erensoy A, Chitale V, Baghaei N (2022) Virtual reality stores: studies on shopper perceptions and behaviors. In: 2022 IEEE Asia-Pacific conference on computer science and data engineering (CSDE). Presented at the 2022 IEEE Asia-Pacific conference on computer science and data engineering (CSDE), IEEE, Gold Coast, Australia, pp 1–6. https://doi.org/10.1109/CSDE56538.2022.10089221

Chapter 5
Personality Associations with Attitudes Toward AI

Jiyoung Park and Sang Eun Woo

Abstract In this chapter, we outline the potential roles of personality in predicting attitudes toward AI. Focusing on the Five-Factor Model of personality (extraversion, agreeableness, conscientiousness, neuroticism, openness) and personal innovativeness in information technology, we summarize findings on how personality is associated with affective (positive and negative emotions) and cognitive (functionality and sociality) dimensions of AI attitudes. We conclude by suggesting several directions for future research in this area.

Keywords Artificial intelligence · Big Five personality traits · Personal innovativeness in information technology · Attitudes

5.1 Introduction

People exhibit vastly different emotional responses to and cognitive evaluations of artificial intelligence (AI). Some express positive sentiments such as excitement, whereas others perceive it as a threat to themselves and human identity (Shank et al. 2019; Złotowski et al. 2017). Some view AI to be warm and inviting, whereas others view it as useful and competent but not relatable (Harris-Watson et al. 2023; Park and Woo 2022). The complexity of attitudes toward AI encompasses multiple dimensions, each uniquely influenced by a variety of factors, ranging from personal to cultural influences (Montag et al. 2024b, c). What is known about personal factors such as age, gender, personality serve as an important basis to understand individuals' attitudes toward AI (Kaya et al. 2024; Park and Woo 2022; Zhang and Dafoe 2019). Understanding individual differences in how people perceive, feel about, and respond to various types of AI is crucial in the design and implementation of AI, as it allows

J. Park (✉)
Department of Psychology, Duksung Women's University, Seoul, South Korea
e-mail: jiyoungpark@duksung.ac.kr

S. E. Woo
Department of Psychological Sciences, Purdue University, West Lafayette, USA

C. Montag and R. Ali (eds.), *The Impact of Artificial Intelligence on Societies*, Studies in Neuroscience, Psychology and Behavioral Economics,
https://doi.org/10.1007/978-3-031-70355-3_5

more personalization that ultimately contributes to enhancing its functionality and promoting well-being for all users.

Among personal factors, personality offers a particularly useful framework for understanding one's attitudes toward an entity (Kenrick and Funder 1988; Moskowitz 1994), providing a systematic lens through which individuals view their surroundings as well as people, objects, and events in them (Moskowitz 1994; Porter et al. 2017). Individuals can be characterized by their differential standings on personality traits that influence patterns of feelings, thoughts, and actions (Baumert et al. 2017; McCrae and Costa 1997; Montag and Elhai 2019). Personality traits reflect individual differences in sensitivity to various stimuli (Gray 1973), and they tend to be relatively stable over time, manifested in consistent and recurrent patterns of behavior (but see recent advances in studying personality changes, Bleidorn et al. 2022). Traits are organized hierarchically in terms of content specificity (see Woo et al. 2015 for a distinction between content vs. contextual specificity in personality measurement). The Five-Factor Model of personality (often interchangeably used as "the Big Five"; Digman 1990; Goldberg 1993; McCrae and Costa 1997) consisting of *extraversion*, *agreeableness*, *conscientiousness*, *neuroticism*, and *openness to experience* (in short, *openness*) posits these dimensions as broad factors of personality traits. The Big Five traits are useful for understanding personality at a high level of abstraction and generality, providing a rough outline of human individuality (McAdams and Pals 2006).

In addition to the broad trait-level personality influences on AI attitudes, researchers have also explored the effects of more context-specific personality constructs such as *personal innovativeness in information technology* (PIIT). PIIT is defined as an individual's willingness to embrace novel information technology (Agarwal and Prasad 1998, p. 206). We view this as a personality construct reflecting one's characteristic adaptations to a technological environment, which is more contextualized to specific environmental influences compared to traits such as the Big Five (McAdams and Pals 2006). Characteristic adaptations are more subject to temporal changes compared to traits, and are influenced by both traits and external factors such as education, training, and social norms (McAdams and Pals 2006). PIIT could positively affect one's belief in their ability to use technological systems successfully and effectively (Kraus et al. 2021) by building more experiences and knowledge related to new technology, which are positively associated with attitudes towards AI (Montag et al. 2023). The beneficial effects of PIIT on attitudes toward new technology have been consistently observed across technology types, cultures, and age groups (e.g., Oostrom et al. 2013; Park and Woo 2022). Thus, examining the role of PIIT along with the Big Five traits can yield useful insights into the overall effects of personality, informing important practical decisions in both the educational and the business sectors.

5.2 Multidimensional Nature of Attitudes Toward AI

As a multidimensional psychological construct, one's attitudes toward an object have affective and cognitive aspects (Breckler 1984). In the same vein, one's attitudes toward AI are best construed as multidimensional, encompassing both affective and cognitive components (Park and Woo 2022; Park et al. 2024). Affective components include generalized mood states such as positive and negative affect, and discrete emotional reactions to an object (Ajzen and Fishbein 2000; Breckler 1984). People's emotional responses to AI range from pleasure (e.g., joy, excitement) to unpleasure (e.g., threat, creepiness), and they can vary depending on the individual's personality, capabilities of the AI tool, and contexts in which the AI is being used (e.g., Koechling et al. 2023; Park and Woo 2022; Shank et al. 2019; Złotowski et al. 2017). One common emotional reaction to AI is the emergence of negative emotions such as fear (Sindermann et al. 2021). A person's experience of fear, often formed through media, negatively affects their ultimate acceptance of AI (Liang and Lee 2017) and can even trigger destructive behaviors toward others in AI-related contexts (Yam et al. 2023). Conversely, individuals also experience positive emotions such as surprise and amazement, when using and interacting with AI, driven by its unique emotional capacity and extraordinary performance (Oh et al. 2018; Shank et al. 2019). Such positive emotional experiences subsequently enhance one's willingness to use AI (Oh et al. 2018) and contribute to more favorable outcomes when AI is applied (Park et al. 2024). It is noteworthy that both negative and positive emotional responses are commonly observed (Liang and Lee 2017; Shank et al. 2019; Yam et al. 2023), and that these emotional responses can have vastly different effects on subsequent outcomes for individual users and organizations that implement the technology.

Cognitive evaluations refer to one's perceptual responses to an object and its characteristics (Breckler 1984). Cognitive attitudes toward AI can be further divided into functionality and sociality aspects. Functionality-related perceptions reflect perceptions of AI performance such as reactivity, flexibility, reliability and quality of outcomes (Park et al. 2024; Rijsdijk et al. 2007). Technology acceptance model (Davis 1989) posits that perceived usefulness and ease of use are two major predictors of new technology acceptance. Functionality-related perceptions have been found as major components of attitudes toward new technology (Venkatesh and Davis 2000), which includes AI (Sohn and Kwon 2020). Positive evaluation of functionality such as perceived usefulness and competence facilitates one's acceptance of AI as well as other related work outcomes (e.g., Harris-Watson et al. 2023; Park et al. 2024).

Another cognitive aspect that emerges as a crucial dimension of attitudes toward AI is sociality (Harris-Watson et al. 2023; Park and Woo 2022). Sociality relates to an agent's relational and ethical characteristics such as friendliness and warmth (Fiske et al. 2007). In interacting with a social agent, humans engage in social cognitive processes that not only involve information about efficiency and competence but also involve relational factors such as warmth and emotions (Fiske et al. 2007). Although people elicit higher interpersonal trust, more positive emotions, and active behaviors toward agents perceived as high in both warmth and competence (Evans and Revelle 2008; Fiske et al. 2007; Montag et al. 2024b, c), warmth perception is a more primary factor than competence in evaluating unfamiliar agents (Fiske et al. 2007). When encountering an unfamiliar agent like AI, people decide whether to approach the agent and ensure it is not harmful (Fiske et al. 2007). In particular, due to the autonomous and self-learning nature of AI, interest and importance of sociality-related attitudes such as humanlikeness is increasing (Glikson and Woolley 2020; Park et al. 2024).

The affective and cognitive attitudes are distinguishable and operate independently in predicting behavioral responses to an object (Breckler 1984). In the context of AI at work, six dimensions (i.e., perceived humanlikeness, perceived adaptability, perceived quality of AI, AI use anxiety, job insecurity and personal utility) emerge as key elements of AI attitudes (Park et al. 2024). Perceived humanlikeness refers to the degree to which individuals believe that AI possess human-like attributes, such as emotions. Perceived adaptability and perceived quality of AI are considered cognitive attitudes. Perceived adaptability reflects an individual's view of AI's ability to self-learn and adjust to uncertain situations, whereas perceived quality of AI denotes one's assessment of AI's functional features, such as accuracy. AI use anxiety and job insecurity are affective attitudes toward AI; AI use anxiety reflects workers' anxiety about the practical usage of AI, while job insecurity represents concerns about AI replacing jobs and affecting workplaces. Personal utility represents an individual's perception of usefulness and satisfaction in using AI, encompassing both the cognitive and affective aspects of attitudes towards AI. These dimensions seem to have unique effects in explaining actual usage of AI (Harris-Watson et al. 2023) and outcomes at work such as a company's recruiting success (Park et al. 2024). For example, perceived warmth of the AI technology has been shown to predict psychological acceptance of AI, whereas perceived competence was positively associated with adoption of the AI's unique expertise and skills in the AI-human teamwork (Harris-Watson et al. 2023). Also, there seem to be some meaningful within-person variations across different dimensions of attitudes. Some individuals exhibit positive perceptions of AI's functionality despite experiencing negative emotions, whereas some do not think much of AI's functionality yet express positive sentiments about the technology (Park and Woo 2022). Taken together, research suggests that these attitudinal dimensions are interconnected *and* expressed distinctly within and across individuals, which underscores the importance of considering specific aspects of AI attitudes.

5.3 The Effects of Personality Factors on AI Attitudes

In this section, we discuss how personality affects AI attitudes, focusing on four key dimensions of AI attitudes: positive emotion, negative emotion, functionality, and sociality. The first two are affective and the other two are cognitive in nature, as discussed above. With regard to personality constructs, we focus on the Big Five traits and PIIT. In doing so, we draw heavily from a recent study we conducted (Park and Woo 2022) where we examined relationships between personality constructs and AI attitudes based on 1530 survey responses from South Korean adults with various demographic characteristics (e.g., gender, age, occupation). In this study, we conceptualized AI as an abstract entity rather than concentrating on specific types of AI. Although there is much practical value in examining people's attitudes toward specific AI technologies (given that there are many notable differences across AI tools and how they are used), taking a generalized approach in measuring AI attitudes as a whole provides a solid foundation for subsequent research on more specific types of AI technology. Some empirical studies have indeed shown that general levels of AI attitudes explained certain variances in trust and willingness to use diverse AI products such as self-driving car, humanoid robots, and digital assistants such as Siri (Sindermann et al. 2021).

In addition, a few other studies have empirically examined the relationships between personality and AI attitudes. For example, a study investigated the effects of the Big Five traits on general positive and negative attitudes toward AI among Turkish adults (Kaya et al. 2024). This research compared the effects of the Big Five traits along with demographic factors and various types of anxiety, such as AI learning anxiety and job replacement anxiety. Another study examined the effects of the Big Five traits on two types of AI attitudes: acceptance of AI and fear of AI among German and Chinese adults (Sindermann et al. 2022). Additionally, a scale development study (Park et al. 2024) identified six attitudinal dimensions of AI (i.e., perceived humanlikeness, perceived adaptability, perceived quality of AI, AI use anxiety, job insecurity and personal utility) and examined their associations with personality variables.

5.3.1 Five-Factor Model of Personality and AI Attitudes

Extraversion is characterized by the tendency to be sociable, cheerful, and agentic (Costa and McCrae 1992). Extraverts tend to engage actively in social activity and are predisposed to experience positive emotions and perceive neutral objects in a more positive light (Costa and McCrae 1992; Watson and Clark 1992). Based on this, one might expect that extraversion would be associated with positive attitudes toward AI in general. However, research to date shows some intriguing patterns of findings. For example, Park and Woo (2022) found that extraversion did not have strong positive associations with various AI attitudinal dimensions. When other personality factors were controlled for, extraversion's positive effect on positive emotion disappeared, and it was in fact associated with more negative emotional responses to AI. Park and Woo (2022) also found that extraverted individuals tended to rate AI's functionality more negatively. Previous research on technology use (defined more broadly) also showed a negative effect of extraversion on actual use of technology (Barnett et al. 2015; Landers and Lounsbury 2006).

Further investigation is needed to unpack this surprising finding, but here is our tentative conjecture: The negative emotional response and lower evaluation on functionality may be attributed to a delicate interplay between reward sensitivity and sociability that may be pronounced among extraverts (Depue and Collins 1999; Lucas et al. 2008). Extraverts tend to engage in a broader range of activities, including social interactions, and they tend to associate people with reward (Wilkowski and Ferguson 2014), and enjoy asserting their dominance over other 'beings.' It is likely that extraverts' desire to manifest assertive abilities in social situations clashes with AI's functionality in possibly surpassing human capabilities. Again, this is an interesting area of further theoretical exploration. Regarding sociality of AI, extraversion does not appear to play a significant role (Park and Woo 2022). The effects of extraversion on sociality attitudes toward new technology have shown inconsistent findings. Some studies found that extraverts frequently engaged in technology-mediated communication (Correa et al. 2010) and it shows the largest correlation with digital footprints that reflect frequent social interaction and engagement through smartphones among the Big Five traits (Marengo et al. 2023). Those high in extraversion reported positive emotions after using social robots (Devaraj et al. 2008; Rice and Markey 2009), whereas other studies have found contrasting results. Those with high extraversion were found to allocate less time to social interactions involving computers because they prefer face-to-face interactions over technology-mediated interactions (Landers and Lounsbury 2006). The discrepancies in findings may partly stem from the nature of technology. Extraversion typically yields favorable attitudes toward technology that facilitates social interaction and personal enjoyment (McElroy et al. 2007; Svendsen et al. 2013). However, it may have negative effects on technology supplanting social interaction (Barnett et al. 2015). Thus, the effects of extraversion on sociality of AI may be positive when AI augments social interaction and serves as a tool for human interaction rather than replacing it.

Agreeableness is characterized as the tendency to maintain social harmony and to defer to others during interpersonal conflicts (Costa and McCrae 1992; Graziano et al. 1996; McCrae and Costa 1997). Given this, it is possible that agreeable people may downward-regulate their negative emotions toward AI effectively while upward-regulating positive emotions, and evaluate AI's functionality and sociality in a generally positive light.

Research indeed suggests that agreeableness may be meaningfully associated with various emotional and cognitive responses toward AI (e.g., Kaya et al. 2024; Park et al. 2024; Stein et al. 2024). However, empirical findings in the literature appear to be somewhat mixed. For instance, Turkish adults with high agreeableness were found to hold more positive AI attitudes both emotionally and cognitively (Kaya et al. 2024; Stein et al. 2024). Notably, Kaya et al. found that agreeableness was the only Big Five trait predicting less negative attitudes towards AI after accounting for demographical factors and the other Big Five traits (Kaya et al. 2024). Similarly, adults with high agreeableness showed higher levels of general positive attitudes towards AI (Babiker et al. 2024; Stein et al. 2024), and lower levels of negative emotional responses toward AI such as AI use anxiety and job insecurity (Park et al. 2024). In another study, agreeableness was negatively associated with fear toward AI and positively with AI acceptance among Chinese, but such associations were not found among Germans (Sindermann et al. 2022). Park and Woo (2022) found that agreeableness predicted positive emotional response toward AI. In terms of cognitive attitudes, agreeableness appears to have positive effects on both functionality and sociality dimensions of AI, although the effects appear to be rather modest in magnitude (Park and Woo 2022; Park et al. 2024). This said, inventories to assess AI attitudes also differed across the studies, making the direct comparison difficult. This is also true for remaining comparison of findings in this context.

Conscientiousness is a trait marked by strong achievement striving and high levels of aspiration as well as diligence and dependability (McCrae and Costa 1997). Individuals with high conscientiousness tend to value competence and efficiency, and thus are likely to embrace AI if they believe that it can enhance their task efficiency and competence. Conscientious people tend to exhibit lower levels of negative emotional responses such as concerns about job replacement and AI use anxiety (Kaya et al. 2024; Park and Woo 2022; Park et al. 2024). The strong belief in their ability to perform effectively may contribute experiencing lower negative emotions and more positive reactions toward AI.

Conscientiousness is generally associated with higher recognition of AI's functionality (e.g., Barnett et al. 2015; Park and Woo 2022; Park et al. 2024) and positively related to general positive AI attitudes among Arab samples (Babiker et al. 2024). Given their heightened sensitivity toward opportunities to show their capabilities, highly conscientious individuals may perceive AI's functionality as an opportunity to enhance their own strengths and performance. At the same time, interestingly, those with high conscientiousness do not appear to view AI as sociable or relatable (e.g., Park and Woo 2022; Park et al. 2024). Studies with Turkish and German adults did not yield consistent findings (Kaya et al. 2024; Sindermann et al. 2022).

Neuroticism is characterized as a tendency to experience negative emotions (McCrae and Costa 1997). Individuals with high neuroticism are predisposed to higher sensitivity and to threats and punishment (DeYoung et al. 2007). Due to their tendency to withdraw and inhibit behaviors in response to stimuli (DeYoung et al. 2007), they often resist and are less open to new changes (Barnett et al. 2015). Consistent with these characteristics, those with high neuroticism consistently reported lower ratings on diverse negative emotional aspects such as general negative emotional response toward AI (Kaya et al. 2024; Park and Woo 2022; Sindermann et al. 2022), AI use anxiety (Park et al. 2024), and job insecurity caused by AI (Park et al. 2024). Research that investigates primary emotional systems likely underlying neuroticism, such as FEAR, SADNESS, and ANGER, and their associations with attitudes towards AI has also revealed similar findings. These three emotional systems had positive associations with job insecurity caused by AI and the perceived threat to human identity posed by AI (Montag et al. 2024a). According to this research, the negative attitudes towards AI were most strongly associated with the SADNESS system, which is often triggered by social separation or a lack of group cohesion. This suggests that the underlying SADNESS facet of neuroticism might drive negative attitudes towards AI (Montag et al. 2024a).

However, interestingly, those with high neuroticism tend to positively evaluate AI's sociality. They perceived AI as warm and friendly, even if they may not necessarily believe it to be functionally useful (Park and Woo 2022). Another study also found that neuroticism was negatively associated with functionality-related attitudes, such as perceived quality of AI (Park et al. 2024). The positive effects of neuroticism on cognitive evaluation seem to be primarily confined to the sociality aspect of AI. These findings align with previous research indicating that neurotic individuals display a more positive attitude toward using internet for socialization (Hamburger and Ben-Artzi 2000) and utilize technology to establish a sense of connectedness in online activities (Amiel and Sargent 2004). The positive association between neuroticism and AI's sociality may reflect neurotic individuals' need to belong via technology.

Openness is characterized as a need for variety, novelty, growth, and change (McCrae and Costa 1997; Woo et al. 2014). Individuals high on openness are described as intellectually and culturally curious, and they are inclined to seek new experiences (DeYoung et al. 2007; Woo et al. 2014). These characteristics lead them to embrace novel information and technology (McElroy et al. 2007; Sindermann et al. 2022; Svendsen et al. 2013). Openness has been found to predict positive emotional responses to AI across studies (e.g., Kaya et al. 2024; Park and Woo 2022; Park et al. 2024). Those with high openness also showed positive evaluations of AI's functionality such as perceived adaptability and quality of AI (Park and Woo 2022; Park et al. 2024). However, it does not appear that highly open people view AI as particularly sociable or relatable (Park and Woo 2022; Park et al. 2024). However, when accounting for a more context-specific personality factor such as PIIT, the effects of openness tends to weaken. It is plausible that openness, as a dispositional trait, precedes the characteristic adaptations that involve exploring new technology and prior experience of using AI (for further discussions on how traits and characteristic adaptations relate to one another, see McAdams and Pals 2006).

5.3.2 Personal Innovativeness in IT and Attitudes Toward AI

Research suggests a consistent, positive influence of PIIT on AI attitudes across affective and cognitive dimensions. It has been found that PIIT accounts for significant variances in individuals' four attitudinal dimensions after accounting for the effects of the Big Five traits, demographical factors, and prior experience of using AI (Park and Woo 2022). Studies—based on South Korean and American adults—have demonstrated that those with high PIIT showed more positive and less negative emotional attitudes (Park and Woo 2022; Park et al. 2024). In Park and Woo's (2022) study, the beneficial effects of PIIT on emotional response were more pronounced in predicting positive emotions than negative emotions. Although PIIT had a weaker effect on negative emotions compared to neuroticism, PIIT demonstrated relatively stronger effects on positive emotions compared to the Big Five traits. Another study also found that those with high PIIT reported less negative emotional responses when using AI or facing realistic threat of being replaced by AI (Park et al. 2024), highlighting the consistent beneficial effect of PIIT on negative emotional response to AI.

The effects of PIIT on cognitive evaluation were also positive. Individuals high on PIIT gave higher ratings on both functionality and sociality (Park and Woo 2022). Similar patterns have been observed in research using American working adults. Individuals with high PIIT tend to positively evaluate functionality-related aspects of AI, such as personal utility of AI and perceived quality of AI, and their effects are relatively stronger compared to the effects of the other Big Five traits such as conscientiousness (Park et al. 2024). Overall, these findings suggest that PIIT has a strong association with how one evaluates and feels about AI technology, which is stronger than the effects of broader dimensions of personality traits. Also, characteristics adaptations related to technology such as PIIT and technology self-efficacy tend to correlate more strongly with positive attitudes towards AI than negative attitudes (Montag et al. 2023; Park and Woo 2022). This underscores the importance of considering characteristic adaptations in understanding personality and attitudes toward AI.

5.4 Implications and Future Research Suggestions

Personality constructs, such as the Big Five traits and PIIT, have distinct and varied effects on both affective and cognitive attitudes toward AI. Differential roles of the Big Five traits and PIIT are particularly noteworthy. Although some of the Big Five traits (e.g., neuroticism) may influence affective attitudes more strongly than cognitive attitudes, PIIT may have stronger (and more proximal) effects on AI's functionality.

As we discussed above, research on the roles of personality in AI attitudes remains scarce and rather fragmented. This is (at least in part) due to inconsistent measurement practices and insufficient consideration of cultural and environmental contexts that likely play a key role in understanding the phenomenon. More systematic research is needed to fully integrate personality theories into existing theories of technology acceptance, taking into account both individual- and environmental-level factors affecting one's attitudes toward AI and AI acceptance.

Research on personality and AI attitudes provides a number of practical implications on how to design and implement AI to enhance individuals' well-being. For instance, interventions or designs that alleviate negative emotions and highlight AI's sociality would be beneficial for neurotic individuals, whereas conscientious individuals would prefer AI promoting task efficiency rather than focusing on social connectedness. Developing and utilizing explainable AI, which produces details and reasons to make its functioning easy to understand for users, would help eliminate fear and negative emotions, such as privacy concerns (Arrieta et al. 2020). Also, considering PIIT's positive effects on various attitudes toward AI, educational and training programs focusing on promoting one's willingness to try out new technology may be effective in shaping their students' and employees' positive attitudes toward AI. Lastly, there has been a continuous call for a valid measure to capture multidimensional and nuanced aspects of AI attitudes. Inconsistent and inconclusive findings in the field of personality factors and AI attitudes are partly due to the lack of a comprehensive measure. Although Park and colleagues (2024) developed a six-factor scale to measure workers' attitudes towards AI application at work, more research is needed to assess AI attitudes among the general population and to measure AI literacy using objective ability tests (Montag et al. 2024b, c).

Based on our review of the literature on personality and attitudes toward AI, we offer some ideas for future research directions. First and foremost, attitudes toward AI are multidimensional and attitudes toward AI can differ depending on the domains (e.g., work, consumer contexts), thus whether and to what extent the results are generalized awaits future research. According to Park et al. (2024) research focusing on AI attitudes at work, functionality-related attitudes and negative emotional attitudinal dimensions emerge as major attitudinal dimensions, whereas positive emotional reactions were less prominent. Future research needs to investigate other types of attitudinal dimensions besides the four attitudes included in this chapter, to gain a more comprehensive understanding on attitudes toward AI.

Second, attitudes toward AI vary by contexts. For example, anthropomorphic and autonomous features elicit positive emotional responses such as excitement among consumers (Shank et al. 2019), but increasing workers' negative emotional response such as job insecurity and incivility toward their colleagues (Yam et al. 2023). The interactive effects of personality and situational contexts need further investigation.

Third, personality also interacts with cultural and environmental factors in shaping attitudes toward AI. A small but increasing body of research suggests that cultural variances exist in interpreting and perceiving AI (Awad et al. 2018; Mantello et al. 2023). Research on the Big Five traits and AI attitudes have revealed differing effects across German and Chinese adults (Sindermann et al. 2022). Scholars propose that collectivists tend to hold more positive attitudes toward AI compared to individualists, likely due to a heightened perception of humanlikeness (Folk et al. 2023). Further exploration into how personality factors shape attitudes toward AI, and how these dynamics interact with cultures remains an important area for research in the coming years.

References

Agarwal R, Prasad J (1998) A conceptual and operational definition of personal innovativeness in the domain of information technology. Inf Syst Res 9(2):204–215. https://doi.org/10.1287/isre.9.2.204

Ajzen I, Fishbein M (2000) Attitudes and the attitude-behavior relation: reasoned and automatic processes. Eur Rev Soc Psychol 11(1):1–33. https://doi.org/10.1080/14792779943000116

Amiel T, Sargent SL (2004) Individual differences in Internet usage motives. Comput Hum Behav 20(6):711–726. https://doi.org/10.1016/j.chb.2004.09.002

Arrieta AB, Díaz-Rodríguez N, Del Ser J, Bennetot A, Tabik S, Barbado A, Herrera F (2020) Explainable Artificial Intelligence (XAI): concepts, taxonomies, opportunities and challenges toward responsible AI. Inf Fusion 58:82–115. https://doi.org/10.1016/j.inffus.2019.12.012

Awad E, Dsouza S, Kim R, Schulz J, Henrich J, Shariff A, Rahwan I (2018) The moral machine experiment. Nature 563(7729):59–64. https://doi.org/10.1038/s41586-018-0637-6

Babiker A, Alshakhsi S, Supti TI, Ali R (2024, June) Do personality traits impact the attitudes towards artificial intelligence? In: The 11th international conference on behavioural and social computing (BESC'24), Harbin, China

Barnett T, Pearson AW, Pearson R, Kellermanns FW (2015) Five-factor model personality traits as predictors of perceived and actual usage of technology. Eur J Inf Syst 24(4):374–390. https://doi.org/10.1057/ejis.2014.10

Baumert A, Schmitt M, Perugini M, Johnson W, Blum G, Borkenau P, Wrzus C (2017) Integrating personality structure, personality process, and personality development. Eur J Pers 31(5):503–528. https://doi.org/10.1002/per.2115

Bleidorn W, Schwaba T, Zheng A, Hopwood CJ, Sosa SS, Roberts BW, Briley DA (2022) Personality stability and change: a meta-analysis of longitudinal studies. Psychol Bull 148(7–8):588–619. https://doi.org/10.1037/bul0000365

Breckler SJ (1984) Empirical validation of affect, behavior, and cognition as distinct components of attitude. J Pers Soc Psychol 47(6):1191–1205. https://doi.org/10.1037/0022-3514.47.6.1191

Correa T, Hinsley AW, De Zuniga HG (2010) Who interacts on the Web? The intersection of users' personality and social media use. Comput Hum Behav 26(2):247–253. https://doi.org/10.1016/j.chb.2009.09.003

Costa PT, McCrae RR (1992) Normal personality assessment in clinical practice: the NEO personality inventory. Psychol Assess 4(1):5–13. https://doi.org/10.1037/1040-3590.4.1.5

Davis FD (1989) Perceived usefulness, perceived ease of use, and user acceptance of information technology. MIS Q 13(3):319–340. https://doi.org/10.2307/249008

Depue RA, Collins PF (1999) Neurobiology of the structure of personality: dopamine, facilitation of incentive motivation, and extraversion. Behav Brain Sci 22(3):491–517. https://doi.org/10.1017/S0140525X99002046

Devaraj S, Easley RF, Crant JM (2008) How does personality matter? Relating the Five-Factor Model to technology acceptance and use. Inf Syst Res 19(1):93–105. https://doi.org/10.1287/isre.1070.0153

DeYoung CG, Quilty LC, Peterson JB (2007) Between facets and domains: 10 aspects of the Big Five. J Personality Social Psychol 93(5):880–896. https://doi.org/10.1037/0022-3514.93.5.880

Digman JM (1990) Personality structure: emergence of the five-factor model. Annu Rev Psychol 41(1):417–440. https://doi.org/10.1146/annurev.ps.41.020190.002221

Evans AM, Revelle W (2008) Survey and behavioral measurements of interpersonal trust. J Res Pers 42:1585–1593. https://doi.org/10.1177/0146167217742886

Fiske ST, Cuddy AJC, Glick P (2007) Universal dimensions of social cognition: warmth and competence. Trends Cogn Sci 11(2):77–83. https://doi.org/10.1016/j.tics.2006.11.005

Folk D, Wu C, Heine S (2023) Cultural variation in attitudes towards social chatbots. https://osf.io/preprints/psyarxiv/wc895

Goldberg LR (1993) The structure of phenotypic personality traits. Am Psychol 48(1):26–34. https://doi.org/10.1037/0003-066X.48.1.26

Glikson E, Woolley AW (2020) Human trust in artificial intelligence: review of empirical research. Acad Manag Ann 14(2):627–660. https://doi.org/10.5465/annals.2018.0057

Graziano WG, Jensen-Campbell LA, Hair EC (1996) Perceiving interpersonal conflict and reacting to it: the case for agreeableness. J Pers Soc Psychol 70(4):820–835. https://doi.org/10.1037/0022-3514.70.4.820

Gray JA (1973) Causal theories of personality and how to test them. In: Royce JR (ed) Multivariate analysis and psychological theory. Academic Press, pp 409–463

Hamburger YA, Ben-Artzi E (2000) The relationship between extraversion and neuroticism and the different uses of the Internet. Comput Hum Behav 16(4):441–449. https://doi.org/10.1016/S0747-5632(00)00017-0
Harris-Watson AM, Larson LE, Lauharatanahirun N, DeChurch LA, Contractor NS (2023) Social perception in Human-AI teams: warmth and competence predict receptivity to AI teammates. Comput Hum Behav 145:107765
Kaya F, Aydin F, Schepman A, Rodway P, Yetişensoy O, Demir Kaya M (2024) The roles of personality traits, AI anxiety, and demographic factors in attitudes toward artificial intelligence. Int J Human-Comp Interact 40(2):497–514. https://doi.org/10.1080/10447318.2022.2151730
Kenrick DT, Funder DC (1988) Profiting from controversy: lessons from the person-situation debate. Am Psychol 43(1):23–34. https://doi.org/10.1037/0003-066X.43.1.23
Koechling A, Wehner MC, Warkocz J (2023) Can I show my skills? Affective responses to artificial intelligence in the recruitment process. RMS 17(6):2109–2138. https://doi.org/10.1007/s11846-021-00514-4
Kraus J, Scholz D, Baumann M (2021) What's driving me? Exploration and validation of a hierarchical personality model for trust in automated driving. Hum Factors 63(6):1076–1105. https://doi.org/10.1177/0018720820922653
Landers RN, Lounsbury JW (2006) An investigation of Big Five and narrow personality traits in relation to Internet usage. Comput Hum Behav 22(2):283–293. https://doi.org/10.1016/j.chb.2004.06.001
Liang Y, Lee SA (2017) Fear of autonomous robots and artificial intelligence: evidence from national representative data with probability sampling. Int J Soc Robot 9(3):379–384. https://doi.org/10.1007/s12369-017-0401-3
Lucas RE, Le K, Dyrenforth PS (2008) Explaining the extraversion/positive affect relation: sociability cannot account for extraverts' greater happiness. J Pers 76(3):385–414. https://doi.org/10.1111/j.1467-6494.2008.00490.x
Mantello P, Ho MT, Nguyen MH, Vuong QH (2023) Bosses without a heart: socio-demographic and cross-cultural determinants of attitude toward Emotional AI in the workplace. AI Soc 38(1):97–119. https://doi.org/10.1007/s00146-021-01290-1
Marengo D, Elhai JD, Montag C (2023) Predicting Big Five personality traits from smartphone data: a meta-analysis on the potential of digital phenotyping. J Pers 91(6):1410–1424. https://doi.org/10.1016/j.chbr.2023.100315
McAdams DP, Pals JL (2006) A new big five: fundamental principles for an integrative science of personality. Am Psychol 61(3):204–217. https://doi.org/10.1037/0003-066X.61.3.204
McCrae RR, Costa PT (1997) Personality trait structure as a human universal. Am Psychol 52(5):509–516. https://doi.org/10.1037/0003-066X.52.5.509
McElroy JC, Hendrickson AR, Townsend AM, DeMarie SM (2007) Dispositional factors in Internet use: personality versus cognitive style. MIS Q 31(4):809–820. https://doi.org/10.2307/25148821
Moskowitz DS (1994) Cross-situational generality and the interpersonal circumplex. J Pers Soc Psychol 66(5):921–933. https://doi.org/10.1037/0022-3514.66.5.921
Montag C, Elhai JD (2019) A new agenda for personality psychology in the digital age? Personality Individ Differ 147:128–134. https://doi.org/10.1016/j.paid.2019.03.045
Montag C, Kraus J, Baumann M, Rozgonjuk D (2023) The propensity to trust in (automated) technology mediates the links between technology self-efficacy and fear and acceptance of artificial intelligence. Comp Human Behav Reports 11:100315
Montag C, Ali R, Davis KL (2024a) Affective neuroscience theory and attitudes towards artificial intelligence. AI Soc, 1–8. https://doi.org/10.1007/s00146-023-01841-8
Montag C, Becker B, Li BJ (2024b) On trust in humans and trust in artificial intelligence: a study with samples from Singapore and Germany extending recent research. Comput Human Behav: Artif Humans:100070. https://doi.org/10.1016/j.chbah.2024.100070
Montag C, Nakov P, Ali R (2024c) On the need to develop nuanced measures assessing attitudes towards AI and AI literacy in representative large-scale samples. AI Soc, 1–2. https://doi.org/10.1007/s00146-024-01888-1

Oh C, Song J, Choi J, Kim S, Lee S, Suh B (2018, April) I lead, you help but only with enough details: understanding user experience of co-creation with artificial intelligence. In: Proceedings of the 2018 CHI conference on human factors in computing systems, pp 1–13. https://doi.org/10.1145/3173574.3174223

Oostrom JK, Van Der Linden D, Born MP, Van Der Molen HT (2013) New technology in personnel selection: how recruiter characteristics affect the adoption of new selection technology. Comput Hum Behav 29(6):2404–2415. https://doi.org/10.1016/j.chb.2013.05.025

Park J, Woo SE (2022) Who likes artificial intelligence? Personality predictors of attitudes toward artificial intelligence. J Psychol 156(1):68–94. https://doi.org/10.1080/00223980.2021.2012109

Park J, Woo SE, Kim J (2024) Attitudes toward AI application at work: scale development and validation. J Occup Organ Psychol. https://doi.org/10.1111/joop.12502

Porter CM, Parrigon SE, Woo SE, Saef RM, Tay L (2017). Cultural and intellectual openness differentially relate to social judgments of potential work partners: cultural and intellectual openness. J Pers 85(5):632–642. https://doi.org/10.1111/jopy.12266

Rice L, Markey PM (2009) The role of extraversion and neuroticism in influencing anxiety following computer-mediated interactions. Personality Individ Differ 46(1):35–39. https://doi.org/10.1016/j.paid.2008.08.022

Rijsdijk SA, Hultink EJ, Diamantopoulos A (2007) Product intelligence: its conceptualization, measurement and impact on consumer satisfaction. J Acad Mark Sci 35(3):340–356. https://doi.org/10.1007/s11747-007-0040-6

Shank DB, Graves C, Gott A, Gamez P, Rodriguez S (2019) Feeling our way to machine minds: people's emotions when perceiving mind in artificial intelligence. Comput Hum Behav 98:256–266. https://doi.org/10.1016/j.chb.2019.04.001

Sindermann C, Sha P, Zhou M, Wernicke J, Schmitt HS, Li M, Montag C (2021) Assessing the attitude towards artificial intelligence: introduction of a short measure in German, Chinese, and English language. KI-Künstliche Intelligenz 35(1):109–118. https://doi.org/10.1007/s13218-020-00689-0

Sindermann C, Yang H, Elhai JD, Yang S, Quan L, Li M, Montag C (2022) Acceptance and fear of artificial intelligence: associations with personality in a German and a Chinese sample. Discover Psychol 2(1):8. https://doi.org/10.1007/s44202-022-00020-y

Sohn K, Kwon O (2020) Technology acceptance theories and factors influencing artificial Intelligence-based intelligent products. Telematics Inform 47:101324. https://doi.org/10.1016/j.tele.2019.101324

Stein JP, Messingschlager T, Gnambs T, Hutmacher F, Appel M (2024) Attitudes towards AI: measurement and associations with personality. Sci Rep 14(1):2909. https://doi.org/10.1038/s41598-024-53335-2

Svendsen GB, Johnsen J-AK, Almås-Sørensen L, Vittersø J (2013) Personality and technology acceptance: the influence of personality factors on the core constructs of the technology acceptance model. Behav Inf Technol 32(4):323–334. https://doi.org/10.1080/0144929X.2011.553740

Venkatesh V, Davis FD (2000) A theoretical extension of the technology acceptance model: four longitudinal field studies. Manage Sci 46(2):186–204. https://doi.org/10.1287/mnsc.46.2.186.11926

Watson D, Clark LA (1992) On traits and temperament: General and specific factors of emotional experience and their relation to the five-factor model. J Pers 60(2):441–476. https://doi.org/10.1111/j.1467-6494.1992.tb00980.x

Wilkowski BM, Ferguson EL (2014) Just loving these people: extraverts implicitly associate people with reward. J Res Pers 53:93–102. https://doi.org/10.1016/j.jrp.2014.08.006

Woo SE, Chernyshenko OS, Longley A, Zhang Z, Chiu C-Y, Stark SE (2014) Openness to experience: its lower-level structure, measurement, and cross-cultural equivalence. J Pers Assess 96(1):29–45

Woo SE, Jin J, LeBreton JM (2015) Specificity matters: criterion-related validity of contextualized and facet measures of conscientiousness in predicting college student performance. J Pers Assess 97(3):301–309. https://doi.org/10.1080/00223891.2014.1002134

Yam KC, Tang PM, Jackson JC, Su R, Gray K (2023) The rise of robots increases job insecurity and maladaptive workplace behaviors: multimethod evidence. J Appl Psychol 108(5):850–870. https://doi.org/10.1037/apl0001045

Złotowski J, Yogeeswaran K, Bartneck C (2017) Can we control it? Autonomous robots threaten human identity, uniqueness, safety, and resources. Int J Hum Comput Stud 100:48–54. https://doi.org/10.1016/j.ijhcs.2016.12.008

Zhang B, Dafoe A (2019). Artificial intelligence: American attitudes and trends. Available at SSRN. https://doi.org/10.2139/ssrn.3312874

Chapter 6
Will AI Jeopardize the Uniqueness of a Patient? Challenges for Patients' Acceptance of AI in Medicine

Kalya M. Kee, Peter J. Schulz, and Joseph J. Y. Sung

Abstract In this chapter we discuss the challenges related to the integration of AI into healthcare, and its impacts on patients who want to be recognized as unique individuals. AI has the potential to change the way that healthcare is delivered and can increase the efficiency of healthcare services. However, there are still challenges that have yet to be addressed. As healthcare has developed, the perspectives and wants of patients have been overlooked. Therefore, the chapter focuses on the impact of AI use in healthcare on patients. We discuss the challenges for AI integration from three perspectives: epistemological, psychological, and ethical. We conclude our chapter with points that should be considered regarding the inevitable integration of AI in healthcare.

Key points	• The increased use of AI in healthcare will change fundamental aspects of patient-clinician relationships and even some facets of what it means to be an individual, unique, human. • Healthcare systems are traditionally centered on patients and should continue to be patient-centered. With the onset of AI and its incorporation into healthcare, this may not always be the case. • In some extreme cases, the integration of AI into healthcare may even lead to the denial of a patient's "humanness" or dehumanization
Needs	• In patients want to be seen as unique individuals. Despite the development and advancements in healthcare, this still needs to be recognized. • There remain significant ethical and legal concerns that need to be addressed regarding its implementation and use. Some ethical concerns include bias in the responses generated by AI, and privacy

(continued)

K. M. Kee (✉)
Lee Kong Chian School of Medicine, Nanyang Technological University, Singapore, Singapore
e-mail: kalyamar001@e.ntu.edu.sg

P. J. Schulz · J. J. Y. Sung
Wee Kim Wee School of Communication and Information, Lee Kong Chian School of Medicine
Nanyang Technological University, Singapore, Singapore
e-mail: peterj.schulz@ntu.edu.sg

J. J. Y. Sung
e-mail: josephsung@ntu.edu.sg

C. Montag and R. Ali (eds.), *The Impact of Artificial Intelligence on Societies*, Studies in Neuroscience, Psychology and Behavioral Economics,
https://doi.org/10.1007/978-3-031-70355-3_6

(continued)

Recommendations	• In incorporating AI into healthcare, catering to a patient's need for a sense of uniqueness will also increase patient satisfaction with, and foster personal involvement in their own healthcare. • In protecting the interests of patients, designated parties need to be accountable and responsible for the use of AI in healthcare

6.1 Introduction

As technology in healthcare progresses, healthcare practitioners may become increasingly disconnected from their patients. Technological advances in the past decades have significantly contributed to the development and refinement of medical procedures, contributing to advancing the treatment and diagnosis of various diseases, across various specialties. These healthcare advances have made healthcare irrefutably more efficient and allowed for the enhancement of procedures across all healthcare domains. However, there are divergences between technological advances and patient needs, particularly regarding the importance for doctors to consider individual patient traits and contexts. This highlights the importance of studies to understand problems developing from a growing technology-based medicine not putting the patients and their needs in the focus.

One technological advancement that is rapidly being integrated into healthcare is Artificial Intelligence (AI). There is great potential for the use of AI in healthcare. For instance, AI-assisted imaging techniques can, in some cases, outperform the judgment of experienced medical professionals (Davenport and Kalakota 2019; Lee and Yoon 2021). However, there exist multiple challenges that need to be overcome to integrate AI fully and successfully into healthcare systems. Patient concerns are one of the key barriers to AI integration. Medical devices that utilize AI claim to have positive impacts on patients (Hassan et al. 2023), but is this really the case? It has even been suggested that AI can lead to the dehumanization of patients (Formosa et al. 2022). AI itself does not promote interaction between humans (such as between doctors and a patient) and cannot respect human identity (Jotterand and Bosco 2021; Palmer and Schwan 2022). In some cases, the decisions that AI appears to make in relation to a patient's healthcare treatment may be seen to be dehumanizing (Formosa et al. 2022). The use of AI in healthcare can make patients feel as if they are simply being reduced to a percentage and being 'seen' as just a number (Binns et al. 2018; Lee and Yoon 2021).

Healthcare systems are traditionally centered on patients; however, this may not always be the case with the use of AI. Some concerns surrounding its use are as follows:

1. What does the use of AI mean for medical treatment of patients and their needs as unique individuals?

2. How will patients, as unique individuals with their personal needs, feel towards the use of AI in their own healthcare?
3. In protecting the interests of patients, who will be responsible for the use of AI in healthcare?

With these questions in mind, this chapter aims to bring together concepts and ideas from multiple domains, to formulate some understanding regarding what it means to be a unique patient in the age of AI. In the context of the IMPACT model connecting the chapters of this book (Interplay of Modality, Person, Area, Country/Culture and Transparency variables) and helping to understand AI attitude formation, we believe that the uniqueness concept of this chapter relates to the Person variable, stressing the important of personal characteristics shaping attitudes towards AI. We first give some context to the concept of uniqueness in medicine. We then discuss the challenges that AI poses from three perspectives: epistemological, psychological, and ethical. We then conclude our chapter with points that should be considered regarding the future with the inevitable integration of AI in healthcare.

6.2 The Changing Role of Patients in Medicine—How Doctor-Patient Interactions Have Evolved Throughout History

In the field of medicine, human interactions and relationships are vital. These relationships include those between doctors and their patients, nurses, and patients, and even doctors and nurses. The relationship between doctor and patient is not only based on patients' trust in clinical knowledge and skills that a doctor possesses (Morgan 2018). Being able to see and communicate with patients physically also contributes to this relationship. These relationships have a deep-rooted history in medical practices.

Hippocrates is often credited as the father of modern or scientific medicine, and his views have shaped what is referred to as "Hippocratic" medicine (Grammaticos and Diamantis 2008; Kleisiaris et al. 2014). His writings have greatly shaped medicine of today and are reflected in variations of the Hippocratic Oath that medical students take in some countries (Green 2017; Sritharan et al. 2001). According to this philosophy, there are two things that doctors must do regarding diseases "to help, or at least to do no harm" (Fabre 1997; Kleisiaris et al. 2014; Smith 1994). In other words, through medical practice, clinicians must, above all, ensure the health of their patients. Additionally, Hippocrates asserted that medicine should rely on and be based upon detailed observations, reasoning, and experience to establish diagnosis and determine treatment plans (Kleisiaris et al. 2014). This oath may be considered impossible to meet to fullest extent and may become harder to realize as medicine advances. As the line between the 'business' of healthcare and patient care blurs, it is hard to ascertain if living up to oath is still possible (Abbasi 2019).

The changes in the doctor-patient relationships and interactions can be linked to three timeframes that characterize developments in medicine (Jewson 1976; Morgan

2018). These timeframes are named "bedside medicine", "hospital medicine", and "laboratory medicine" (Jewson 1976). Personalized medical care was established in the late eighteenth century (the late 1700s), as established in the first framework of "bedside medicine". At this time, patients were often in the upper classes of society and were able to afford to see physicians. Doctors and patients shared an extremely close relationship, as the number of patients that they tended to were small. Doctors and patients shared a close bond, and doctors likely recognized their patients as unique, separate, individuals who were shaped by their own lived experiences. The doctor-patient relationship became less personal in "hospital medicine" of the early nineteenth century (early 1800s). During this time medical practitioners (specifically, surgeons) started running hospitals, which were initially run by governors who were laymen. Hospitals, rather than homes, became the key sites for medical practice, making healthcare more centralized (Morgan 2018). With this change, wards became a "training ground" (Nicolson 2009). Where patients were once viewed as individuals that doctors served, patients were gradually treated as "clinical material" (Nicolson 2009). Patients increasingly "lost control of their own bodies, forfeiting the validity of their own concepts of health, illness and physicality" (Evenden 1992; Fissell and Fissell 2002; Jewson 1976; Lindemann and Fissell 1993; Nicolson 2009). The third phase, "laboratory medicine", emerged around the mid-nineteenth century (roughly from the 1840s to 1860s). Developments in this phase were led by the practice of 'scientific' medicine, methodology, and processes. This sought disease at the cellular level and intensified the reductionist tendencies of the preceding stage. The laboratory was the site for the advancement and application of medical knowledge (Gillam 2016). Scientists working in laboratories gradually became even more detached from patients. There was a greater focus on utilizing objective measures and rigorous processes, compared to the earlier centuries, where doctors sought to acquire knowledge about individual patients and a patient's perception of their illness (Morgan 2018). The frameworks established by Jewson (1976), of "bedside medicine", "hospital medicine", and "laboratory medicine") suggest that there was a gradual shift away from the patient as an individual with unique circumstances. During the age of "laboratory medicine", patients were viewed as sources of information for more medical knowledge to contribute towards medical and scientific advancements.

While medical practice may have shifted away from patients at the core, patients still wish to feel that their circumstances and emotions are being considered. Patients view themselves as unique, and special, and expect their doctors to consider their traits, such as background and socio-demographic characteristics (Launer 2003). Despite the need for patients to be recognized as unique individuals with equally distinct medical conditions, advancements in medicine have moved focus away from the patient. Modern-day medical developments, particularly related to advances in technology, have increased this distance. Despite changes in medical practices throughout history, one key facet has remained: Medicine still involves interactions between patient and doctor, and the intentionality of doctors to treat/diagnose patients. However, the expanding integration of AI into healthcare is likely to challenge this key characteristic of healthcare.

In healthcare, fields where imaging techniques are being utilized represent pioneers of AI integration. One such specialty is gastroenterology. Globally, colorectal cancer is a leading cause of mortality and morbidity and is a major public health issue (Favoriti et al. 2016; Sung et al. 2021). It is the third most commonly diagnosed cancer and is the third highest cause of cancer death (Sung et al. 2021). AI has immense potential to benefit patients in the field of gastroenterology. AI will affect patients by preventing potential human errors in disease detection (Hassan et al. 2023). Due to its heavy usage of image-based diagnosis (e.g. CT, MRI, endoscopy, and histology) and surgical/endoscopic intervention, AI is already being used and integrated into current medical practice. AI can be used in various ways, for multiple applications in gastroenterology beyond its use in medical imaging for lesion identification and detection (Kröner et al. 2021). In this field, AI use in polyp detection can reduce the polyp miss rate among patients (Haslam et al. 2007; Le Berre et al. 2020). AI is also being used to develop scoring systems for risk stratification, to predict treatment responses, and to evaluate the quality of endoscopic examinations (Kröner et al. 2021; Sung and Poon 2020). From our view, advances in healthcare intrinsically change the dynamic between patient and clinician and need to be addressed to ensure that patient needs remain the key focus of healthcare.

6.3 An Epistemological Perspective Regarding Challenges in AI Integration into Healthcare

In discussing the involvement of AI in the healthcare sector, a short epistemological observation concerning medicine, specifically medical practice, is required. Medicine is what has been described as a practical science, meaning its ultimate goal lies in a specific action, not in general recognition (Broadbent 2019). What drives medicine is not about being more knowledgeable, but the goal to help individual people. In other words, the outcome of medical practice is the well-being of individual people. As a practical discipline, medicine deals directly with individuals, specifically with the condition of an individual at a particular point in time. It is essential for a diagnosis that this assessment takes place at a specific point in time. In contrast to the conditions present in theoretical statements, a diagnosis can be deficient not only when it is factually incorrect but also when it is made too late (Gandhi et al. 2006).

Humans are social by nature, being "social animals". Considering human behavior, it has been recognized that we strive for social connections and relationships with others in our environments (Seppala et al. 2013). In seeking such connections, humans change or adapt their behaviors to fit into groups (Fiske 2010). In some ways, this is contradictory. While each person wants to feel a sense of belonging within groups, individuals also strive to be unique from their peers. Uniqueness is a fundamental aspect of an individual's identity. Being unique means that we possess a personal sense of experiencing the self (or our self) that can only be recognized by the individual person (Şimşek and Yalınçetin 2010). We (as humans) often feel a desire to shape our personal identity that is special, distinct, and different from others (Schumpe and Erb 2015). Uniqueness can be defined in several dimensions, and viewed from different lenses, including philosophical and psychological.

What makes me, *me*? What defines *my* personal identity? These questions have been explored in-depth by philosophers throughout history. Philosophers have sought to understand the complex question in numerous ways. One commonly cited way to explain the formation of personal identity was proposed by John Locke in the seventeenth century. Locke posits that personal identity is constantly and repeatedly updated through psychological continuity. He proposes that humans begin with an "empty" mind (or a tabula rasa) which is then shaped by individual experiences (Locke 1948). He also asserts that the sources for our thoughts and ideas are sensations from our experiences and reflections of our experiences.

We do not exist in isolation. As social creatures, we interact with other human beings. The way we interact with each other reflects our identity. Philosopher, Immanuel Kant, proposed that, as living persons, we should treat humanity "never simply as a means, but always at the same time as an end". In other words, we must have respect for persons. We can treat other people as a means to our own ends, but at the same time, we must also treat other individuals as ends in themselves (Wood 1998). However, this is not always the case. We often use other people to meet our own ends. This is particularly evident in client-facing jobs, such as in healthcare. For instance, in going for a doctor's appointment, we go for our own sakes, to get a diagnosis, and to receive advice from the doctor. We are not approaching the doctor to be of service to them. However, although we see a doctor to meet our own needs, we still need to address the doctor's personal, 'human', needs. So, we treat the doctors with respect and consideration. On the flip side, service providers, such as doctors, need to treat their clients (i.e. patients) as fellow humans, rather than a work-related quota that needs to be fulfilled. It is important to recognize an individual's worth as a person, rather than focusing only on an individual's own needs and wants.

Another philosopher, Charles Taylor, takes the concepts of individualism further. He states that authenticity is a way that we define our identities. In being authentic, individuals are autonomous, which is reflected in their thoughts and subsequent actions or behavior (Taylor 2005). The concept of "authenticity" has important implications for ethics, particularly in healthcare. As individuals strive for autonomy, systems need to provide spaces where individuals can pursue their goals. By facilitating means for individuals to act as they desire, and respecting their individuality, we, therefore, can honor the value of "respect for persons" (White 2018). As part of the human experience, and for decisions that individuals decide for themselves, patients want to be recognized as 'themselves'. In the desire to be recognized, patients want a doctor or clinician who can relate to their personal needs and empathize with their circumstances.

One concern regarding health-specific AI relates to the general lack of diversity, specifically in terms of race and gender, in tests conducted using AI, suggesting that the algorithm concept is inherently skewed or biased. Reviews have found that authors of most studies related to AI were conducted in high-income countries, from the USA, and non-clinicians (Alberto et al. 2023; Celi et al. 2022). Similar under representations have been observed in psychological research, that has, for a long time, focused on participants with Western, educated, industrialized, rich, democratic (WEIRD) backgrounds (Henrich et al. 2010).

The aforementioned studies suggest that there is a lack of representation for various other populations, which could lead to biases in the results reported regarding AI. Other inherent biases exist due to the selective nature of trials, particularly randomized control trials, that are used to test or develop AI tools. For instance, studies have shown that the nature of trials leads to a disproportionate number of healthy men being selected over any other population (Rothwell 2006). As a consequence, women, the elderly, those with chronic conditions, and pregnant women are excluded from testing. However, as AI is generally trained using data that may be inherently biased, this is especially concerning. It is evident that individuals who are not male and are from different medical, racial, social, and economic backgrounds are at risk for different diseases and conditions. Individuals who do not fall under the 'healthy man' category may be misdiagnosed by an AI. This sentiment is also a concern of existing patients. In a qualitative study that was conducted among 15 patients, one concern expressed by our participants was specific to the information that has been 'inputted' to the AI. The participants, who were all from Singapore, expressed concerns related to AI tools that are developed in Western countries (refer to the WEIRD problem above). Participants expressed the need for AI tools to be 'localized' for specific contexts and cultures (Kee et al. 2024). This is also reflected in the overarching IMPACT framework in this book, pronouncing the relevance of culture variables to understand AI attitudes (Montag et al. 2024a, b). The concern that the majority 'voices' will dominate and determine the results that are provided is a concern for all involved, including health professionals and patients (Chen et al. 2024).

6.4 A Psychological Perspective Regarding Challenges in AI Integration into Healthcare

Getting a better understanding of patients to deliver diagnoses is important for both patients and their doctors. Doctors are knowledgeable regarding well-defined patterns of diseases, particularly in their specialties. Through personal interactions with patients, they can apply the patterns that they know to their individual, unique, patients. This is a crucial process in healthcare, where diagnoses are based on doctors' judgments, including their personal knowledge, and understanding of their patients. A diagnosis is specific to a certain individual based on a doctor's broad understanding. Patients' uniqueness and need to feel unique are considered. To our understanding, AI of today does not take into consideration potential contextual variables that an individual may have experienced. Rather, AI fits individuals into pre-established 'boxes' that it has established based on datasets that have been fed to the technology. AI does not 'care' or intend to seek the "best" care for an individual patient. What does the integration of AI mean for a treatment that should be tailored to unique individuals? To best answer this, we first need to understand why individuals desire to feel a sense of uniqueness.

In the realm of psychology, the phenomenon of striving for uniqueness to define one's personal identity is often referred to as the "Need for Uniqueness" (Snyder and Fromkin 1977, 2012). The "Need for Uniqueness" is defined as the desire to seek differentiation from others (Snyder 1992; Wang et al. 2019). Feeling unique, and having a personal sense of uniqueness, is an important aspect of being human. A sense of uniqueness can moderate the relationship associations of extraversion and openness to experience an individual's happiness (Koydemir et al. 2014). While the "Need for Uniqueness" theory is often associated with consumer behavior (i.e., having a need for uniqueness will motivate consumers to prefer products that foster individuality), it can be applied to many other domains, including healthcare.

Beyond psychology, in the realm of healthcare, it is essential for individual patients to feel unique. Patients seeking medical attention want to feel that their personal, individual, and special needs are being considered by healthcare providers. When confronted with any health challenges or indications, such as experiencing flu-like symptoms that are worrying, individuals may question: "Am *I* really having COVID-19?" While many others may have similar symptoms, individuals believe that they are different and that their unique circumstances distinguish them from 'everyone else'. This experience may be even more intensified in the case of severe diseases. Patients want to feel that their personal needs are being addressed. It has been identified that a patient's sense of uniqueness affects the level of acceptance of medical AI. One study identified that participants who felt a higher sense of uniqueness had higher levels of acceptance for medical AI which improve their experience of healthcare services (Cai et al. 2023).

Feeling a sense of uniqueness has positive effects on mental and physical well-being. In healthcare, being able to foster a patient's personal sense of uniqueness is extremely important, as it may affect their own health moving forward. It has been identified that delivering health-related information in a more personalized manner makes patients feel like they are distinct individuals and are unique. This has various implications for healthcare. A sense of uniqueness can have influence on deliberate health behaviors. For instance, it may lead to higher adherence to the medication regimens prescribed by their doctors (Veazie and Cai 2007). Patients who have a higher sense of their own uniqueness are more likely to believe that they belong to statistically-based minorities (Veazie and Cai 2007). For example, take the following scenario. If a patient were to be told the following true statement, namely, that an AI used in adenoma rate detection can detect adenoma almost 30% of the time (Sung et al. 2021; Wang et al. 2019). A patient who feels more unique or believes that they are a more unique individual is likely to believe that they belong to the minority. Thus, they are likely to accept the use of AI in their diagnostic colonoscopy, as their AI-detected diagnosis be true. However, the acceptance of AI use in healthcare may depend on the application where it is utilized. Patients with a higher sense of uniqueness appear to have a lower acceptance of AI use in diagnosis and treatment (Cai et al. 2023). However, if patients perceive that the AI displays empathy in the human–machine interaction, this may mediate the relationship, and increase acceptance of AI use in diagnosis and treatment (Cai et al. 2023). One study that evaluated the preferences for chatbot or physician responses even found that their participants preferred the chatbot-generated responses, and felt that these responses were more empathetic (Ayers et al. 2023). The relationship between the need for uniqueness and acceptance of AI use is complex. However, patients want to be seen and feel that their doctors recognize, and empathize with, their personal traits and individual contexts.

In extreme cases, the integration of AI into healthcare may lead to the dehumanization of patients. In essence, dehumanization refers to the denial of an individual's "humanness" (Haslam et al. 2007). The mind is often defined from two dimensions: (1) experiences, and the capacity to feel, and (2) agency, and the capacity to exert choices and make decisions (Gray et al. 2007). Dehumanization can sometimes be subtle, and not immediately obvious or explicit. The dehumanization of patients has persisted, perhaps unintentionally. Dehumanization in medicine has been attributed to nonfunctional causes, such as deindividuating practices, impaired patient agency, and clinician-patient dissimilarity, and functional causes, such as mechanization of practices, reduced empathy, and moral disengagement (Haque and Waytz 2012). The integration of AI into healthcare likely will only exacerbate the factors that are associated with dehumanizing patients. AI may move clinicians further away from their patients, resulting in a loss of human connection and recognition of patients as individual humans.

6.5 An Ethical Perspective Regarding Challenges in AI Integration into Healthcare

While the use of AI in healthcare holds great promise, there remain significant ethical and legal concerns that need to be addressed regarding its implementation and use. The increased use of AI will change fundamental aspects of patient-clinician relationships and even some facets of what it means to be an individual, unique, human (Jotterand and Bosco 2021). Some ethical concerns include bias in the responses generated, privacy, and authorship (Limna et al. 2023; Montag et al. 2020; Zhou et al. 2023).

Clinicians report contradictory reactions toward the use of AI in healthcare practice. One systematic review reported that clinicians believe that a majority of patients have supportive attitudes toward clinical AI (Chen et al. 2022). Furthermore, it has been reported that clinicians are unclear about the views of their patients towards AI. Some studies reported that clinicians see a perceived benefit of AI integration as being able to focus on interacting with their patients (Chen et al. 2022). Some clinicians expected that the use of AI (specifically clinical decision support systems) may reduce time spent with patients (Lambert et al. 2023). However, if AI were to be used for autonomous diagnoses, a clinician may not be physically present with the patient during their encounter and interaction with AI (Hassan et al. 2023; Lambert et al. 2023). In specialties that may require close human interaction, healthcare practitioners (specifically nurses) emphasized that utilizing AI in healthcare delivery would reduce human touch and connection, and subsequently would have a negative effect on patients (Lambert et al. 2023). These points suggest that AI that does not consider patient needs can be detrimental to AI integration into healthcare, and potentially cause unexpected harm to patients.

Navigating the integration of AI into healthcare is a complex challenge, and governance frameworks need to be put in place to protect patients, as unique individuals, in the age of AI. The frameworks should protect humans in various rights, including the right to personal identity, free will, mental privacy, equal access to mental augmentation, and protection from algorithmic bias (Jotterand and Bosco 2021). Despite the pressing need for frameworks to be put in place to safeguard patients as AI becomes integrated into healthcare, there are still limited numbers of formal frameworks that directly address AI in healthcare (Gama et al. 2022). In addition, existing frameworks are limited in the scope of guidance provided. Most frameworks only focus on AI transparency and effectiveness (Crossnohere et al. 2022). However, fewer are focused on the engagement of patients, such as on the opinions of and personal values that patients have regarding AI use in their healthcare (Crossnohere et al. 2022). From an ethics perspective, there are still many challenges to be addressed regarding the use of AI in patient-focused healthcare. For instance, what if a patient can provide information regarding every detail of their life (such as family history, personal interactions, etc.) to an AI to accurately "map" them for a more accurate diagnosis? What are the implications of allowing AI to access this information? How will this threaten the doctor-patient relationship, and consequently patients' sense of uniqueness? Without established frameworks, these unanswered questions, and challenges regarding AI integration into healthcare will persist and require urgent attention.

6.6 Conclusions Regarding the Integration of AI into Healthcare

Patients are the key group of individuals that should be protected and supported. Their personal needs need to be addressed. While the role of the doctors will change with the integration of AI into healthcare, the needs of patients remain the same. Doctors should remain as moderators between AI systems and patients. On top of doctors, healthcare systems, and governing bodies to protect the needs of patients. A central aspect of medical practice is the establishment of a diagnosis. What is determined in the diagnosis is the presence of a typical condition, a pathological entity that exhibits constant characteristics and operates under fixed regularities. Every diagnosis is, by its logical status, a statement, and specifically, a statement of a certain kind. Through it, a specific disease concept is assigned to a particular individual patient at a specific point in time. Upon closer examination of AI's role in medicine, one encounters quantified statements, shifting away from medical practice and towards general pathological or nosological knowledge.

As to the question of the individual ("unique") perspective of the own life of a patient: The individual patient typically has an idea of what is ailing them. They not only objectively identify their ailment but also consistently assess and evaluate it. When a patient seeks medical help, they often arrive with complaints they've already interpreted in their own way. Moreover, patients are not merely satisfied with receiving a diagnosis; they also seek meaningful insights into what that diagnosis signifies for their future. Hence, the concept of prognosis becomes paramount in such contexts. And in the context of these questions, the perception of uniqueness for the patient becomes even more evident.

There is no doubt that AI will improve healthcare. It can sharpen precision health and provide a better understanding of regularities. However, AI today provides information on a general level, based on the information that it "knows". It is hard to say if it actually does address the specific needs of an individual, based on the factors that make each patient distinct. Instead, AI integrates an individual into a broader pool of data. Thus, there needs to be a consensus regarding the use of AI in healthcare that does not hinder research or threaten the challenges faced by individual patients.

Patients will be the key recipients of treatments or diagnoses from AI. Some studies have noted that the public is generally optimistic towards the use of AI in healthcare, such as AI being used to help doctors and to reform medical care (Gao et al. 2020). However, when it comes to the intention to use AI in their healthcare, there are still concerns among the public related to trust in AI (Gao et al. 2020; Liu and Tao 2022). There is apprehension regarding the removal of a 'human' or patient-centered healthcare as AI becomes increasingly used (Benda et al. 2021). Patients are worried that they are being reduced to being "just a number" (Lee and Yoon 2021), and, in the same thread, that their healthcare treatment is not being specialized for them. Without the personalized (perceived or not) treatment that is prescribed by a trusted doctor, a patient may feel that they are not being recognized as an individual who is unique, with unique problems and situations. A doctor's trust and belief in AI can affect their own attitudes towards AI in healthcare practice (Schulz et al. 2023). The trust of healthcare practitioners regarding AI in healthcare can also influence the acceptance of their patients. A review identified that physicians' acceptance of an AI system is positively associated with patients' satisfaction with an AI system (Lambert et al. 2023). This finding is promising for the future of AI integration, as it suggests that clinicians still consider the opinions of their patients in medicine. Their consideration may also suggest to patients that clinicians have their interests at heart. While treatment plans may not be, in reality, personalized, the perceived lack of empathy and recognition makes future patients wary of AI being used in healthcare.

In various parts of the world, new physicians continue to recite the Hippocratic oath as they enter the medical domain. Part of the oath states that "Into whatsoever houses I enter, I will enter to help the sick, and I will abstain from all intentional wrong-doing and harm (Davey 2001)." Medical practitioners, new and old, utilize the oath as a guide towards the ethics they use in the medical domain, and how they approach treatment of their patients. Similarly, patients expect that their doctors are following these principles, and have their best interests at the forefront, without having any ulterior motives. The oath also states that doctors "will use treatment to help the sick according to my ability and judgment (Davey 2001)." Patients trust that their doctors will do everything they can to help them. They trust a doctor's capacity to observe and understand what they are experiencing and living through. They also trust that their doctors are being authentic in wanting to treat them. However, with the integration of AI, it becomes less clear whether patients are truly receiving treatments with empathy and compassion as unique human beings. Ultimately, catering to a patient's need for a sense of uniqueness will also increase patient satisfaction with, and foster personal involvement in their healthcare.

Medicine and medical systems should be patient-centered. There is a critical need to refocus technology-driven healthcare around the patient. Stakeholders of healthcare (such as healthcare practitioners, AI developers, policymakers, etc.) should come together to ensure that patient interests are protected. Shelley (Shelley 2016) cited healthcare consultant, Bill Kirkup, who stated that "we have lost something of the art of medicine in a headlong rush to embrace the science". Although, in the future, AI may appear to show empathy or consideration, the AI of today is not yet able to provide 'real' compassionate care or support for patients. In this vein, we should strive for AI driven medical care to prioritize the patient to the forefront. AI systems, such as personalized systems and precision medicine, need to consider more 'human' aspects of healthcare. With the inevitable integration of AI into healthcare, healthcare professionals should collaborate with AI, and AI developers, to enhance patient care and provide the best possible outcomes.

References

Abbasi K (2019) First do no harm: the impossible oath. BMJ 366:l4734. https://doi.org/10.1136/bmj.l4734

Alberto IRI, Alberto NRI, Altinel Y, Blacker S, Binotti WW, Celi LA, Chua T, Fiske A, Griffin M, Karaca G, Mokolo N, Naawu DKN, Patscheider J, Petushkov A, Quion J, Senteio C, Taisbak S, Tırnova İ, Tokashiki H, Yap K et al (2023) Who does the fairness in health AI community represent? medRxiv. https://doi.org/10.1101/2023.03.20.23287471

Ayers JW, Poliak A, Dredze M, Leas EC, Zhu Z, Kelley JB, Faix DJ, Goodman AM, Longhurst CA, Hogarth M, Smith DM (2023) Comparing physician and artificial intelligence chatbot responses to patient questions posted to a public social media forum. JAMA Intern Med 183(6):589–596. https://doi.org/10.1001/jamainternmed.2023.1838

https://doi.org/10.1093/jamia/ocab238

Binns R, Kleek MV, Veale M, Lyngs U, Zhao J, Shadbolt N (2018) 'It's reducing a human being to a percentage': perceptions of justice in algorithmic decisions. In: Proceedings of the 2018 CHI conference on human factors in computing systems, Montreal QC, Canada. https://doi.org/10.1145/3173574.3173951

Broadbent A (2019) The goal of medicine. In: Philosophy of medicine. Oxford University Press. https://doi.org/10.1093/oso/9780190612139.003.0002

Cai Z, He H, Huo W, Xu X (2023) More unique, more accepting? Integrating sense of uniqueness, perceived knowledge, and perceived empathy with acceptance of medical artificial intelligence. Int J Human–Computer Interact:1–14. https://doi.org/10.1080/10447318.2023.2291616

Celi LA, Cellini J, Charpignon M-L, Dee EC, Dernoncourt F, Eber R, Mitchell WG, Moukheiber L, Schirmer J, Situ J, Paguio J, Park J, Wawira JG, Yao S (2022). Sources of bias in artificial intelligence that perpetuate healthcare disparities—a global review. PLOS Digit Health 1(3):e0000022. https://doi.org/10.1371/journal.pdig.0000022

Chen M, Zhang B, Cai Z, Seery S, Gonzalez MJ, Ali NM, Ren R, Qiao Y, Xue P, Jiang Y (2022) Acceptance of clinical artificial intelligence among physicians and medical students: a systematic review with cross-sectional survey [Original Research]. Front Med 9. https://doi.org/10.3389/fmed.2022.990604

Chen K, Shao A, Burapacheep J, Li Y (2024) Conversational AI and equity through assessing GPT-3's communication with diverse social groups on contentious topics. Sci Rep 14(1):1561. https://doi.org/10.1038/s41598-024-51969-w

Crossnohere NL, Elsaid M, Paskett J, Bose-Brill S, Bridges JFP (2022) Guidelines for artificial intelligence in medicine: literature review and content analysis of frameworks [Review]. J Med Internet Res 24(8):e36823. https://doi.org/10.2196/36823

Davenport T, Kalakota R (2019) The potential for artificial intelligence in healthcare. Future Healthc J 6(2):94–98. https://doi.org/10.7861/futurehosp.6-2-94

Davey LM (2001) The oath of Hippocrates: an historical review. Neurosurgery 49(3):554–566. https://journals.lww.com/neurosurgery/fulltext/2001/09000/the_oath_of_hippocrates__an_historical_review.2.aspx

Evenden DA (1992) Patients, power and the poor in eighteenth-century Bristol [Book review]. Canadian J Hist 27:551+. https://link.gale.com/apps/doc/A13374182/AONE?u=googlescholar&sid=googleScholar&xid=cdae0457

Fabre J (1997) Hip, hip, Hippocrates: extracts from the Hippocratic doctor. BMJ 315(7123):1669–1670. https://doi.org/10.1136/bmj.315.7123.1669

Favoriti P, Carbone G, Greco M, Pirozzi F, Pirozzi REM, Corcione F (2016) Worldwide burden of colorectal cancer: a review. Updat Surg 68(1):7–11. https://doi.org/10.1007/s13304-016-0359-y

Fiske ST (2010) Social beings: a core motives approach to social psychology, 2nd ed. J. Wiley

Fissell ME, Fissell ME (2002) Patients, power and the poor in eighteenth-century Bristol. Cambridge University Press. https://books.google.com.sg/books?id=mbr0C5LnwbIC

Formosa P, Rogers W, Griep Y, Bankins S, Richards D (2022) Medical AI and human dignity: contrasting perceptions of human and artificially intelligent (AI) decision making in diagnostic and medical resource allocation contexts. Comp Human Behav 133:107296. https://doi.org/10.1016/j.chb.2022.107296

Gama F, Tyskbo D, Nygren J, Barlow J, Reed J, Svedberg P (2022) Implementation frameworks for artificial intelligence translation into health care practice: scoping review [Review]. J Med Internet Res 24(1):e32215. https://doi.org/10.2196/32215

Gandhi TK, Kachalia A, Thomas EJ, Puopolo AL, Yoon C, Brennan TA, Studdert DM (2006) Missed and delayed diagnoses in the ambulatory setting: a study of closed malpractice claims. Ann Intern Med 145(7):488–496. https://doi.org/10.7326/0003-4819-145-7-200610030-00006

Gao S, He L, Chen Y, Li D, Lai K (2020) Public perception of artificial intelligence in medical care: content analysis of social media [Original Paper]. J Med Internet Res 22(7):e16649. https://doi.org/10.2196/16649

Gillam S (2016) The reappearance of the sick man: a landmark publication revisited. Br J Gen Pract 66(653):616–617. https://doi.org/10.3399/bjgp16X688153

Grammaticos PC, Diamantis A (2008) Useful known and unknown views of the father of modern medicine, Hippocrates and his teacher Democritus. Hell J Nucl Med 11(1):2–4

Gray HM, Gray K, Wegner DM (2007) Dimensions of mind perception. Science 315(5812):619–619. https://doi.org/10.1126/science.1134475

Green B (2017) Use of the Hippocratic or other professional oaths in UK medical schools in 2017: practice, perception of benefit and principlism. BMC Res Notes 10(1):777. https://doi.org/10.1186/s13104-017-3114-7

Haque OS, Waytz A (2012) Dehumanization in medicine: causes, solutions, and functions. Perspec Psychol Sci 7(2):176–186. https://www-jstor-org.remotexs.ntu.edu.sg/stable/41613554

Haslam N, Loughnan S, Reynolds C, Wilson S (2007) Dehumanization: a new perspective. Social Person Psychol Compass 1(1):409–422. https://doi.org/10.1111/j.1751-9004.2007.00030.x

Hassan C, Repici A, Sharma P (2023) Incorporating artificial intelligence into gastroenterology practices. Clin Gastroenterol Hepatol 21(7):1687–1689. https://doi.org/10.1016/j.cgh.2023.02.008

Henrich J, Heine SJ, Norenzayan A (2010) Most people are not WEIRD. Nature 466(7302):29–29. https://doi.org/10.1038/466029a

Jewson ND (1976) The disappearance of the sick-man from medical cosmology, 1770–1870. Sociology 10(2):225–244. https://doi.org/10.1177/003803857601000202

Jotterand F, Bosco C (2021) Artificial intelligence in medicine: a sword of Damocles? J Med Syst 46(1):9. https://doi.org/10.1007/s10916-021-01796-7

Kee KM, Choo CM, Kim C, Schulz PJ, Goh WWB, Sung JJY (2024, 26–28 June) "It's also a double-edged sword": a qualitative study on the perspectives of patients towards artificial intelligence in healthcare [poster presentation]. In: 22nd International and interdisciplinary conference on communication, medicine and ethics, Brescia, Italy

Kleisiaris CF, Sfakianakis C, Papathanasiou IV (2014) Health care practices in ancient Greece: the Hippocratic ideal. J Med Ethics Hist Med 7:6

Koydemir S, Şimşek ÖF, Demir M (2014) Pathways from personality to happiness: sense of uniqueness as a mediator. J Humanist Psychol 54(3):314–335. https://doi.org/10.1177/0022167813501226

Kröner PT, Engels MM, Glicksberg BS, Johnson KW, Mzaik O, van Hooft JE, Wallace MB, El-Serag HB, Krittanawong C (2021) Artificial intelligence in gastroenterology: a state-of-the-art review. World J Gastroenterol 27(40):6794–6824. https://doi.org/10.3748/wjg.v27.i40.6794

Lambert SI, Madi M, Sopka S, Lenes A, Stange H, Buszello C-P, Stephan A (2023) An integrative review on the acceptance of artificial intelligence among healthcare professionals in hospitals. NPJ Digit Med 6(1):111. https://doi.org/10.1038/s41746-023-00852-5

Launer J (2003) Uniqueness and conformity. QJM: Int J Med 96(8):615–616. https://doi.org/10.1093/qjmed/hcg099

Le Berre C, Sandborn WJ, Aridhi S, Devignes M-D, Fournier L, Smaïl-Tabbone M, Danese S, Peyrin-Biroulet L (2020) Application of artificial intelligence to gastroenterology and hepatology. Gastroenterology 158(1):76–94.e72. https://doi.org/10.1053/j.gastro.2019.08.058

Lee D, Yoon SN (2021) Application of artificial intelligence-based technologies in the healthcare industry: opportunities and challenges. Int J Environ Res Public Health 18(1). https://doi.org/10.3390/ijerph18010271

Limna P, Kraiwanit T, Jangjarat K, Klayklung P, Chocksathaporn P (2023) The use of ChatGPT in the digital era: perspectives on chatbot implementation. J Appl Learn Teach 6(1)

Lindemann M, Fissell ME (1993) Patients, power, and the poor in eighteenth-century Bristol. Am Hist Rev 98:164

Liu K, Tao D (2022) The roles of trust, personalization, loss of privacy, and anthropomorphism in public acceptance of smart healthcare services. Comp Human Behav 127:107026. https://doi.org/10.1016/j.chb.2021.107026

Locke J (1948). An essay concerning human understanding, 1690. In: Readings in the history of psychology. Appleton-Century-Crofts, pp 55–68. https://doi.org/10.1037/11304-008

Montag C, Sindermann C, Baumeister H (2020) Digital phenotyping in psychological and medical sciences: a reflection about necessary prerequisites to reduce harm and increase benefits. Curr Opin Psychol 36:19–24. https://doi.org/10.1016/j.copsyc.2020.03.013

Montag C, Ali R, Al-Thani D, Hall BJ (2024a) On artificial intelligence and global mental health. Asian J Psychiatr 91:103855. https://doi.org/10.1016/j.ajp.2023.103855

Montag C, Nakov P, Ali R (2024b) Considering the IMPACT framework to understand the AI-well-being-complex from an interdisciplinary perspective. Tele Inform Reports 13:100112. https://doi.org/10.1016/j.teler.2023.100112
Morgan M (2018) The doctor-patient relationship. In: Sociology as applied to medicine, 7th ed. Palgrave, London, pp 77–98
Nicolson M (2009) Commentary: Nicholas Jewson and the disappearance of the sick man from medical cosmology, 1770–1870. Int J Epidemiol 38(3):639–642. https://doi.org/10.1093/ije/dyp183
Palmer A, Schwan D (2022) Beneficent dehumanization: Employing artificial intelligence and carebots to mitigate shame-induced barriers to medical care. Bioethics 36(2):187–193. https://doi.org/10.1111/bioe.12986
Rothwell PM (2006) Factors that can affect the external validity of randomised controlled trials. PLoS Clin Trials 1(1):e9. https://doi.org/10.1371/journal.pctr.0010009
Schulz PJ, Lwin MO, Kee KM, Goh WWB, Lam TYT, Sung JJY (2023) Modeling the influence of attitudes, trust, and beliefs on endoscopists' acceptance of artificial intelligence applications in medical practice [Original Research]. Front Public Health 11. https://doi.org/10.3389/fpubh.2023.1301563
Schumpe BM, Erb H-P (2015) Humans and uniqueness. Sci Prog 98(1):1–11. https://doi.org/10.3184/003685015X14205597448201
Seppala E, Rossomando T, Doty JR (2013) Social connection and compassion: important predictors of health and well-being. Social Res 80(2):411–430. http://www.jstor.org/stable/24385608
Shelley BP (2016) Re-humanizing "high-tech, no touch" medicine: narrative medicine and cineme-ducation perspectives. Arch Med Health Sci 4(1):1–5. https://doi.org/10.4103/2321-4848.183367
Şimşek ÖF, Yalınçetin B (2010) I feel unique, therefore I am: the development and preliminary validation of the personal sense of uniqueness (PSU) scale. Person Indiv Diff 49(6):576–581. https://doi.org/10.1016/j.paid.2010.05.006
Smith WD (1994) Hippocrates, vol 7. Harvard University Press
Snyder CR (1992) Product scarcity by need for uniqueness interaction: a consumer catch-22 carousel? Basic Appl Soc Psychol 13(1):9–24. https://doi.org/10.1207/s15324834basp1301_3
Snyder CR, Fromkin HL (1977) Abnormality as a positive characteristic: the development and validation of a scale measuring need for uniqueness. J Abnorm Psychol 86(5):518–527. https://doi.org/10.1037/0021-843X.86.5.518
Snyder CR, Fromkin HL (2012) Uniqueness: the human pursuit of difference. Springer Science and Business Media
Sritharan K, Russell G, Fritz Z, Wong D, Rollin M, Dunning J, Morgan P, Sheehan C (2001) Medical oaths and declarations. BMJ 323(7327):1440–1441. https://doi.org/10.1136/bmj.323.7327.1440
Sung JJY, Poon NCH (2020) Artificial intelligence in gastroenterology: where are we heading? Front Med 14(4):511–517. https://doi.org/10.1007/s11684-020-0742-4
Sung H, Ferlay J, Siegel RL, Laversanne M, Soerjomataram I, Jemal A, Bray F (2021) Global cancer statistics 2020: GLOBOCAN estimates of incidence and mortality worldwide for 36 cancers in 185 countries. CA: A Cancer J Clin 71(3):209–249. https://doi.org/10.3322/caac.21660
Taylor JS (2005) Personal autonomy: new essays on personal autonomy and its role in contemporary moral philosophy. Cambridge University Press
Veazie PJ, Cai S (2007) A connection between medication adherence, patient sense of uniqueness, and the personalization of information. Med Hypotheses 68(2):335–342. https://doi.org/10.1016/j.mehy.2006.04.077
Wang P, Berzin TM, Glissen Brown JR, Bharadwaj S, Becq A, Xiao X, Liu P, Li L, Song Y, Zhang D, Li Y, Xu G, Tu M, Liu X (2019) Real-time automatic detection system increases colonoscopic polyp and adenoma detection rates: a prospective randomised controlled study. Gut 68(10):1813–1819. https://doi.org/10.1136/gutjnl-2018-317500

White L (2018) The need for authenticity-based autonomy in medical ethics. HEC Forum 30(3):191–209. https://doi.org/10.1007/s10730-017-9335-2

Wood A (1998) The final form of Kant's practical philosophy. South J Philos 36(S1):1–20. https://doi.org/10.1111/j.2041-6962.1998.tb01774.x

Zhou J, Müller H, Holzinger A, Chen F (2023) Ethical ChatGPT: concerns, challenges, and commandments. arXiv preprint arXiv:2305.10646

Chapter 7
Utilizing Artificial Intelligence to Support Autism Research

Elizabeth B. Varghese, Marwa Qaraqe, and Dena Al-Thani

Abstract Autism, categorized under the umbrella term autism spectrum disorder (ASD), poses significant challenges in communication, learning, and social interaction due to delayed brain development. Individuals with ASD face lifelong challenges, necessitating specialized education and interventions. The intersection of autism and Artificial Intelligence (AI) offers promising solutions, leveraging AI's capabilities in processing data, recognizing patterns, and adapting to individual needs to revolutionize the understanding, diagnosis, and support of individuals with ASD. This chapter is intended to analyze the support of AI in providing solutions to early diagnosis, therapy, intervention, and education. The promising role of AI in addressing the complex needs of individuals with ASD is also discussed while acknowledging current limitations and prospects.

Keywords Autism spectrum disorder (ASD) · Artificial intelligence (AI) · Diagnosis · Therapy · Intervention · Education

7.1 Introduction

Autism, characterized by the delay in neuroplasticity (i.e. delayed brain development), presents challenges in communication, learning, emotional expression, and situation adaptation (Ghosh et al. 2021) In 2013, the American Psychiatric Association consolidated four separate autism diagnoses into a comprehensive

E. B. Varghese (✉) · M. Qaraqe · D. Al-Thani
Division of Information and Computing Technology, College of Science and Engineering, Hamad Bin Khalifa University, Qatar Foundation, Doha, Qatar
e-mail: evarghese@hbku.edu.qa

M. Qaraqe
e-mail: mqaraqe@hbku.edu.qa

D. Al-Thani
e-mail: dalthani@hbku.edu.qa

C. Montag and R. Ali (eds.), *The Impact of Artificial Intelligence on Societies*, Studies in Neuroscience, Psychology and Behavioral Economics,
https://doi.org/10.1007/978-3-031-70355-3_7

umbrella known as autism spectrum disorder (ASD) (Roehr 2013). This amalgamation included the previous individual diagnoses of autistic disorder, pervasive developmental disorder—not otherwise specified (PDD-NOS), childhood disintegrative disorder, and Asperger syndrome. As such, ASD is a neurological disorder that often leads to social isolation due to difficulties in interacting effectively with others and exhibits restricted repetitive behavior patterns (Roehr 2013).

Over the past three decades, there has been a global rise in the prevalence of ASD. As per the World Health Organization (WHO), on a global scale, one child out of 100 is diagnosed with autism each year (Zeidan et al. 2022). Individuals with ASD face persistent challenges from early childhood throughout their lives, requiring specialized education, sessions, and tailored approaches to interaction. While there is no cure for autism, various therapies, including speech, behavioral interventions, and emotion-focused, may enhance their condition and foster integration into society (Ghosh et al. 2021). The signs of autism typically become apparent within the initial three years of a child's life, and its impact extends into the later stages of life (Kanner 1943). The behavior of each child with autism differs; one might be highly verbal, bright, and socially engaged, while another could be non-verbal and face intellectual challenges (Whalon and Hart 2011).

Recently, Artificial Intelligence (AI) has emerged as a transformative force across various domains, revolutionizing the way we approach complex challenges. Technologies based on AI, Machine Learning (ML), and Deep Learning (DL) have demonstrated their capabilities in facilitating real-world applications. Within the realm of healthcare, AI has increasingly played a pivotal role in reshaping diagnostic and intervention strategies. In recent years, the intersection of autism and AI has emerged as a promising avenue for addressing these challenges. AI, with its capacity to process vast datasets, recognize patterns, and adapt to individual needs, holds the potential to revolutionize our approach to understanding, diagnosing, and supporting individuals with ASD.

This synergy between AI and autism research unfolds across various dimensions. AI algorithms, which can detect subtle behavioral cues from neuroimaging, eye-tracking, sensor, and video data, enhance early detection and diagnosis—often crucial for effective intervention (Ghosh et al. 2021). Personalized intervention programs, tailored to the distinct learning styles of individuals with ASD, are made possible through adaptive AI-driven educational tools (Cognoa, n.d). Moreover, the integration of AI extends into social skills training, with Virtual Reality (VR) environments offering controlled spaces for practicing real-world interactions (Banire et al. 2021). Emotion recognition through facial expression analysis and the development of assistive technologies, including AI-driven virtual assistants, contribute to enhancing the daily lives of individuals with ASD.

In this chapter, we present an overview of diverse AI-based techniques designed for early diagnosis, therapeutic interventions, and educational support. Section 7.2 outlines the utilization of AI in the diagnosis of autism. Following that, Sect. 7.3 delves into the details of AI-assisted therapy and intervention for ASD. The subsequent section, Sect. 7.4, discusses various methods employed for educational purposes aimed at assisting individuals with autism. The detailed organization of

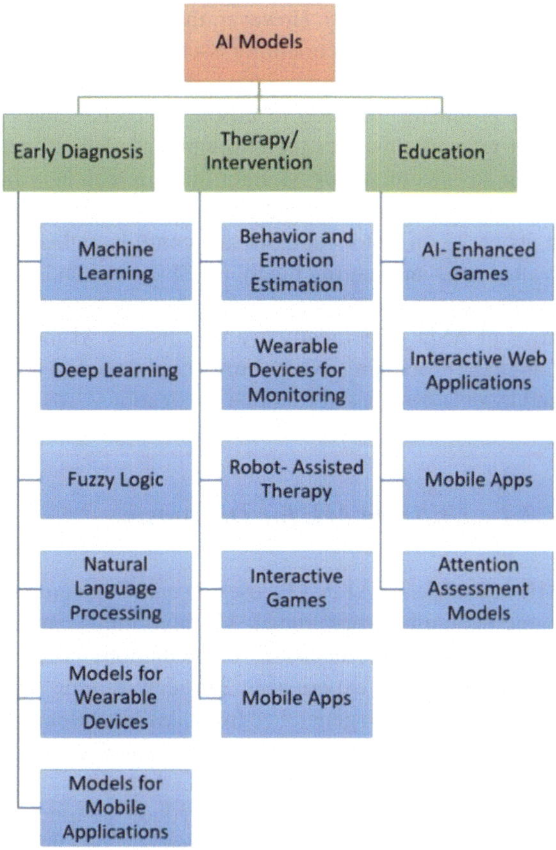

Fig. 7.1 Organization of the chapter—mainly focusing on the AI approaches for ASD diagnosis, therapy/intervention, and education

these sections is shown in Fig. 7.1. The chapter is wrapped up with a concise discussion of the existing approach's limitations and a glimpse into potential future perspectives.

7.2 AI Models for Early Diagnosis of Autism

Early diagnosis of ASD involves identifying symptoms and developmental delays in children during infancy or toddlerhood, which is crucial for timely interventions that can improve developmental outcomes and quality of life. Traditional diagnostic methods, such as Autism Diagnostic Observation Schedule (ADOS) (Lord et al. 2006) and Autism Diagnostic Interview-Revised (ADI-R) (Rutter et al. 2003), while accurate, are often time-consuming, complex, and require specialized clinicians. To address these challenges, researchers have developed screening tools like the Modified Checklist for Autism in Toddlers (M-CHAT) and the self-report scale,

Autism Quotient (AQ). However, these tools still have limitations, such as lengthy questionnaires and accessibility issues (Bone et al. 2016; Little et al. 2019; Thabtah 2019b).

A promising solution to tackle these challenges and streamline ASD assessment referrals involves the development of intelligent screening methods. Leveraging advancements in AI algorithms, researchers have sought to create accurate pre-diagnostic screening and classification approaches capable of predicting autistic traits based on historical cases and controls, rather than relying solely on manually crafted rules and scoring functions (Shahamiri and Thabtah 2020). This section aims to uncover the methods and techniques utilizing AI in the literature for early diagnosis of ASD. Specifically, we will discuss AI models based on ML, DL, Natural Language Processing (NLP), Fuzzy Logic, models leveraging Wearable Device Data, and models designed for mobile applications.

7.2.1 Utilizing ML for Diagnosis

ML is a subset of AI that focuses on enabling computers to learn from data without being explicitly programmed. ML algorithms can analyze large datasets, identify patterns, and make decisions or predictions based on the information they have learned from past experiences. Through training on labeled or unlabeled datasets, ML models learn to generalize from past examples and make predictions or decisions about new, unseen data (Varghese and Thampi 2021). Figure 7.2 shows the general workflow of ML algorithms for ASD diagnosis.

Early ML approaches aimed to reduce the time-consuming procedure of autism screening associated with standard diagnostic tools like ADOS and the ADI-R. (Wall et al. 2012) introduced a data-driven method using the Alternating Decision Tree (ADTree) algorithm to streamline the process by identifying a subset of questions from these tools. They found that only 8 of the 29 questions in ADOS module 1 and 7 of the 93 items in ADI-R were necessary for accurate autism diagnosis. These findings significantly reduced the length of these assessments without compromising accuracy. Further studies used ADI-R and ADOS-2 records to train ML models, such as the Decision Forest (DF) algorithm employed by Abbas et al. (2018). They integrated critical features into a parental questionnaire (PQ) and annotation-based video-tagging modules, combining responses using L2-regularized logistic regression (LR) for classification. Enhancing this method, Abbas et al. (2020) introduced a clinician questionnaire module, resulting in a three-module screener leveraging the Gradient Boosting Decision Tree (GBDT) algorithm, which outperformed previous outcomes within a shorter timeframe.

Researchers have increasingly turned to brain imaging for early diagnosis due to the limitations of conventional test-based methods. Neuroimaging techniques, especially Magnetic Resonance Imaging (MRI), have been instrumental in identifying ASD at younger ages (Chaddad et al. 2021). Features from brain images, such as the cerebral cortex's surface area and structural anomalies in white matter as assessed

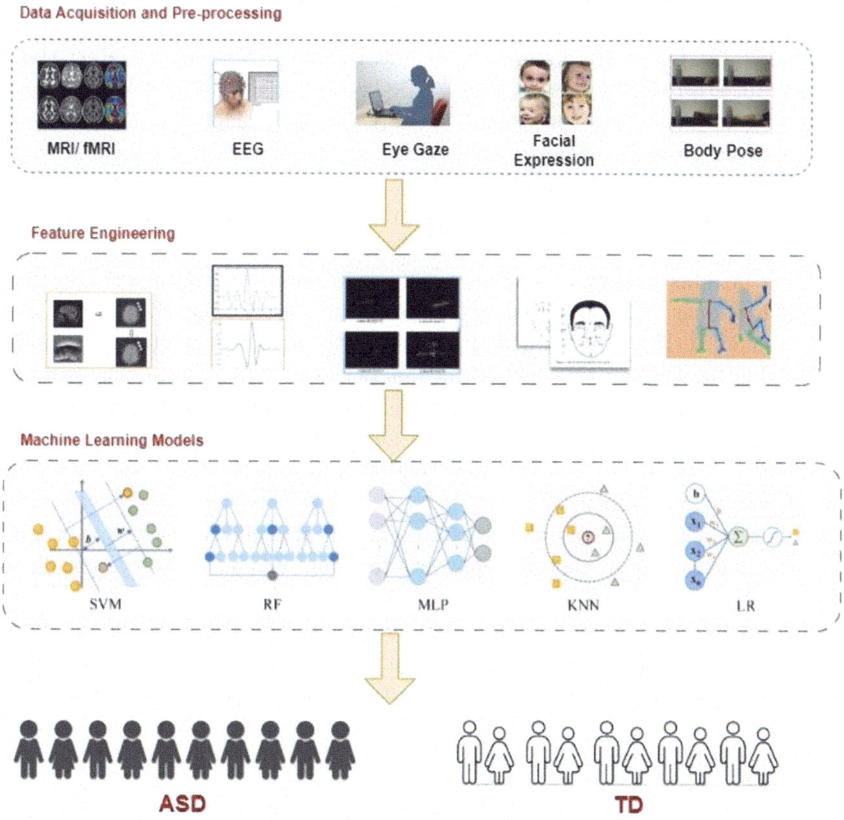

Fig. 7.2 General workflow of ML algorithms for ASD diagnosis

with diffusion tensor imaging, are analyzed using ML algorithms to develop classification models. Support Vector Machines (SVMs) are commonly used in these studies demonstrating the efficacy of MRI in early ASD detection. Segovia et al. (2014) applied SVM to classify participants into three categories based on sMRI data—(i) unaffected siblings of children with ASD, (ii) Typically Developing (TD) children, and (iii) children with ASD. Their study indicated that siblings of children with ASD have an increased likelihood of having ASD. Additionally, other ML algorithms such as Random Forest (RF) and Gradient Boosting Method (GBM) have also been employed in this domain (Katuwal et al. 2016). The study proposed by Xiao et al. (2017) utilized RF and Naive Bayes (NB) algorithms for the classification of toddlers into ASD or TD categories using MRI brain features.

Brain biomarkers like Electroencephalogram (EEG) have emerged as promising tools for diagnosing ASD traits in young individuals. EEG captures the brain's electrical activity, and ML models extensively analyze features from these signals for classification. SVM is the predominant algorithm used in this domain, appearing in about 50% of related studies (Abou-Abbas et al. 2021; Heunis et al. 2018; Kang et al. 2018; Li et al. 2022b; Peketi and Dhok 2023; Tawhid et al. 2020; Wadhera and Mahmud 2022). Other ML algorithms, such as K-nearest Neighbor (KNN) (Abou-Abbas et al. 2021; Ibrahim et al. 2018), RF (Jayarathna et al. 2019; Wadhera and Mahmud 2022), and Artificial Neural Network (ANN) (Hadoush et al. 2019), are also employed for early diagnosis using EEG data, indicating diverse approaches in leveraging brain activity for ASD detection.

Technological advancements have led to the use of eye-tracking technology for early ASD diagnosis. This method captures eye movements and gaze patterns, providing insights into visual attention and social interaction behaviors (Jeyarani and Senthilkumar 2023). AI analyzes these patterns to distinguish children with ASD, with SVM (Kang et al. 2020b; Lai et al. 2020; Oliveira et al. 2021; Zhao et al. 2021) being the leading ML method for this purpose. Studies have demonstrated significant differences in eye fixation patterns between children with ASD and TD children, using various algorithms such as LDA (Zhao et al. 2021), K-Means Clustering (Kang et al. 2020a), and Decision Tree (DT) (Kanhirakadavath and Chandran 2022) to enhance diagnostic accuracy.

Moreover, behavioral features and genetic factors also play a crucial role in ASD diagnosis. AI techniques capture behavioral features such as voice, eye gaze, and facial expressions during simulated social interactions or playtime, and use classifiers like RF and SVM for autism spectrum status detection (Drimalla et al. 2019). Motor deficits, as outlined in the Diagnostic and Statistical Manual of Mental Disorders (DSM-5), were evaluated using smart tablet devices to record gesture patterns, and analyzed with various ML algorithms (Li et al. 2017). Additionally, genetic research reveals that approximately 80% of ASD susceptibility is hereditary (Genovese and Butler 2023). ML algorithms predict autism risk genes from genetic models and gene expression data, with SVM and RF showing promise in forecasting language impairment (Lin et al. 2021) and identifying risk genes (Brueggeman et al. 2020; Lin et al. 2020), highlighting the potential of genomics as a valuable medical marker for ASD.

In a nutshell, this section discussed various methodologies employed in streamlining autism screening processes, leveraging brain imaging techniques for early diagnosis, and utilizing technological advancements such as eye tracking for ASD assessment. Additionally, it highlights the significance of SVM as a prominent ML algorithm in ASD diagnosis, both from EEG and MRI data and eye tracking data. The literature also mentions the use of other ML algorithms such as RF, GBM, K-NN, ANN, NB, and DT in ASD classification tasks. Furthermore, the review touches upon the exploration of AI in capturing behavioral features to establish objective ASD diagnosis methods.

7.2.2 *Leveraging DL for Early Diagnosis*

The proliferation of data volume and advancements in computer hardware have led to the rise of DL approaches in autism identification, surpassing traditional ML methods that rely on pre-defined features (Varghese and Thampi 2021). DL algorithms, particularly Convolutional Neural Networks (CNNs), have become prominent in early diagnosis strategies using neuroimaging techniques like MRI and fMRI (Anirudh and Thiagarajan 2019; El Gazzar et al. 2019; El-Gazzar et al. 2019). CNNs, inspired by the visual cortex of the human brain, employ a multi-level learning process that hierarchically analyzes patterns in raw data. This capability allows for extracting generalized abstractions from MRI images, enabling accurate ASD classification, as demonstrated by various studies utilizing multi-channel CNN architectures (Khosla et al. 2018) and graph CNNs (Anirudh and Thiagarajan 2019). A sample CNN framework is portrayed in Fig. 7.3.

DL approaches also comprise various types of Autoencoders (Eslami et al. 2019; Eslami and Saeed 2019; Kong et al. 2019; Wang et al. 2019) and Recurrent Neural Networks (RNNs), including Long Short-Term Memory (LSTM) (Dvornek et al. 2019) networks, for analyzing fMRI and sMRI data. Autoencoders, being unsupervised networks, reduce the dimensionality of input data to extract meaningful features, which aids in ASD diagnosis. RNNs and LSTMs are designed to handle sequential data, process inputs of variable length, and capture long-term dependencies, making them suitable for fMRI analysis. Studies have shown the efficacy of these DL methods in extracting critical features and achieving high classification accuracy in ASD detection.

When examining the DL techniques for ASD diagnosis from EEG data, CNNs have demonstrated significant effectiveness in feature extraction from EEG signals (Ari et al. 2022; Tawhid et al. 2020). Transfer learning, where pre-trained models like AlexNet, GoogLeNet, SqueezeNet, and MobileNet are repurposed for ASD identification, has further enhanced diagnostic accuracy and efficiency (Mohi ud Din and Jayanthy 2022; Stamate et al. 2021). Specialized networks like EEGNet, designed for EEG-based brain-computer interfaces, and combined models like Bi-directional LSTM (B-LSTM) with CNNs have shown promising results in automatic ASD identification, highlighting the potential of DL frameworks in this domain (Ali et al. 2022; Wadhera et al. 2021).

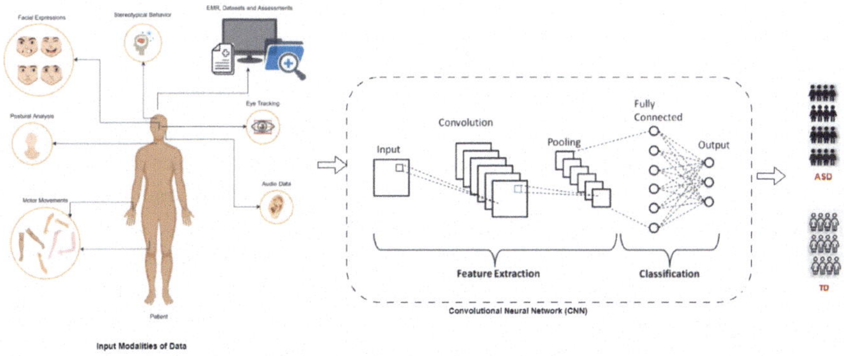

Fig. 7.3 Sample CNN framework for ASD diagnosis

Advancements in technology have also facilitated the use of computer vision and DL techniques to analyze behavioral patterns and biomarkers for objective ASD screening. Researchers have leveraged facial analysis, gaze estimation, and audio recordings to capture differences between ASD and TD subjects. Methods such as facial expression recognition (Carpenter et al. 2021; Zhao and Lu 2020), head pose estimation (Kojovic et al. 2021; Ramirez-Duque et al. 2019), and gaze pattern analysis using customized CNNs, and LSTMs have proven effective in diagnosing ASD from images and videos. Studies employing networks like Conformer (Song et al. 2022) and AttentionGazeNet (Li et al. 2022a), along with gradient-weighted class activation mapping, have provided significant insights into the diagnostic process, showcasing the potential of DL in early and accurate ASD detection.

While DL is widely regarded as a promising technique, traditional ML approaches still play a crucial role in ASD identification (Li et al. 2024). The selection of a particular method should be carefully considered, taking into account factors such as dataset size, problem complexity, and the need for model interpretability (Li et al. 2024).

7.2.3 Fuzzy Logic, Natural Language Processing (NLP), Wearable Devices for ASD Diagnosis

Fuzzy logic, a branch of AI that handles reasoning under uncertainty by using degrees of truth, has been effectively applied in autism diagnosis to assess and categorize symptom severity. Studies have utilized Fuzzy Rule-Based Systems (FRB) (Kaur and Kakkar 2019), combining neural networks with fuzzy logic (Van Hieu and Hien 2018), and Fuzzy Cognitive Maps (FCM) (Peketi and Dhok 2023) to develop models that evaluate patient symptoms and predict the presence of ASD, ADHD, and Intellectual Disability (ID). Techniques like the Fuzzy Delphi Method (FDM) and Fuzzy-Weighted Zero-Inconsistency (FWZIC) method have also been used to prioritize diagnostic criteria and classify patients into severity levels, enhancing the precision and efficiency of early autism diagnosis and treatment planning (Joudar et al. 2023). These advancements emphasize the significant potential of AI in improving clinical decision-making and patient outcomes in ASD diagnosis.

Natural Language Processing (NLP), a computer science field focused on computer–human language interaction, enables computers to understand and interpret human languages (Kao and Poteet 2007). It utilizes techniques like analyzing parts of speech and integrating grammar rules and lexicons (Kao and Poteet 2007). NLP aids early autism diagnosis in various ways. For example, a chatbot developed by Mujeeb et al. (2017) assists clinicians by interacting with users, extracting keywords, and generating diagnoses based on user responses. Elbattah et al. (2020) converted eye-tracking data into textual representations to train classification models for ASD detection. Mukherjee et al. (2023) analyzed parental dialogues from social platforms using ML models and sentiment analysis to detect ASD symptoms. Yuan et al. (2016) developed an NLP-based system for extracting and processing information from medical forms to diagnose autism. Additionally, speech data analysis using ML models has also been explored for ASD prediction, highlighting NLP's potential in improving autism diagnosis (Ramesh and Assaf 2021).

Wearable devices are increasingly being utilized for health diagnostics by incorporating sensors like accelerometers, gyroscopes, and heart rate monitors to gather physiological and behavioral data. In the realm of ASD diagnosis, these devices can track metrics such as movement patterns, sleep quality, and heart rate variability, which may provide critical insights into ASD symptoms. For instance, the WearSense device leverages smartwatches to detect stereotypical behaviors in children with autism by using accelerometer data and ML algorithms to identify and classify repetitive behaviors, achieving a 96.7% accuracy rate in detecting autistic behaviors (Amiri et al. 2017). Additionally, research has investigated the detection of sensory-motor movements (SMM) like hand flapping and rocking using wearable accelerometers (Goodwin et al. 2014). While these methods have not been directly used for ASD diagnosis, they highlight the potential for AI technologies to utilize SMM data from wearable devices, potentially leading to more precise and efficient diagnostic tools and earlier interventions for individuals with ASD.

7.2.4 AI Powered Mobile Applications

Integrating mobile applications (apps) into the detection and screening of ASD represents a promising advancement in healthcare, by utilizing AI algorithms to analyze behavioral data collected through questionnaires and device sensors. For instance, the Mobile Autism Risk Assessment (MARA) app developed by Duda et al. (2014) uses a 7-item questionnaire to assess a child's social and communication skills, achieving a sensitivity of 89.86% in detecting ASD. Similarly, the ASDTests app by Thabtah (2019a) provides user-friendly tests for various age groups, collecting data for research and optimizing predictive accuracy with ML algorithms. The SenseToKnow app from Duke University utilizes a tablet's sensors to analyze facial expressions, gaze patterns, and motor skills, predicting the likelihood of an autism diagnosis without requiring additional equipment (SensetoKnow, n.d). Another innovative app, Cognoa, developed by Tariq et al. (2018) combines ML and video analysis to screen for ASD by analyzing uploaded videos of children's behavior, providing a non-invasive and accessible monitoring tool for parents.

AI-powered mobile apps like Autism AI, proposed by Shahamiri and Thabtah (2020) use DL algorithms to screen for ASD by capturing questionnaire data and analyzing it with CNNs. While numerous apps exist for ASD screening via questionnaires, only a few leverage AI for generating screening outcomes, indicating that this area is still nascent with opportunities for advancement. AI has the potential to identify learning disabilities early, assisting clinicians in decision-making and identifying a child's risk of spectrum disorders through the analysis of longitudinal behavioral data (Rehman et al. 2021). DL enables pattern recognition among diverse features, aiding in trait identification that may elude human observation, and highlighting the untapped potential of AI in mobile apps for early screening and diagnosis.

7.3 AI-Assisted Therapy/Intervention for Autism Disorders

Early intervention for ASD, ideally starting as early as 3 years of age, is crucial for better long-term outcomes and skill development. Traditional therapies like Applied Behavior Analysis (ABA) and speech therapy, although effective, are often expensive and inaccessible, especially in rural or underserved areas (Ghosh et al. 2021). AI technologies present a cost-effective alternative, utilizing devices such as cameras, sensors, and virtual reality for continuous behavior analysis and therapy. These AI-enabled tools support skill acquisition, social skills development, and constant monitoring, reducing the need for specialized personnel and making essential treatments more accessible and affordable (Ghosh et al. 2021). This section reviews the research on using AI for autism monitoring, intervention, and therapy.

7.3.1 Behavior and Emotion Estimation

Individuals with ASD often struggle with recognizing and expressing emotions, which impacts their social interactions and emotional regulation. Accurate estimation of their emotional states and atypical behaviors can enable therapists and caregivers to tailor interventions, promote emotional regulation, and support social skill development. Innovations such as the therapy strategy developed by Stanford Medicine using Google Glass and AI to interpret facial expressions into emotions have shown promising results in improving social skills for children with autism (Stanford, n.d). Other research, like that by Sebe et al. (2006) utilized visual and audio cues with Bayesian Networks to enhance emotion recognition accuracy, aiding children with ASD in comprehending emotions. Similarly, Piana et al. (2019) developed a system using RGB-D sensors to help children with ASD recognize and express emotions through full-body movements, demonstrating the potential of AI in emotional and behavioral interventions.

ML and DL models have also been employed to detect atypical behaviors in children with ASD for targeted interventions. Techniques like those proposed by Vyas et al. (2019) used video data and pose estimation to track and analyze children's movements, categorizing them as typical or atypical using CNN. Rad et al. (2015) developed a CNN-based model to identify motor movements with real-time classification of accelerometer signals, distinguishing between SMM and non-SMM behaviors. Despite the progress, the simplistic framing of basic emotions in AI systems poses significant challenges, such as cultural and contextual inaccuracies and biases (Barrett et al. 2019). Ethical implications, including privacy concerns and reinforcement of stereotypes, urge a more nuanced and culturally sensitive approach to representing human emotions in AI technologies (Crawford 2021).

7.3.2 Wearable Devices, Interactive Games, and Mobile Apps

Wearable devices are increasingly vital in autism monitoring, offering continuous and non-invasive tracking of physiological and behavioral parameters such as heart rate, skin conductance, sleep patterns, and activity levels (El Arbaoui et al. 2023). These devices support remote monitoring, enabling caregivers and therapists to observe progress and make informed care decisions from a distance. Mamun et al. (2019) proposed a system that integrates ML techniques with 5G networks to monitor health parameters in autism centers, utilizing wearable devices to collect data and employing SVM algorithms to detect abnormalities, triggering alerts and emergency responses when needed. Similarly, Alwakeel et al.'s Autistic Child Sensor and Assistant System (ACSA) (Alwakeel et al. 2015) uses wearable sensors to monitor motion and behavior, alerting parents to potential risks such as self-injury through a connected mobile application and ML analysis. Additionally, the open computing platform by Rahman and Bhuiyan (2015) help parents and caregivers manage daily activities by collecting and analyzing physiological signals with AI and ML techniques. This platform facilitates continuous health assessment through a modular approach that supports various activities. Masino et al. (2019) developed an ML-based method to detect stress in children with ASD by analyzing heart rate data and beat-to-beat intervals, achieving high accuracy in stress recognition through induced stress tasks and physiological monitoring.

Interactive games have emerged as a valuable tool for engaging individuals with autism in therapeutic activities by incorporating fun and rewarding elements, motivating them to practice essential skills (Rouhi et al. 2019). These games can be tailored to meet each individual's unique needs, enhancing the effectiveness of personalized interventions. For instance, the therapeutic tool, sensory paint, developed by Ringland et al. (2014) utilizes whole-body interactions to support autism interventions, while the web-based game, Emotify, (Rouhi et al. 2019) focuses on teaching emotional behavior through animations and voice tone recognition, using RF-based classifiers to detect emotions from speech data. These interactive tools not only aid in the recognition and expression of emotions but also support the development of motor, language, social, and cognitive functions, demonstrating the broad potential of interactive games in autism therapy.

Mobile apps for autism intervention are versatile tools designed to support individuals with autism in various developmental and daily life aspects, including skill development, behavior management, communication, sensory regulation, and education. The AaB app (Thabtah 2019a), developed by Duke University and Apple, aids parents in identifying mental health challenges in young children through modules of questionnaires and videos, though it is limited in scope and lacks instant screening capabilities. Cognoa, (Kanne et al. 2018) designed to assess autism risk in children aged 18 months to 5 years, uses a two-phase evaluation process involving parent questionnaires and video assessments, demonstrating promising accuracy in identifying autism risk. These apps offer interactive, customizable experiences, catering to the diverse needs of individuals with autism and their support networks.

7.3.3 AI-Based Robot Assisted Therapy

An interesting application of AI in therapy involves the development of robots designed to enhance social skills and emotional recognition. The humanoid robot NAO, developed by SoftBank Robotics (Robotics, n.d), is an emotional robot that helps children with ASD by providing opportunities to practice recognizing facial expressions and responding to social cues, ultimately improving social skills and self-esteem. NAO, with its ability to express emotions through various mechanisms like changing eye color and voice tone, promotes acceptance of special education in regular classrooms. At MIT, researchers have developed a robot that uses data from video, audio, and physiological measurements to tailor interactions to individual children, employing DL to perceive and respond to their affective states and engagement levels during therapy (Rudovic et al. 2018). Other innovative approaches include robotic therapies that assess emotions from audio signals and visual attention capabilities. For instance, Kim et al. (Kim et al. 2017) used SVM models to evaluate emotional states from audio data during interactions, while another study (Di Nuovo et al. 2018) employed DL to determine visual attention on robots as an engagement indicator.

AI represents a promising tool for autism management, yet current research on its effectiveness remains limited. While AI-based robots and apps offer support for children's learning, they also present certain drawbacks. For instance, robots are costly to produce and utilize, and apps require children to possess reading skills, follow instructions, and maintain motivation—a challenge for many autistic children. Moreover, while some children may engage more readily with a robot, it's unclear whether these interaction skills will transfer to human interactions. Additionally, the integration of apps into typical settings like therapy sessions and schools is still in its infancy, indicating a need for further development and adoption.

7.4 AI for Educational Purposes

AI is rapidly transforming various facets of our lives, including education, where it holds great promise, particularly for children with autism. Through personalized instruction, support, and data-driven analysis, AI has the potential to revolutionize the learning experience for these children, addressing their unique needs in a tailored manner. This section aims to highlight existing approaches that can assist children with autism in their educational journey.

7.4.1 AI-Enhanced Games

AI-enhanced educational games represent a promising avenue for revolutionizing the learning experience of children with ASD. The utilization of advanced AI technologies, in an educational game by Brain Power, LLC' (BrainPower, n.d), facilitates real-time feedback and support for the unique needs of children with ASD. By employing computer vision and facial recognition algorithms, the game assists in social-emotional learning by analyzing facial expressions and guiding appropriate social interactions, thereby targeting improvements in social communication skills and self-regulation. Similarly, the educational game by Cognoa Inc.' (Cognoa, n.d) harnesses AI features to provide personalized learning experiences that adapt to each child's strengths, challenges, and learning preferences. Through AI algorithms, the game customizes content and activities, focusing on specific skills such as communication and problem-solving, to foster holistic growth and development in children with ASD.

Beyond traditional educational games, innovative approaches such as social scenario game platforms and personalized assistive robots further demonstrate the transformative potential of AI in education for children with ASD. Platforms like the social scenario game (Riedl et al. 2009) provide adolescents with high-functioning ASD opportunities to practice social skills autonomously, thereby promoting skill acquisition and confidence-building. Additionally, personalized assistive robots like Kiwi (Kiwi, n.d) from the University of Southern California deliver math lessons and social skill development activities, offering personalized feedback and instruction based on individual progress and engagement levels. These AI-driven interventions showcase significant improvements in both academic and social domains for children with ASD, highlighting the invaluable role of AI in enhancing educational outcomes and facilitating the holistic development of individuals with autism.

7.4.2 Interactive Web Applications and Mobile Apps

Radwan et al. (2017) proposed an active ML framework designed to teach object recognition to children with ASD via a web application. This approach involves training the classifier with a small initial dataset and subsequently selecting informative instances from unlabeled data, requesting labels from experts. Uncertainty regarding object recognition was quantified using parameters such as response correctness, response latency, and the number of required auditory stimulus repeats, which were combined using a weighted approach to determine the uncertainty value. Objects with the highest uncertainty values were prioritized for teaching in subsequent iterations, facilitating an adaptive and personalized learning experience for the children.

The mobile app developed by Amante et al. (2015) aimed at educating autistic individuals about first-aid procedures. The application consisted of six stages, each comprising multiple sublevels, with characters integrated using AI. Users advanced through the game by completing sublevels, accumulating knowledge as they progressed, and receiving a scorecard at the end of each sublevel to assess their performance.

7.4.3 Attention Assessment Models

Assessing attention patterns in children with ASD is crucial for delivering effective interventions and providing individualized attention during learning. Studies conducted by Esqueda-Elizondo et al. (2022) utilized EEG data to assess attention levels in ASD children, employing ML models to classify features extracted from EEG signals. Moreover, research exploring the potential of virtual reality (VR) for attention assessment in ASD and TD children (Banire et al. 2021, 2023; Varghese et al. 2023) employed objective and non-invasive methods using VR-based classroom setups and continuous performance tasks (CPT) (Fig. 7.4). ML algorithms were utilized to analyze visual and eye-tracking data, leading to the development of person-specific and generalized models for attention detection, with findings suggesting the superiority of gaze-based models and the importance of personalized approaches in ASD research. Furthermore, attention assessment models were developed using video data, employing DL techniques to extract head pose parameters and movement patterns for attention assessment (Varghese et al. 2023) and utilized head pose and gaze parameters to quantify the attention level of children with ASD (Varghese et al. 2024). These interdisciplinary approaches highlight the potential of EEG, VR, and video data combined with ML and DL methods to gain insights into attentional processes in children with ASD and inform personalized interventions and support strategies.

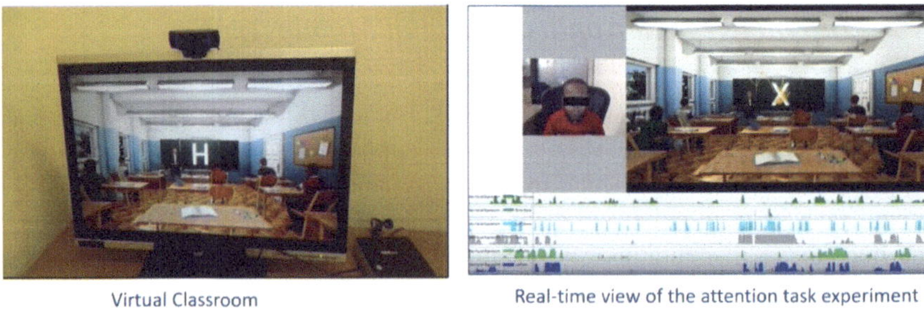

Fig. 7.4 VR-based classroom setup and CPT for attention assessment (Banire et al. 2021, 2023; Varghese et al. 2023, 2024)

7.5 Conclusion and Future Perspectives

AI is the simulation of human intelligence processes by machines, particularly computer systems. In recent years, researchers have widely utilized the capabilities of AI to support autism. In this chapter, we unveil how AI bolsters the possibilities in the early diagnosis of ASD. Moreover, we discuss how the support of AI helps in the intervention/therapy strategies and educational tactics to enhance the quality of life of individuals with ASD. Specifically, through techniques such as ML, DL, fuzzy logic, NLP, etc. AI technologies offer valuable tools for early detection and diagnosis, alleviating the burden on families, clinicians, and children undergoing evaluation. By reducing waiting times, processing large datasets, and achieving high levels of accuracy, AI-enabled applications enhance diagnostic processes, providing clinicians with safer decisions and a clearer understanding of each child's needs. Additionally, AI applications have the potential to lower assessment costs and increase accessibility for families, ultimately aiming to ensure timely interventions and inclusive participation for individuals with autism in society.

Furthermore, AI holds immense promise in revolutionizing the education of children with autism, offering customized learning experiences, supporting communication and social skills development, aiding sensory processing, and facilitating data-driven analysis. Despite challenges related to cost, equity, ethics, and AI bias, when deployed conscientiously and ethically, AI can serve as a potent instrument in delivering inclusive and impactful education for children with autism. By harnessing the advantages of AI alongside evidence-based approaches and human support, we can unleash the inherent potential of children with autism and empower them to excel in their educational pursuits. The inferences and future perspectives derived from the review are as follows:

- *Fusion of multimodal data*: While numerous studies have primarily concentrated on processing RGB data from images or videos, there is great potential in combining information from multiple modalities. Researchers should explore the integration of various data types, including audio, depth, and sensor data, to obtain more comprehensive insights and improve the effectiveness of their approaches. Besides, AI demonstrates remarkable potential in utilizing a wide array of behavioral and biological markers to predict and diagnose ASD. The accuracy of these predictions may fluctuate based on the types and sources of data employed. Nevertheless, integrating multiple modalities allows the unique strengths of each marker type to complement one another, compensating for individual limitations and offering a more comprehensive assessment of ASD.
- *Benchmark datasets*: The advancement of AI heavily relies on data, yet benchmark datasets remain scarce in autism research. Hence, establishing a collaborative research framework is crucial to improve existing datasets and develop new ones to share research outcomes globally. This initiative encourages collaborations among academics from various nations, fostering fair comparisons of technical solutions, joint experiments, and thorough empirical validation of studies on a worldwide scale

Ethics and data privacy

- Researchers ought to prioritize policy-level initiatives involving stakeholders to develop study designs rooted in the FATE (Fairness, Accountability, Transparency, and Ethics) framework for utilizing AI in ASD research (Kohli et al. 2022). The study by Erb et al. (2021) sheds light on the intricate balance between data sharing and privacy concerns within the realm of open science. While sharing data is crucial for advancing scientific knowledge and fostering collaboration, it also poses significant risks to individual privacy. The potential for unauthorized access, re-identification of individuals from anonymized datasets, and ethical dilemmas surrounding informed consent and the protection of vulnerable populations highlight the complexities of navigating data sharing in an open science landscape. To address these challenges, robust privacy protocols and governance frameworks are necessary, comprising measures such as encryption, anonymization, access controls, and a commitment to responsible data stewardship. Thus, embracing and enforcing robust regulations, policies, data protection and privacy legislation are crucial to mitigate the risk of inadvertent data leakage, promoting confidence among stakeholders.
- *Personalized educational tools*: Children with ASD require personalized support strategies in their learning process, as what works for one child may not be effective for another (Banire et al. 2023). This personalized approach enables interventions tailored to each child's unique needs and characteristics, highlighting the importance of applying AI to develop personalized tools for improving learning outcomes. By providing personalized assistive educational tools, we can enhance educational outcomes for individuals with ASD, facilitating their integration into society and reducing stigma, isolation, and instances of bullying (Barua et al. 2022).

References

Abbas H, Garberson F, Glover E, Wall DP (2018) Machine learning approach for early detection of autism by combining questionnaire and home video screening. J Am Med Inform Assoc 25(8):1000–1007

Abbas H, Garberson F, Liu-Mayo S, Glover E, Wall DP (2020) Multi-modular AI approach to streamline autism diagnosis in young children. Scientific Rep 10(1):5014

Abou-Abbas L, van Noordt S, Desjardins JA, Cichonski M, Elsabbagh M (2021) Use of empirical mode decomposition in ERP analysis to classify familial risk and diagnostic outcomes for autism spectrum disorder. Brain Sci 11(4):409

Ali NA, Syafeeza AR, Jaafar AS, Nor NK (2022) ConVnet BiLSTM for ASD classification on EEG brain signal. I. Int J Online Biomed Eng 18(11)

Alwakeel SS, Alhalabi B, Aggoune H, Alwakeel M (2015) A machine learning based WSN system for autism activity recognition. Paper presented at the 2015 IEEE 14th international conference on machine learning and applications (ICMLA), pp 771–776

Amante VS, de Vera CJR, Espinosa JAL, Reyes SPP, Agregado G (2015) AIDISM: an android-based game to educate individuals with autism on basic first aid using artificial intelligence. Int J Concep Comput Inf Technol 3(3):2345– 9808

Amiri AM, Peltier N, Goldberg C, Sun Y, Nathan A, Hiremath SV, Mankodiya K (2017) WearSense: detecting autism stereotypic behaviors through smartwatches. Healthcare 5(1):11

Anirudh R, Thiagarajan JJ (2019) Bootstrapping graph convolutional neural networks for autism spectrum disorder classification. Paper presented at the ICASSP 2019–2019 IEEE international conference on acoustics, speech and signal processing (ICASSP), pp 3197–3201

Ari B, Sobahi N, Al ccin OF, Sengur A, Acharya UR (2022) Accurate detection of autism using Douglas-Peucker algorithm, sparse coding based feature mapping and convolutional neural network techniques with EEG signals. Comput Biol Med 143:105311

Banire B, Al Thani D, Qaraqe M, Mansoor B (2021) Face-based attention recognition model for children with autism spectrum disorder. J Healthc Inform Res 5(4):420–445

Banire B, Al Thani D, Qaraqe M (2023) One size does not fit all: detecting attention in children with autism using machine learning. User Modeling and User-Adapted Interaction, 1–33.

Barrett LF, Adolphs R, Marsella S, Martinez AM, Pollak SD (2019) Emotional expressions reconsidered: challenges to inferring emotion from human facial movements. Psychol Sci Publ Int 20(1):1–68

Barua PD, Vicnesh J, Gururajan R, Oh SL, Palmer E, Azizan MM, Kadri NA, Acharya UR (2022) Artificial intelligence enabled personalised assistive tools to enhance education of children with neurodevelopmental disorders—a review. Int J Environ Res Public Health 19(3):1192

Bone D, Bishop SL, Black MP, Goodwin MS, Lord C, Narayanan SS (2016) Use of machine learning to improve autism screening and diagnostic instruments: effectiveness, efficiency, and multi-instrument fusion. J Child Psychol Psychiatry 57(8):927–937

BrainPower. Empowered brain. https://brain-power.com/empowered-brain/. Accessed 17 Mar 2024

Brueggeman L, Koomar T, Michaelson JJ (2020) Forecasting risk gene discovery in autism with machine learning and genome-scale data. Sci Rep 10(1):4569

Carpenter KL, Hahemi J, Campbell K, Lippmann SJ, Baker JP, Egger HL, Espinosa S, Vermeer S, Sapiro G, Dawson G (2021) Digital behavioral phenotyping detects atypical pattern of facial expression in toddlers with autism. Autism Res 14(3):488–499

Chaddad A, Li J, Lu Q, Li Y, Okuwobi IP, Tanougast C, Desrosiers C, Niazi T (2021) Can autism Be diagnosed with artificial intelligence? A narrative review. Diagnostics 11(11):2032

Cognoa. Empowering the healthcare community to do more sooner for children and their families. https://cognoa.com/technology/. Accessed 17 Mar 2024

Crawford K (2021) The atlas of AI: power, politics, and the planetary costs of artificial intelligence. Yale University Press

Di Nuovo A, Conti D, Trubia G, Buono S, Di Nuovo S (2018) Deep learning systems for estimating visual attention in robot-assisted therapy of children with autism and intellectual disability. Robotics 7(2):25

Drimalla H, Landwehr N, Baskow I, Behnia B, Roepke S, Dziobek I, Scheffer T (2019) Detecting autism by analyzing a simulated social interaction. Paper presented at the machine learning and knowledge discovery in databases: European conference, ECML PKDD 2018, Dublin, Ireland, September 10–14, 2018, Proceedings, Part I 18, pp 193–208

Duda M, Kosmicki JA, Wall DP (2014) Testing the accuracy of an observation-based classifier for rapid detection of autism risk. Transl Psychiatry 4(8):e424

Dvornek NC, Li X, Zhuang J, Duncan JS (2019) Jointly discriminative and generative recurrent neural networks for learning from fMRI. Paper presented at the machine learning in medical imaging: 10th international workshop, MLMI 2019, held in conjunction with MICCAI 2019, Shenzhen, China, October 13, 2019, Proceedings 10, pp 382–390

El Arbaoui FEZ, El Hari K, Saidi R (2023) A review on the application of the Internet of Things in monitoring autism and assisting parents and caregivers. Computational Intelligence for Medical Internet of Things (MIoT) Applications, pp 123–142

El Gazzar A, Cerliani L, van Wingen G, Thomas RM (2019) Simple 1-D convolutional networks for resting-state fMRI based classification in autism. Paper presented at the 2019 international joint conference on neural networks (IJCNN), pp 1–6

El-Gazzar A, Quaak M, Cerliani L, Bloem P, van Wingen G, Mani Thomas R (2019) A hybrid 3DCNN and 3DC-LSTM based model for 4D spatio-temporal fMRI data: an ABIDE autism classification study. Paper presented at the international workshop on OR 2.0 context-aware operating theaters, pp 95–102

Elbattah M, Guerin J, Carette R, Cilia F, Dequen G (2020) Nlp-based approach to detect autism spectrum disorder in saccadic eye movement. Paper presented at the 2020 IEEE symposium series on computational intelligence (SSCI), pp 1581–1587

Erb B, Bosch C, Herbert C, Kargl F, Montag C (2021) Emerging privacy issues in times of open science. https://doi.org/10.31234/osf.io/u236e

Eslami T, Saeed F (2019) Auto-ASD-network: a technique based on deep learning and support vector machines for diagnosing autism spectrum disorder using fMRI data. Paper presented at the Proceedings of the 10th ACM international conference on bioinformatics, computational biology and health informatics, pp 646–651

Eslami T, Mirjalili V, Fong A, Laird AR, Saeed F (2019) ASD-DiagNet: a hybrid learning approach for detection of autism spectrum disorder using fMRI data. Front Neuroinform 13:70.

Esqueda-Elizondo JJ, Juarez-Ramirez R, Lopez-Bonilla OR, Garcia-Guerrero EE, Galindo-Aldana GM, Jimenez-Beristain L, Serrano-Trujillo A, Tlelo-Cuautle E, Inzunza-Gonzalez E (2022) Attention measurement of an autism spectrum disorder user using EEG signals: a case study. Math Comput Appl 27(2):21

Genovese A, Butler MG (2023). The autism spectrum: behavioral, psychiatric and genetic associations. Genes 14(3): 677

Ghosh T, Al Banna MH, Rahman MS, Kaiser MS, Mahmud M, Hosen AS, Cho GH (2021) Artificial intelligence and internet of things in screening and management of autism spectrum disorder. Sustain Cities Soc 74:103189

Goodwin MS, Haghighi M, Tang Q, Akcakaya M, Erdogmus D, Intille S (2014) Moving towards a real-time system for automatically recognizing stereotypical motor movements in individuals on the autism spectrum using wireless accelerometry. Paper presented at the proceedings of the 2014 ACM international joint conference on pervasive and ubiquitous computing, pp 861–872

Hadoush H, Alafeef M, Abdulhay E (2019) Automated identification for autism severity level: EEG analysis using empirical mode decomposition and second order difference plot. Behav Brain Res 362:240–248

Heunis T, Aldrich C, Peters JM, Jeste SS, Sahin M, Scheffer C, De Vries PJ (2018) Recurrence quantification analysis of resting state EEG signals in autism spectrum disorder—a systematic methodological exploration of technical and demographic confounders in the search for biomarkers. BMC Med 16:1–17

Ibrahim S, Djemal R, Alsuwailem A (2018) Electroencephalography (EEG) signal processing for epilepsy and autism spectrum disorder diagnosis. Biocybern Biomed Eng 38(1):16–26

Jayarathna S, Jayawardana Y, Jaime M, Thapaliya S (2019) Electroencephalogram (EEG) for delineating objective measure of autism spectrum disorder. In: Computational models for biomedical reasoning and problem solving. IGI Global, pp 34–65

Jeyarani RA, Senthilkumar R (2023) Eye tracking biomarkers for autism spectrum disorder detection using machine learning and deep learning techniques. Res Autism Spectr Disord 108:102228

Joudar SS, Albahri AS, Hamid RA (2023) Intelligent triage method for early diagnosis autism spectrum disorder (ASD) based on integrated fuzzy multi-criteria decision-making methods. Inform Med Unlocked 36:101131

Kang J, Zhou T, Han J, Li X (2018) EEG-based multi-feature fusion assessment for autism. J Clin Neurosci 56:101–107

Kang J, Han X, Hu J, Feng H, Li X (2020a) The study of the differences between low-functioning autistic children and typically developing children in the processing of the own-race and other-race faces by the machine learning approach. J Clin Neurosci 81:54–60

Kang J, Han X, Song J, Niu Z, Li X (2020b) The identification of children with autism spectrum disorder by SVM approach on EEG and eye-tracking data. Comput Biol Med 120:103722
Kanhirakadavath MR, Chandran MSM (2022) Investigation of eye-tracking scan path as a biomarker for autism screening using machine learning algorithms. Diagnostics 12(2):518
Kanne SM, Carpenter LA, Warren Z (2018) Screening in toddlers and preschoolers at risk for autism spectrum disorder: evaluating a novel mobile-health screening tool. Autism Res 11(7):1038–1049
Kanner LAO (1943) Autistic disturbances of affective contact. Nerv Child 2(3):217–250
Kao A, Poteet SR (2007) Natural language processing and text mining. Springer
Katuwal GJ, Baum SA, Cahill ND, Michael AM (2016) Divide and conquer: sub-grouping of ASD improves ASD detection based on brain morphometry. PloS One 11(4):e0153331
Kaur G, Kakkar D (2019) Fuzzy based integrated diagnostic system for neurodevelopmental disorders. Paper presented at the 2019 6th international conference on signal processing and integrated networks (SPIN), pp 132–136
Khosla M, Jamison K, Kuceyeski A, Sabuncu MR (2018) 3D convolutional neural networks for classification of functional connectomes. Paper presented at the international workshop on deep learning in medical image analysis, pp 137–145
Kim JC, Azzi P, Jeon M, Howard AM, Park CH (2017) Audio-based emotion estimation for interactive robotic therapy for children with autism spectrum disorder. Paper presented at the 2017 14th international conference on ubiquitous robots and ambient intelligence (URAI), pp 39–44
Kiwi. Robot uses AI to personalize teaching of autistic children. https://thenextweb.com/news/robot-uses-ai-to-personalize-teaching-of-autistic-children. Accessed 27 Mar 2024
Kohli M, Kar AK, Sinha S (2022) The role of intelligent technologies in early detection of autism spectrum disorder (asd): a scoping review. IEEE Access 10:104887–104913
Kojovic N, Natraj S, Mohanty SP, Maillart T, Schaer M (2021) Using 2D video-based pose estimation for automated prediction of autism spectrum disorders in young children. Sci Rep 11(1):15069
Kong Y, Gao J, Xu Y, Pan Y, Wang J, Liu J (2019) Classification of autism spectrum disorder by combining brain connectivity and deep neural network classifier. Neurocomputing 324:63–68
Lai M, Lee J, Chiu S, Charm J, So WY, Yuen FP, Kwok C, Tsoi J, Lin Y, Zee B (2020) A machine learning approach for retinal images analysis as an objective screening method for children with autism spectrum disorder. EClinicalMedicine, 28
Li B, Sharma A, Meng J, Purushwalkam S, Gowen E (2017) Applying machine learning to identify autistic adults using imitation: an exploratory study. PloS One 12(8):e0182652
Li J, Chen Z, Zhong Y, Lam H, Han J, Ouyang G, Li X, Liu H (2022a) Appearance-based gaze estimation for ASD diagnosis. IEEE Trans Cybern 52(7):6504–6517
Li Q, Weiland RF, Konvalinka I, Mansvelder HD, Andersen TS, Smit DJ, Begeer S, Linkenkaer-Hansen K (2022b) Intellectually able adults with autism spectrum disorder show typical resting-state EEG activity. Sci Rep 1 12(1):19016
Li J, Kong X, Sun L, Chen X, Ouyang G, Li X, Chen S (2024) Identification of autism spectrum disorder based on electroencephalography: a systematic review. Comput Biol Med 108075
Lin Y, Afshar S, Rajadhyaksha AM, Potash JB, Han S (2020) A machine learning approach to predicting autism risk genes: validation of known genes and discovery of new candidates. J Child Adolesc Psychiatr Nurs 11:500064
Lin P, Moni MA, Gau SS, Eapen V (2021) Identifying subgroups of patients with autism by gene expression profiles using machine learning algorithms. Front Psychiatry 12:637022
Little SG, Akin-Little A, Harris GM (2019) Autism spectrum disorder: screening and diagnosis. In Little SG and Akin-Little A (eds) Behavioral interventions in schools: evidence-based positive strategies, 2nd ed. American Psychological Association, pp 191–203. https://doi.org/10.1037/0000126-011
Lord C, Risi S, DiLavore PS, Shulman C, Thurm A, Pickles A (2006) Autism from 2 to 9 years of age. Arch Gen Psychiatry 63(6):694–701
Mamun MI, Rahman A, Khaleque MA, Hamid MA, Mridha MF (2019) Autilife: a healthcare monitoring system for autism center in 5g cellular network using machine learning approach. Paper

presented at the 2019 IEEE 17th international conference on industrial informatics (INDIN), 1, pp 1501–1506
Masino AJ, Forsyth D, Nuske H, Herrington J, Pennington J, Kushleyeva Y, Bonafide CP (2019) M-Health and autism: recognizing stress and anxiety with machine learning and wearables data. Paper presented at the 2019 IEEE 32nd international symposium on computer-based medical systems (CBMS), pp 714–719
Mohi ud Din Q, Jayanthy AK (2022) Automated classification of autism spectrum disorder using EEG signals and convolutional neural networks. Biomed Eng: Appl 34(02):2250020
Mujeeb S, Javed MH, Arshad T (2017) Aquabot: a diagnostic chatbot for achluophobia and autism. Int J Adv Comput Sci Appl 8(9):209–216
Mukherjee P, Sadhukhan S, Godse M, Chakraborty B (2023) Early detection of autism spectrum disorder (ASD) using traditional machine learning models. Int J Adv Comput Sci Appl 14(6)
Oliveira JS, Franco FO, Revers MC, Silva AF, Portolese J, Brentani H, Machado-Lima A, Nunes FL (2021) Computer-aided autism diagnosis based on visual attention models using eye tracking. Sci Rep 11(1):10131
Peketi S, Dhok SB (2023) Machine learning enabled P300 classifier for autism spectrum disorder using adaptive signal decomposition. Brain Sci 13(2):315
Piana S, Malagoli C, Usai MC, Camurri A (2019) Effects of computerized emotional training on children with high functioning autism. IEEE Trans Affect Comput 12(4):1045–1054
Rad NM, Bizzego A, Kia SM, Jurman G, Venuti P, Furlanello C (2015) Convolutional neural network for stereotypical motor movement detection in autism. arXiv Preprint arXiv:1511.01865
Radwan AM, Birkan B, Hania F, Cataltepe Z (2017) Active machine learning framework for teaching object recognition skills to children with autism. Int J Dev Disabil 63(3):158–169
Rahman MA, Bhuiyan M (2015) IOT enabled sensor in multimodal intelligent applications for children with special needs. Paper presented at the 2015 internet technologies and applications (ITA), pp 352–357
Ramesh V, Assaf R (2021) Detecting autism spectrum disorders with machine learning models using speech transcripts. arXiv Preprint arXiv:2110.03281
Ramirez-Duque AA, Frizera-Neto A, Bastos TF (2019) Robot-assisted autism spectrum disorder diagnostic based on artificial reasoning. J Intell Robot Syst 96(2):267–281
Rehman IU, Sobnath D, Nasralla MM, Winnett M, Anwar A, Asif W, Sherazi HHR (2021) Features of mobile apps for people with autism in a post COVID-19 scenario: current status and recommendations for apps using AI. Diagnostics 11(10):1923
Riedl M, Arriaga R, Boujarwah F, Hong H, Isbell J, Heflin J (2009) Graphical social scenarios: toward intervention and authoring for adolescents with high functioning autism. Paper presented at the 2009 AAAI fall symposium series
Ringland KE, Zalapa R, Neal M, Escobedo L, Tentori ME, Hayes GR (2014) SensoryPaint: a natural user interface supporting sensory integration in children with neurodevelopmental disorders. In: CHI'14 extended abstracts on human factors in computing systems, pp 1681–1686
Robotics S (2024) World Autism Awareness Day: humanoid robots helping children with autism. https://www.aldebaran.com/sites/default/files/press/PR_SBRE_NAO-26Autism.pdf. Accessed 17 Mar 2024
Roehr B (2013) American psychiatric association explains DSM-5. BMJ 346
Rouhi A, Spitale M, Catania F, Cosentino G, Gelsomini M, Garzotto F (2019) Emotify: emotional game for children with autism spectrum disorder based-on machine learning. Paper presented at the proceedings of the 24th international conference on intelligent user interfaces: companion, pp 31–32
Rudovic O, Lee J, Dai M, Schuller B, Picard RW (2018) Personalized machine learning for robot perception of affect and engagement in autism therapy. Sci Robot 3(19):1–11
Rutter M, Le Couteur A, Lord C et al (2003) Autism diagnostic interview-revised, Vol. 29. Western Psychological Services, p 30

Sebe N, Cohen I, Gevers T, Huang TS (2006) Emotion recognition based on joint visual and audio cues. Paper presented at the 18th international conference on pattern recognition (ICPR'06), pp 1136–1139

Segovia FI, Holt R, Spencer M, Gorriz JM, Ramirez J, Puntonet CG, Phillips C, Chura L, Baron-Cohen S, Suckling J (2014) Identifying endophenotypes of autism: a multivariate approach. Front Comput Eurosci 8:60

SensetoKnow.App can screen for autism in 10 minutes. https://sites.duke.edu/sensetoknow/. Accessed 13 Mar 2024

Shahamiri SR, Thabtah F (2020) Autism AI: a new autism screening system based on artificial intelligence. Cogn Comput12(4):766–777

Song C, Li J, Ouyang G (2022) Early diagnosis of ASD based on facial expression recognition and head pose estimation. Paper presented at the 2022 IEEE international conference on systems, man, and cybernetics (SMC), pp 1248–1253

Stamate C, Magoulas GD, Thomas MS, BASIS Team (2021) Deep learning topology—preserving EEG—based images for autism detection in infants. Paper presented at the international conference on engineering applications of neural networks, pp 71–82

Stanford. Google Glass helps kids with autism read facial expressions. https://med.stanford.edu/news/all-news/2018/08/google-glass-helps-kids-with-autism-read-facial-expressions.html. Accessed 27 Mar 2024

Tariq Q, Daniels J, Schwartz JN, Washington P, Kalantarian H, Wall DP (2018) Mobile detection of autism through machine learning on home video: a development and prospective validation study. PLoS Med 15(11):e1002705

Tawhid M, Siuly S, Wang H (2020). Diagnosis of autism spectrum disorder from EEG using a time-frequency spectrogram image-based approach. Electron Lett 56(25): 1372–1375.

Thabtah F (2019a) An accessible and efficient autism screening method for behavioural data and predictive analyses. Health Inform J 25(4):1739–1755

Thabtah F (2019b) Machine learning in autistic spectrum disorder behavioral research: a review and ways forward. Inform Health Soc Care 44(3):278–297

Van Hieu N, Hien NLH (2018) Artificial neural network and fuzzy logic approach to diagnose autism spectrum disorder. Int Res J Eng Technol 5(6):1–7

Varghese EB, Thampi SM (2021) Towards the cognitive and psychological perspectives of crowd behaviour: a vision-based analysis. Connect Sci 33(2):380–405

Varghese EB, Qaraqe M, Al Thani D, Ekenel HIK (2023) Attention assessment in children with autism using head pose and motion parameters from real videos. Paper presented at the GLOBECOM 2023–2023 IEEE global communications conference, pp 6462–6468

Varghese EB, Qaraqe M, Al-Thani D (2024) Attention level evaluation in children with autism: leveraging head pose and gaze parameters from videos for educational intervention. IEEE Trans Learn Technol 17:1777–1793

Vyas K, Ma R, Rezaei B, Liu S, Neubauer M, Ploetz T, Oberleitner R, Ostadabbas S (2019) Recognition of atypical behavior in autism diagnosis from video using pose estimation over time. Paper presented at the 2019 IEEE 29th international workshop on machine learning for signal processing (MLSP), pp 1–6

Wadhera T, Mahmud M (2022) Brain functional network topology in autism spectrum disorder: a novel weighted hierarchical complexity metric for electroencephalogram. IEEE J Biomed Health Inform 2727(4):1718–1725

Wadhera T, Kakkar D, Rani R (2021) Behavioral modeling using deep neural network framework for ASD diagnosis and prognosis. In: Emerging Technologies for Healthcare: Internet of Things and Deep Learning Models, 279–298

Wall DP, Dally R, Luyster R, Jung J, DeLuca TF (2012) Use of artificial intelligence to shorten the behavioral diagnosis of autism. Plos One. https://doi.org/10.1371/journal.pone.0043855

Wang C, Xiao Z, Wang B, Wu J (2019) Identification of autism based on SVM-RFE and stacked sparse auto-encoder. IEEE Access 7:118030–118036

Whalon KJ, Hart JE (2011) Children with autism spectrum disorder and literacy instruction: an exploratory study of elementary inclusive settings. Rem Spec Educ 32(3):243–255

Xiao X, Fang H, Wu J, Xiao C, Xiao T, Qian L, Liang F, Xiao Z, Chu KK, Ke X (2017) Diagnostic model generated by MRI-derived brain features in toddlers with autism spectrum disorder. Aut Res 10(4):620–630

Yuan J, Holtz C, Smith T, Luo J (2016) Autism spectrum disorder detection from semi-structured and unstructured medical data. EURASIP J Bioinformatics Syst Biol 2017:1–9

Zeidan J, Fombonne E, Scorah J, Ibrahim A, Durkin MS, Saxena S, Yusuf A, Shih A, Elsabbagh M (2022) Global prevalence of autism: a systematic review update. Aut Res 15(5):778–790

Zhao W, Lu L (2020) Research and development of autism diagnosis information system based on deep convolution neural network and facial expression data. Libr Hi Tech 38(4):799–817

Zhao Z, Tang H, Zhang X, Qu X, Hu X, Lu J (2021) Classification of children with autism and typical development using eye-tracking data from face-to-face conversations: machine learning model development and performance evaluation. J Med Internet Res 23(8):e29328

Chapter 8
Artificial Intelligence in Education: the Importance of Metacognitive Monitoring

Patrick Albus and Tina Seufert

Abstract The integration of emerging technologies in educational contexts has evolved significantly over recent decades, extending from basic multimedia applications to advanced virtual reality and, more recently, text-generating artificial intelligence (AI). This chapter explores the competencies needed to effectively use AI in educational contexts, with an emphasis on transforming and extending traditional cognitive and metacognitive skills. We begin by examining the traditional learning process to establish a basic understanding, followed by a discussion of how these processes are redefined when AI is incorporated. We focus on how AI affects both the object level, where AI assists in the processing of learning content, and the meta level, where AI assists in the regulation and monitoring of learning strategies. Through this discussion, we highlight the need for educators and learners to develop specific competencies to maximize the potential of AI as a supportive tool rather than a replacement for human cognitive effort. The implications for future educational practices, the role of educators, and the design of AI-supported learning environments are explored, suggesting a greater focus on learning processes rather than just learning outcomes. Significant changes in education systems are needed to leverage the full potential of AI, advocating a balance between technology and traditional educational values to improve teaching and learning.

8.1 Introduction

In recent decades, the integration of new technologies into teaching and learning contexts has progressed continuously. This development ranges from simple multimedia applications to virtual reality and, more recently, text-generating artificial intelligence (AI; Chen et al. 2020). These new technologies can create amazing

P. Albus (✉) · T. Seufert
Department Learning and Instruction, Institute of Psychology and Education, Ulm University, Lise-Meitner-Straße 16, 89081 Ulm, Germany
e-mail: patrick.albus@uni-ulm.de

C. Montag and R. Ali (eds.), *The Impact of Artificial Intelligence on Societies*, Studies in Neuroscience, Psychology and Behavioral Economics,
https://doi.org/10.1007/978-3-031-70355-3_8

learning materials, but it is important not to forget the underlying learning processes, as these new technological possibilities also bring their own challenges for learners.

A few years ago, the term AI in educational research was primarily associated with intelligent artificial tutors. Today, with the development and broad accessibility of Large Language models like ChatGPT, AI includes a much broader range of capabilities, including adaptive features, personalisation, problem solving and reasoning (de Witt et al. 2023; Chen et al. 2020). The integration of AI into teaching and learning processes has significant implications for didactic concepts. While AI can perform tasks that traditionally require human cognitive processes, its role is not to replace educators or take over independent human learning. Instead, AI should be thought of as a supporting force that complements and enriches teaching and learning processes (Mah et al. 2023; Yau et al. 2021). The challenges arising from this interplay highlight the need for both educators and learners to develop specific competencies in order to make the most of AI's capabilities.

This chapter focuses on the competencies required to effectively use AI as an optimal support in the learning process. This can be also seen against the proposed IMPACT framework postulating that the influence of AI depends also on the Area, where it is integrated, here the education sector (Montag et al. 2024a, b). Further, the chapter aims to provide an overview of how the learning process and the required competencies evolve and adapt when AI is integrated into learning. To this end, it first outlines the traditional learning process and the traditional competencies required to provide a basis for understanding subsequent developments. It then discusses how these competencies can be transformed, adapted or extended through the inclusion of AI. Implications for the future design of learning environments will be drawn from this discussion, and a forecast will be made of how educational systems will need to evolve to fully exploit the potential of AI in teaching and learning contexts.

8.2 Learning in the Age of AI

8.2.1 Fundamentals of the General Learning Process

To fully understand the implications of integrating AI into the learning process, it is first necessary to examine the fundamentals of the learning process in general, without the involvement of AI. This examination provides the foundation upon which the specific changes and enhancements resulting from the integration of AI technologies can be detailed later. In general, two levels of cognitive learning processes can be distinguished: the object level and the meta level, which we will examine in more detail below (de Bruin et al. 2020; Nelson 1990).

8.2.1.1 Learning on the Object Level

When learners invest mental resources in processing the content of the learning material, this is referred to as the object level (Nelson 1990). To develop an in-depth understanding of how learners process information on the object level, it is helpful to refer to Atkinson and Shiffrin's (1968) three-store model of memory. This model, which divides information processing into three successive stages, allows a structured analysis of the different stages through which information passes: the sensory register, short-term memory and long-term memory.

First, sensory information from the environment enters the sensory register, where it remains for a very short time, a few seconds. This information is highly ephemeral and only those elements that attract attention move on to the next stage of information processing (Atkinson and Shiffrin 1968). The selected information is then transferred via separate pathways for text and image processing into working memory, which serves as an active processing site. Here, information is processed through cognitive processes such as rehearsal, organisation, and making connections with previously known knowledge. These processes are crucial because the capacity of working memory is limited, both in terms of the amount of information it can hold and the length of time it can be held (Baddeley 2000). If information is only processed superficially here, it corresponds to the knowledge level in Bloom's Taxonomy of Educational Objectives (Bloom 1956). At this level, information can be recalled but not understood and cannot be explained in one's own words. Only when it is processed more deeply and linked to prior knowledge can higher levels such as comprehension, application or even evaluation be achieved (Bloom 1956). Finally, information that has been sufficiently processed in working memory is transferred to long-term memory. This is characterised by its almost unlimited capacity and its ability to store information for long periods of time. The successful transfer of knowledge to long-term memory is facilitated by processes such as repeated practice, deep processing, and making meaningful connections (Schnotz and Bannert 2003).

8.2.1.2 Necessary Competences for the Object Level

In order to structure the process of learning and understanding content effectively, specific competences are needed to enable learners to acquire and process information efficiently. These skills include both the selection and use of different media and the integration of new knowledge into existing knowledge structures.

The ability to choose the most appropriate media for each learning situation is crucial. Learners should understand which media formats (such as images, text, video or podcasts) are most effective for different types of information. Choosing the appropriate medium depends on the learner's understanding of the advantages and disadvantages of each format and how these can affect knowledge acquisition.

Effective reading strategies for text and images are essential for processing and understanding information. Learners need to be able to critically analyse text and interpret images in order to fully comprehend the content. These skills are particularly important when text and images are combined to convey complex information (Schlag et al. 2007). Structuring strategies, such as mind mapping, help to make connections between text and image information (Merchie and Van Keer 2012; Seufert 2019). These techniques help learners to develop a deeper understanding of the material and promote the organisation of knowledge in a way that facilitates long-term retention.

Optimal integration of information into long-term memory requires a certain level of prior knowledge and openness to new knowledge. Critical reflection on the alignment of new and existing knowledge is also essential to avoid misunderstandings and to assess the relevance of new knowledge in the context of what has already been learned (Seufert 2003).

8.2.1.3 Learning on the Meta Level

The meta level, often referred to as metacognition, involves planning, monitoring and regulating one's own learning process (Nelson 1990). This is where the content learning process at object level is observed and controlled from a meta perspective. At this meta level, learners reflect on their learning strategies, assess how effectively they are learning and adjust their approaches as necessary. This level therefore involves awareness of and control over one's own cognitive processes. It involves setting learning goals, planning learning activities, monitoring understanding and progress, and evaluating learning outcomes. Metacognition enables learners to adapt their learning process to changing circumstances or new demands (Zimmerman 2002).

8.2.1.4 Necessary Competences for the Meta Level

The ability to plan, monitor, and regulate one's own learning process enables learners to make their learning more effective. To successfully navigate this metacognitive process, certain essential competencies are required.

Learners must establish clear, well-defined objectives, which is fundamental to the planning stage of metacognitive learning. The use of Bloom's Taxonomy makes it possible to formulate concrete learning objectives at different cognitive levels, from simple recall to evaluation (Bloom 1956). This initial planning stage is crucial because it lays the foundation for the success of the learning process. Clear goal setting helps learners to choose effective learning strategies aimed at achieving specific learning objectives. This strategic knowledge includes the selection of appropriate methods and techniques that match both the content and the learner's personal strengths and weaknesses for a personalized learning experience. In addition, the monitoring phase requires learners to objectively assess their progress. During the monitoring phase, learners continually evaluate whether they are achieving their set goals and whether they are on the right track. This involves self-assessment of their progress and determining whether the chosen learning strategy is appropriate or needs to be adjusted. This phase is critical because it directly influences self-regulation and requires constant reflection (Zimmerman 2002). In the regulating phase, learners adjust their strategies on the basis of what they have learned in the monitoring phase. This requires a high level of motivation to change and detailed strategic knowledge. The ability to adapt is crucial for effective learning as it enables learners to respond flexibly to challenges and changes in the learning process (Zimmerman and Schunk 2001).

8.2.2 How Does the Learning Process Change with AI Assistance?

We now consider the integration of AI into the learning process at both levels. When learners interact with AI based systems for learning, it is crucial that they use AI to gather information and deepen their understanding of the learning content, e.g. by discussing and refining their knowledge with an AI Chatbot. Interactive AI tools can also serve as a learning partner for planning and reflection, e.g. by asking for feedback, new strategies, motivational hints etc. We therefore assume that changes of the learning process will occur at both, the object and meta level, requiring adaptation and expansion of the required competencies (Mah et al. 2023).

8.2.2.1 The Object Level of AI Assisted Learning

Learning with AI at the object level basically follows the same principles as learning in general. However, the integration of AI technologies requires the adaptation and expansion of the competencies needed for their effective use (Mah et al. 2023).

In the context of AI assisted learning, the focus shifts from choosing the optimal media to choosing the optimal AI tool. It is critical for learners to choose the right AI tool that meets their specific learning needs and goals. This requires not only an understanding of the technological options available, but also the ability to assess their potential for one's own learning process.

Another important aspect of learning with AI is the development of prompt competency. AI systems, especially those based on natural language processing, require precise inputs or "prompts" to generate appropriate responses. Therefore, the ability to formulate effective prompts is essential to achieve desired outcomes (Zamfirescu-Pereira et al. 2023). This involves formulating the prompt, checking the relevance and accuracy of the response, and adjusting the prompt if necessary. It is critical to recognize that AI will sometimes generate responses that do not accurately reflect factual information. Addressing this issue is essential, as discussed in Sect. 8.2.3.1, which emphasizes the critical role of human review of AI output.

Learners also need a basic understanding of the specific domain in which AI is being used. Without this foundational understanding, it is difficult to ask relevant questions or assess the adequacy of the AI's output. This competency is critical to ensuring that interactions with AI are productive and that learners can verify the accuracy of the information they receive.

This means that in addition to specific skills, general AI knowledge is also important. Understanding how AI systems work, how they are trained, why they may produce incorrect information, and how they process information and generate responses is fundamental to realizing their full potential. This knowledge not only influences the efficiency of tool use, but also improves the quality of learning experiences and outcomes. It underscores the importance of developing AI literacy in order to become effective learners. Recent literature underscores this need at various levels of education. For example, Casal-Otero et al. (2023) provide a systematic literature review on AI literacy in K-12 education, identifying key trends and gaps in current research. Su et al. (2023) explore the challenges and opportunities of AI literacy in early childhood education, highlighting foundational skills for young learners. In addition, Fathahillah et al. (2023) analyze AI literacy within the blended learning model in higher education, providing insights into the effective integration of AI tools. Collectively, these studies highlight the critical role of AI literacy in optimizing educational outcomes in diverse learning environments.

8.2.2.2 The Meta Level of AI Assisted Learning

At the meta level, the integration of AI into learning processes also requires the adaptation and expansion of necessary competencies (Mah et al. 2023). These adaptations enable learners to effectively integrate AI into their learning process and maximize the benefits of the interplay between human and AI.

In the planning phase, goal clarity remains critical. Learners need to be able to clearly define their learning objectives. Understanding the capabilities and limitations of the AI in reaching these goals is critical. Questions such as "What can I expect from the AI?" and "What tasks can the AI assist with?" must be answered to ensure an efficient task sharing between human and machine. This task allocation determines where the AI will support the learning process and when the learner must actively engage. This concept of "augmented intelligence" emphasizes collaboration between human and AI, leveraging the strengths of both to optimize the learning experience (Yau et al. 2021).

During the monitoring phase, the ability to identify, structure, and align learning progress is critical. AI can be used for learning analytics of learning progress and potential deficiencies and providing real-time feedback (Roll and Wylie 2016). This allows learners to continuously review their learning process and ensure that they are on the right track. The ability to interpret the information provided by AI and integrate it into one's own learning context becomes a critical skill of self-regulation (Lim et al. 2023).

When learners recognize the need to adjust their learning process, regulation is required. Regulating the learning process requires motivation to change and advanced knowledge of the AI tool. Learners must be willing to adjust their strategies based on insights gained during the monitoring phase. Understanding how to effectively make adjustments with AI support is essential. This includes knowing how to use feedback from AI tools to modify learning strategies and efficiently manage the learning process (Järvelä et al. 2023).

8.2.3 Implications

In the previous sections, we explored how the integration of AI affects both, the object level and the meta level of learning processes. We have identified specific competencies that learners need to develop or enhance in order to effectively integrate AI into their learning processes. These competencies go beyond those required for traditional non-AI learning and include technological understanding, critical thinking, and advanced metacognitive skills. Below, we highlight two key implications of using AI in education that are particularly relevant in the current era.

8.2.3.1 Human Verification of AI Output

It remains a critical task for humans to verify and evaluate the outputs of AI. This need arises primarily from the current shortcomings of Large Language Model based AI in providing error-free information or accurately citing sources. Therefore, humans must be able to critically evaluate and, if necessary, correct the information generated by AI, which means that they must stay one step ahead of AI in certain aspects. According to Bloom's Taxonomy, learners must consistently reach the highest level, the evaluation level. However, this is by no means easy to achieve, which underscores the complexity of practical AI applications in education. In addition, correcting AI requires a certain level of knowledge about the tool in order to generate appropriate and meaningful prompts. Without this knowledge, it would be difficult to realize the full potential of AI and ensure that its capabilities are used effectively.

8.2.3.2 Prior Knowledge

Prior knowledge plays a critical role in the learning process (Seufert et al. 2024). The effectiveness of AI as a learning tool can vary significantly depending on the learner's level of prior knowledge. The adaptability of learning systems, especially those using AI, is critical in determining how well different learners can be supported. Learners with different levels of prior knowledge require different types of support (Seufert 2003).

Learners with low prior knowledge have a high need for learning assistance, but may struggle to use AI-based systems effectively. They may find it difficult to ask relevant questions or correctly interpret the information generated by the AI. This highlights a significant challenge for the application of AI in educational contexts, as the potential benefits of AI may not be fully realized by those who may need the most support. Conversely, learners with moderate prior knowledge often benefit the most from AI-based learning tools. These learners already have a foundation of both content and understanding of AI that enables them to understand and make sense of the information provided by AI. This intermediate group is well positioned to use AI technologies to enhance their learning experience, as they can effectively interact with and benefit from the adaptive capabilities of AI systems. High prior knowledge learners have the ability to use AI effectively, but require less support because they already have extensive knowledge and can learn independently. These learners can complete tasks more efficiently and effectively to their satisfaction without much assistance. However, their ability to use AI tools effectively underscores the importance of ensuring that all learners reach a level of proficiency where they can fully exploit the potential of AI technologies in their learning processes.

8.2.3.3 Implications for Designing AI Assisted Learning Environments

These observations have several important implications for the design of AI-based learning environments. First, it is essential that learners have a minimum level of both content knowledge and understanding of AI in order to benefit from AI-based learning tools. Educational institutions will need to develop strategies to bring learners up to this baseline level. Furthermore, effective implementation of these strategies will also require supportive political interventions that prioritize educational policies and funding to enhance AI literacy. This could include integrating foundational courses that cover essential subject matter and introductory AI concepts to ensure that all learners have the necessary background to engage effectively with AI tools.

Second, it is critical to address how to effectively support learners with low levels of prior knowledge to reach the intermediate level necessary for meaningful use of AI. This support could be provided through preparatory courses, additional tutoring programs, or the use of adaptive AI specifically tailored to the needs of novices. For example, such AI systems could help novices formulate the right questions to build foundational knowledge, guide them through the initial stages of learning, and progressively introduce more complex concepts as their understanding deepens.

8.3 Looking to the Future

The integration of AI into educational systems requires a rethinking of existing educational practices and structures. Taking into account the considerations outlined in this chapter, in particular the competencies required for learning with AI and their implications, several essential steps are needed for the future of education. Future approaches to education should shift the focus from learning products, i.e. outcomes, to learning processes. On the one hand, AI tools can be used to analyse, visualize, and provide feedback on learning processes; on the other hand, learners need to be aware of the processes themselves. Examinations could therefore include presentations of learning products and their genesis, thereby strengthening students' ability to verbalize their knowledge as well as their learning experiences and strategies. This approach emphasizes the importance of reflection over the mere reproduction of knowledge and promotes deep understanding and critical thinking.

The role of educators will change fundamentally. Instead of their perceived traditional role as primary knowledge providers, educators will increasingly act as learning facilitators, supporting and guiding the learning process. This shift implies a greater emphasis on supporting learners' self-regulation skills and developing their metacognitive abilities. Educators will need to focus on helping students become more autonomous learners, able to effectively manage their own learning with the help of AI technologies.

It is clear that learners need a broad set of competencies to learn effectively with AI. These competencies include not only a technical understanding of AI, but also advanced learning skills that encompass both the object and meta level of learning. Fostering these competencies will be critical to realizing the full potential of AI in education. This includes fostering skills such as critical thinking, problem solving, and effective communication, all of which are essential for interacting with AI systems.

Overall, learning with this new generation of generative AI models is still in its early stages, but offers significant potential for future educational innovation. Further research and development are needed to adapt education systems to fully integrate and leverage the benefits of AI. The future of education will therefore require not only a technological but also a pedagogical reorientation in order to create an optimal learning environment in the age of generative AI.

References

Atkinson, R. C., & Shiffrin, R. M. (1968). Human Memory: A Proposed System and its Control Processes. *In Psychology of Learning and Motivation* (Bd. 2, S. 89–195). Elsevier. https://doi.org/10.1016/S0079-7421(08)60422-3

Baddeley A (2000) The episodic buffer: a new component of working memory? Trends Cogn Sci 4(11):417–423. https://doi.org/10.1016/S1364-6613(00)01538-2

Bloom BS, Engelhart MD, Furst EJ, Hill WH, Krathwohl DR (1956) Taxonomy of educational objectives: the classification of educational goals. In: Handbook 1: cognitive domain. Longman, New York, 1103–1133

Casal-Otero L, Catala A, Fernández-Morante C, Taboada M, Cebreiro B, Barro S (2023) AI literacy in K-12: a systematic literature review. Int J STEM Educ 10(1):29. https://doi.org/10.1186/s40594-023-00418-7

Chen L, Chen P, Lin Z (2020) Artificial intelligence in education: a review. IEEE Access 8:75264–75278. https://doi.org/10.1109/access.2020.2988510

De Bruin ABH, Roelle J, Carpenter SK, Baars M (2020) Synthesizing cognitive load and self-regulation theory: a theoretical framework and research agenda. Educ Psychol Rev 32(4):903–915. https://doi.org/10.1007/s10648-020-09576-4

Fathahillah F, Fakhri MM, Ahmar AS (2023) Analysis of artificial intelligence literacy in the blended learning model in higher education. EduLine: J Educ Learn Inno 3(4):566–575. https://doi.org/10.35877/454RI.eduline2049

Järvelä S, Nguyen A, Molenaar I (2023) Advancing SRL research with artificial intelligence. Comput Hum Behav 147:107847. https://doi.org/10.1016/j.chb.2023.107847

Lim L, Bannert M, Van der Graaf J, Fan Y, Rakovic M, Singh S, Molenaar I, Gašević D (2023) How do students learn with real-time personalized scaffolds? Br J Edu Technol. https://doi.org/10.1111/bjet.13414

Mah D-K, Hense J, Dufentester C (2023) Didaktische Impulse zum Lehren und Lernen mit und über Künstliche Intelligenz. In: Witt C, Gloerfeld C, Wrede SE (eds) Künstliche Intelligenz in der Bildung. Springer, pp 91–108

Merchie E, Van Keer H (2012) Spontaneous mind map use and learning from texts: the role of instruction and student characteristics. Procedia: Soc Behav Sci 69:1387–1394. https://doi.org/10.1016/j.sbspro.2012.12.077

Montag C, Nakov P, Ali R (2024a) Considering the IMPACT framework to understand the AI-well-being-complex from an interdisciplinary perspective. Tele Inform Reports 13:100112. https://doi.org/10.1016/j.teler.2023.100112

Montag C, Ali R, Al-Thani D, Hall BJ (2024b) On artificial intelligence and global mental health. Asian J Psychiatr 91:103855. https://doi.org/10.1016/j.ajp.2023.103855

Nelson TO (1990) Metamemory: a theoretical framework and new findings. In: The psychology of learning and motivation, pp 125–173. https://doi.org/10.1016/s0079-7421(08)60053-5

Roll I, Wylie R (2016) Evolution and revolution in artificial intelligence in education. Int J Artif Intell Educ 26(2):582–599. https://doi.org/10.1007/s40593-016-0110-3

Schlag S, Florax M, Ploetzner R (2007) The use of learning strategies in learning from text and pictures. Front Artificial Intelligence Appl 162:331

Schnotz W, Bannert M (2003) Construction and interference in learning from multiple representation. Learn Instr 13(2):141–156. https://doi.org/10.1016/s0959-4752(02)00017-8

Seufert T (2003) Supporting coherence formation in learning from multiple representations. Learn Instr 13(2):227–237. https://doi.org/10.1016/s0959-4752(02)00022-1

Seufert T (2019) Training for coherence formation when learning from text and picture and the interplay with learners' prior knowledge. Front Psychol 10. https://doi.org/10.3389/fpsyg.2019.00193

Seufert T, Hamm V, Vogt A, Riemer V (2024) The interplay of cognitive load, learners' resources and self-regulation. Educ Psychol Rev 36(2). https://doi.org/10.1007/s10648-024-09890-1

Su J, Ng DTK, Chu SKW (2023) Artificial intelligence (AI) literacy in early childhood education: the challenges and opportunities. Comput Educ: Artificial Intelligence 4:10012. https://doi.org/10.1016/j.caeai.2023.100124

Witt C, Gloerfeld C, Wrede S (2023) Künstliche Intelligenz in der bildung. Springer Fachmedien Wiesbaden GmbH

Yau KLA, Lee HJ, Chong YW, Ling MH, Syed AR, Wu C, Goh HG (2021) Augmented intelligence: surveys of literature and expert opinion to understand relations between human intelligence and artificial intelligence. IEEE Access 9:136744–136761

Zamfirescu-Pereira JD, Wong RY, Hartmann B, Yang Q (2023, April) Why Johnny can't prompt: how non-AI experts try (and fail) to design LLM prompts. In: Proceedings of the 2023 CHI conference on human factors in computing systems, pp 1–21. https://doi.org/10.1145/3544548.3581388

Zimmerman BJ (2002) Becoming a self-regulated learner: an overview. Theory Practice, Digital/Theory Practice 41(2):64–70. https://doi.org/10.1207/s15430421tip4102_2

Zimmerman BJ, Schunk DH (2001) Reflections on theories of self-regulated learning and academic achievement. In: Zimmerman B, Schunk D (eds) Self-regulated learning and academic achievement: theoretical perspectives, 2nd edn. Lawrence Erlbaum Associates, Mahwah, NJ, pp 289–307

Chapter 9
Trust in Automated Driving and the Three Stages of Trust Framework: Takeaways for Designing Human-Centered AI Applications

Johannes Kraus and Martin Baumann

Abstract This chapter focuses on a transfer from research on trust processes in the interaction with automated vehicles to the interaction with current AI systems like Large Language Models (LLMs). After discussing parallels between the domains and transferable research insights, the psychological processes in trust calibration are discussed along the central propositions of the Three Stages of Trust framework (Kraus in Psychological processes in the formation and calibration of trust in automation, 2020). The framework emphasises the dynamic role of trust and the iterative learning about a system's trustworthiness with presented information prior and during system interaction. Furthermore, it underlines the role of situational context and individual user differences. Designing AI systems that support calibrated trust involves transparent communication of capabilities and limitations, integrating human-centered design principles, and offering adaptive information to aid decision-making. These strategies aim to foster a balanced and informed use of AI, eventually fostering an efficient and safe interaction.

Keywords Human-AI interaction · Trust in Automation · Human Factors

9.1 Introduction

While the term artificial intelligence (AI) is recently being used as a term to coin applications of artificial neuronal networks and Large Language Models (LLM) in both professional and private areas, the interaction with intelligent technology has

J. Kraus (✉)
Johannes Gutenberg-University Mainz, Mainz, Germany
e-mail: jokraus@uni-mainz.de

M. Baumann
Ulm University, Ulm, Germany
e-mail: martin.baumann@uni-ulm.de

C. Montag and R. Ali (eds.), *The Impact of Artificial Intelligence on Societies*, Studies in Neuroscience, Psychology and Behavioral Economics,
https://doi.org/10.1007/978-3-031-70355-3_9

long been investigated before the rise of broadly used AI software, such as ChatGPT. One of the areas in which users' understanding and interaction with intelligent, partially autonomous systems has been widely investigated in recent years is (partly) automated vehicles. One of the reasons for the interest in this area is that automated vehicles promise to be one necessary means to significantly increase traffic safety and contribute to the reduction of currently 1.19 million fatalities on global roads per year (WHO 2023). Research in this area led to a huge amount of valuable empirical results to enable efficient, safe and comfortable interaction design. Here, many questions and findings can be directly transferred to the interaction and design of recently deployed AI systems. For all these systems system transparency, system observability and directability (Christoffersen and Woods 2002), and the development of calibrated trust (Walch et al. 2017; Kraus 2020) are essential challenges that have to be met to achieve a safe, efficient, appropriate and satisfactory use of the systems.

This chapter focuses on trust processes in the interaction with intelligent AI systems, using interaction of drivers with automated vehicles as an example area of studying these processes hypothesising that these results can widely be transferred to any domain of human-AI system interaction, because of the commonality of the underlying design challenges and psychological processes. Trust has prominently been conceptualised as a technology-specific attitude that has been found to play a central role for how people think about technical systems in general, how they adopt and use them (Lee and See 2004; Kraus et al. 2021; Sindermann et al. 2021). We will discuss the role of trust for AI adoption in terms of the Three Stages of Trust framework (Kraus 2020) and derive implications for designing information campaigns and interaction concepts for these systems to facilitate the development of human-centered interaction strategies that can support calibrated trust in and eventually a balanced and informed use of current and future AI systems. In this sense this chapter can also be seen through the lenses of the IMPACT framework building the backbone of the present book (e.g., Montag et al. 2024). According to this framework the effect AI on the well-being of human depends on the interplay of several factors, one of which is the Area, that is the product or the domain the AI is built in and used. In this chapter the area that we will focus on is human-automated vehicle interaction and its generalization to human-AI interaction.

9.2 Generalising from Driver-Automated Vehicle Interaction to Human-AI Interaction

As mentioned above, in our days the term AI is strongly associated with deep neural networks, LLMs, such as ChatGPT, and comparable systems. Whatsoever, for decades engineers, computer scientists, and Human Factors specialists among others have been researching and working on the development of intelligent technical systems that can autonomously carry out highly complex tasks in dynamic environments—of which driving with automated driving systems is one of the most prominent ones. Driving is enormously complex, includes about 1600 subtasks (Walker et al. 2015), and requires a substantial amount of time and effort to learn how to be performed safely and efficiently. Nevertheless, there are already systems on the market that can perform this task autonomously, such as the Uber or Waymo self-driving vehicles. For certain manoeuvres and situations such systems pass the Turing test, that is they perform a driving manoeuvre in a way indistinguishable from a human driver (Stanton et al. 2020).

Nevertheless, these intelligent systems are still far away from being able to drive from any starting point to any destination on any roads under any conditions as humans can do. Consequently, it will still take decades for such fully self-driving vehicles to be available ubiquitously (Shladover 2022). But below the level of fully self-driving vehicles there are intelligent automation systems that, at least, are capable of performing the driving task within a defined so-called Operational Design Domain (ODD, SAE International 2018). According to a taxonomy developed by the Society of Automotive Engineers (SAE) one can distinguish six levels of driving automation. In the first three levels of automation, from Level 0 with no automation, Level 1 where the driver is assisted either in lateral or longitudinal control (current Adaptive Cruise Control Systems or Lane Keeping Systems), to Level 2 (Partial Automation) where the system takes over both the lateral and the longitudinal control, the driver always has to monitor the environment and to be prepared to intervene at any time to ensure traffic safety. From Level 3 (Conditional Automation) onwards the system also monitors the environment as long as the system is actively controlling the driving task, that is operating within the defined ODD. At Level 3, the human driver serves as a backup for the automated system. The driver must be able to take back control within a reasonable time period, and the system must allow for this transition time (see Zhang et al. 2019, for a review of 129 studies). At Level 4 automation (High Automation) the system itself must be able to serve as backup within the defined ODD. Level 5 automation then defines fully self-driving cars.

From a Human Factors perspective, the most critical levels of automation are Levels 2 and 3 as on these levels the human driver is no longer in the loop of performing the driving task but is still required to serve as a backup in case of system limits or failures. For this it is essential that the driver performs those actions that are required to constantly monitor the system and the environment (Level 2) or to be prepared to take back control within a rather limited time frame (Level 3), often in critical, non-routine situations. Whether human drivers show this behaviour adequately (and in general interact in a functional, efficient and safe manner with automated vehicles) strongly depends on the adequacy of their mental models, beliefs and the resulting expectations about the capabilities and reliability of the automated system (Kraus 2020). A substantial number of empirical studies investigated factors influencing human driver behaviour when interacting with automated vehicles, especially with Level 2 and Level 3 automation vehicles (see Zhang et al. 2019 for a review). A common theme of many of these studies is the importance of trust as a variable strongly influencing human driver behaviour in the interaction with automated vehicles (e.g., Gold et al. 2015; Kraus 2020; Kraus et al. 2020; Kraus et al. 2019; Manchon et al. 2022; Montag et al. 2023a, b; Mühl et al. 2020; Walker et al. 2018). For example, Manchon et al. (2022) showed that the initial trust level in automated vehicles influences the frequency with which drivers engage in non-driving related tasks or how much they monitor the road while the automation is active. Drivers with a higher initial trust level engaged more in non-driving related tasks and monitored the road less.

The interaction with such partially or conditionally automated vehicles is a prototypical situation that has considerable commonalities with the interaction with current AI systems. In a wide variety of AI application contexts, subtasks of a (cooperative) main task are delegated to the AI system while the human user is still responsible for the overall task performance. Typically, these AI systems are designed to support users in decision-making by providing suggestions and the human user verifies or evaluates these suggestions or recommendations. Consequently, comparable to Level 2 vehicle automation systems, users have to monitor the performance of the system and evaluate the adequacy of its suggestions and output including the decision whether to use the system's outputs at all and if so to which extent. Additionally, in case the AI system reaches a system limit (e.g., because the human user's question requires information the system is not trained with) or it shows a failure (e.g., if AI systems produce invalid outputs like the infamous hallucinations of ChatGPT) users must identify such situations based on their monitoring and intervene or take back control of the subtask. Despite the differences in physical appearance and tasks to be performed, from a user perspective, the challenges and the psychological nature of the familiarisation and interaction processes are in many regards comparable: e.g., learning about the system, understanding it as well as making sense of and interpreting its outputs. In both application domains the human users are confronted with a highly complex technical system whose operating principles are opaque to a major extent, and using the system puts the users into a situation of vulnerability and risk. Therefore, we are convinced that the commonalities between these application areas, despite also some obvious differences, justify the application of the results from studies on driver-automated vehicles interaction to understand the human behaviour in human-AI interaction situations (Montag et al. 2023a, b).

9.3 Trust in Automation

As indicated above, a central variable in the interaction with both automated vehicles and other AI-based systems is trust in automation which has been widely discussed in recent years as a subjective evaluation of intelligent systems relevant for decision-making and reliance on intelligent technology. Defined in the interpersonal domain as a "willingness of a party to be vulnerable to the actions of another party based on the expectation that the other will perform a particular action important to the trustor, irrespective of the ability to monitor or control that other party" (Mayer et al. 1995, p. 712), trust has been transferred to and investigated in different domains in which human interact or work with (more or less) automated systems for the last 35 years (e.g., Muir 1987, 1994; Muir and Moray 1996; Lee and Moray 1992, 1994). Under the label *trust in automation* it is conceived as a psychological variable that serves as a subjective mediator of a trustor's (human operator/user) perception and evaluation of features and characteristics of the technical system (trustee) and their decision to interact with a system and use it (Mayer et al. 1995; Madhavan and Wiegmann 2007). The defining characteristics of trust in the interpersonal domain (Thielmann and Hilbig 2015)—(a) presence of uncertainty and risk, (b) a certain expectation about the trustee, and (c) acceptance of vulnerability—can be readily transferred to the domain of interacting with modern technology, especially to the interaction with automated vehicles and other AI-based systems—for example LLM or recommendation systems.[1] Such systems can be considered as black boxes, making an intuitive understanding of their inner workings and functionality difficult. They are neither transparent nor self-explicatory leaving users uncertain about causal relationships between input and output, their functional scope, capabilities, reliability, strengths and weaknesses. This lack of understanding tendentially hinders users from making informed decisions about whether and how to use the systems' outputs. Trust can in this regard be understood as a psychological currency that allows humans to rely on AI systems even if they do not possess the complete knowledge about them. Trust in automation builds on an expectancy of how these systems might work and behave and the willingness to accept vulnerability in using and relying on them (e.g., Kraus 2020). Importantly, this vulnerability results from the individual risk associated with the task under consideration. In line with this, a prominent definition of trust in automation in the field was brought forward by Lee and See (2004) who define it "as the attitude that an agent will help achieve an individual´s goal in a situation characterized by uncertainty and vulnerability" (p. 51).

Given that trust is based on the formation of expectations towards the system and is an important psychological factor in the decision to rely on a system, it is crucial to understand under which conditions people correctly assess the trustworthiness of a system. In this context, in particular two concepts play a central role: calibrated trust—an optimal level of trust leading to balanced and safe system use—and trust calibration—the psychological process in which information about a system is used to assess its trustworthiness and to adapt the trust level accordingly. Calibrated trust is "a condition in which a user's level of trust is precisely congruent with the system's actual capabilities and performance" (Kraus 2020, p. 19; Muir 1987) theoretically associated to an optimised pattern of system use minimising negative and maximising positive outcomes. This balanced state of trust should theoretically diminish overtrust (trusting a system too much potentially leading to unsafe system use) and distrust (trusting a system too little leading to a situation in which advantages of a system cannot fully play out, Parasuraman and Riley 1997). To understand and facilitate calibrated trust in users through training, system and interface design it is essential

[1] Note that while the two forms of trust discussed here share defining components at a psychological level, their actual relatedness is not conclusively resolved empirically (see for example, Scholz et al. 2024; Montag et al. 2023a, b).

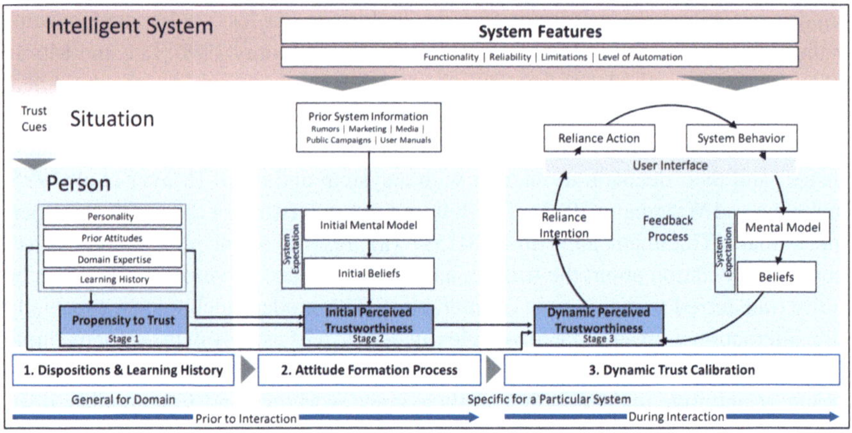

Fig. 9.1 The three stages of trust framework (simplified representation from Kraus 2020)

to understand the psychological process of trust calibration and which role characteristics of users, the system under consideration as well as the task and context it is used in play.

9.4 Three Stages of Trust Framework

In the following, the Three Stages of Trust framework (Kraus 2020, Fig. 9.1) will be discussed along some of its key propositions to illustrate assumptions on variables and psychological processes involved in the trust calibration process in the interaction with intelligent systems. The framework integrates variables and processes from trust research (e.g. Lee and See 2004; Hoff and Bashir 2015) and other psychological domains (interpersonal trust, social cognition and personality psychology; importantly the Theory of Planned Behavior) and serves as a means for orientation of research hypotheses and design as well as considering trust in system interface design. The main assumption of the framework is that trust in automation is built up and calibrated in three consecutive trust layers: (1) the propensity to trust in automation, (2) initial learned trust in automation, (3) dynamic learned trust in automation. While this framework was mainly validated in the domains automated driving systems and social robots, the proposed psychological processes can be extended to human expectation building, decision-making and interaction in any human-AI interaction domain. For this chapter we will discuss seven propositions (taken from Kraus 2020[2]) and implications of the framework in terms of their applicability for current AI systems like decision support and LLM systems.

[2] Note that the assumptions are directly cited from Kraus (2020) but they were selected and put in a different order for fitting the context of this chapter. Altogether 7 propositions are presented.

1. *Trust in automation is formed in a dynamic learning process over time, which begins before the actual interaction with a specific automated system.*

In line with this, it is not sufficient to plan and design for trustworthiness of AI systems only during the interaction phase. Rather, trust calibration begins prior to the interaction and is considerably affected by expectations that are built up prior to system use. In the case of current AI systems, media and especially social media play a crucial role in shaping expectations and attitudes with which users start the interaction with these systems. Also, all kinds of information available prior to acquisition in the early phase of the customer journey need to be carefully designed in terms of the expectations that are brought forward by them. It has been shown that such prior information has a significant influence both on trust development during the interaction phase with the system (Beggiato and Krems 2013), and for protecting trust in the system in situations of system limits (Kraus et al. 2020).

2. *Stage 1: The propensity to trust in automation is formed on the basis of user personality, the individual learning history with technology and automated systems (e.g., experience and domain expertise), as well as general attitudes towards technology and automation.*

The trustworthiness of a system is not only a function of its objective capabilities and technical components. Importantly, these characteristics are perceived and evaluated by humans and thus psychological variables and the context in which information is presented play a crucial role in understanding why a system is trusted in a certain situation or with a certain task. In this, as can be seen in Stage 1 of the framework in Fig. 9.1, dispositional variables of users and their experiential history with technological systems build a reference point for experience formation against which provided information and the experience with unfamiliar new systems is evaluated. This holds several implications for the design and dissemination of current AI systems:

- Know your users: users' attitudes, personality and former experience and expertise play a role and can be addressed both in communication about a system and system design.
- Think about user groups: A single system, method of communicating about it, and user interface may not suffice to address interindividual differences.
- Consider the context: environmental and situational factors like stress, time, noise and illumination can affect how much attention and time users can spend to consider information provided about (prior to interaction) and by the system (during the interaction). In line, provided information should fit the context and its implications for information processing.

Knowledge about the context of use and the user (groups) can be gathered by employing a human-centered design process of AI systems involving users early on in the development process and iteratively evaluating both technical and design solutions of the systems under consideration (e.g., Kauer-Franz and Franz 2022). Exemplary personality variables that might be considered are Extraversion, Emotionality,

Agreeableness, Self-Esteem, Affinity for Technology, and the Propensity to Trust in Automated Technology (e.g., Kraus et al. 2021; Scholz et al. 2024).

3. *Stages 2 and 3: Learned trust in automation is built up and calibrated in two phases—initial learned trust and dynamic learned trust—on the basis of available information (trust cues) and the system expectation (informed by the mental model and beliefs).*
4. *Stage 2: Initial learned trust in automation is formed and calibrated on the basis of prior system information in a process that follows to a substantial extent the mechanisms of attitude formation and change.*

Trust cues are "in some way observable or given pieces of evidence a trustor might use to draw inferences about a trustee's trustworthiness in a specific situation" (Thielmann and Hilbig 2015, p. 21). These trust cues can for example carry information on the reputation, the purpose, process, performance, and appearance of a system (Kraus 2020; Kraus et al. 2019). From this, users build up initial mental models and expectations about the system. In line with the definition of trust as an attitude also the psychological process of searching for, selecting, processing and weighting such information in learning about AI systems might be characterised along the principles of human attitude building and formation. Accordingly, trust cues need to be designed in line with these principles both in the information about the system before the interaction as well as in the displayed information in the context of system use (e.g. interface design). In this the following recommendations can help to enhance calibrated trust:

- Design information to entail trust cues with diagnostic information on the actual scope of function and reliability of system outputs.
- Consider channels, timing and context of the communication.
- Think about the results of information processing and its implications for forming and updating mental models, beliefs, expectations and attitudes.

5.1 *Stage 3: Dynamic learned trust in automation influences reliance decisions as part of a mediation process (mental models, beliefs, attitudes, intention).*
5.2 *Stage 3: Dynamic learned trust in automation is calibrated in a feedback process during the interaction with an automated system along a comparison of the current system expectation and the observed system behaviour and the associated output of the user interface.*

Trust is not a fixed and stable variable, but it develops in a learning process and in this is adapted to an integrative evaluation of available information over time. Therefore, in evaluating trust it is not sufficient to measure it at one point in time but rather measure it repeatedly and assess relative changes in trust over time. At the same time this provides a solution for individual anchoring of what is a low or high level of trust as users might differ considerably in their answering styles to Likert-like scales.

During the interaction, crucially, these expectations and the interpretation of system behaviour and associated occurrences is shaped by the information and explanations presented in the user interfaces or displays. This includes for example information on and the explanation of consequences of errors, presenting probabilities for the success of single operations and the validity of presented information. Above this, it includes the interaction and interface design including factors like the appearance and the communication style of the AI systems. For example, Metzger et al. (2024) found that trust in an LLM chatbot is considerably higher if it uses an authoritative, powerful communication style (as it is the default for example in ChatGPT) as compared to a more powerless language using linguistic features like disclaimers, hedges and polite forms indicating some sort of uncertainty of the provided information. Also, the inclusion of disclaimer information might be used to support trust calibration in users. At the same time, this needs to be presented in a salient way as presenting it once at the beginning of the interaction (as it is a current practice) does not seem to affect trust calibration (Metzger et al. 2024). Again, in line with the perspective of this chapter to take on a perspective of extending domain-specific knowledge of the interaction with intelligent systems to current AI applications, design implications for fostering a human-centered and trustworthy design from other domains—e.g., automated driving—can be transferred to the interaction with these systems (e.g., Ekman et al. 2018; Debernard et al. 2016; Walch et al. 2017; Hoc et al. 2009).

From this, the following take-home messages for trustworthy AI system design can be formulated:

- Trust is not a single shot status assessment of a system quality but rather develops dynamically along provided information.
- In a human-centered design process trust should not be used as a status measurement against a benchmark, rather it should be measured at different points in time in the familiarisation process with a system to allow understanding of which pieces of information (trust cues) support users in trust calibration.
- Trustworthy AI design should follow principles of a human-centered design process and can orient itself besides recent domain-specific resources also on previous scientific findings and existing guidelines from other related domains insofar it is to be expected that the psychological processes of trust calibration and decision-making follow similar mechanisms.
- AI systems need to make their reasoning transparent and can provide details on how they arrived at certain recommendations. Thereby it might in many cases be a more trustworthy approach to present recommendations as hypotheses along with material in support of different decision options.

6. *Stages 2 and 3: Prior system information influences the interpretation of observed system behavior and user interface output at stage 3.*

Expectations guide the interpretation of what is happening during interaction, therefore it seems a feasible strategy to provide as much transparent information on the scope of system functioning (e.g., ODD in automated driving) and system limitations as possible early on in the process—optimally prior to the interaction. In line, it has been found that provided information shapes and alters the interpretation of system behavior during system use (e.g. Kraus et al. 2020; Beggiato and Krems 2013). As expectations are proposed to be based on the mental model and the sum of beliefs of users it makes sense to also consider these variables when aiming to design trustworthy AI systems. This includes information on the inner workings and capabilities of the systems as well as information on its competence and reliability. In line with multi-dimensional trust concepts (e.g. Mayer et al. 1995; Scholz et al. 2024) also information on the system benevolence and integrity might play an important role for making these systems transparent and for aligning expectations with actual experiences users make during the interaction. In this, supposedly negative information about a system is as crucial as positive information in educating users about the trustworthiness of a system as these support users' realistic assessment of the system capabilities and thus building up expectations in line with its actual capabilities and limitations. This is supported by findings from the domain of automated driving that trust only temporarily decreases after the experience of a system error and tends to be reinstated in the course of continuous error-free interaction with the system (e.g., Kraus et al. 2020).

Taken together the following recommendations for system design can be drawn:

- During the interaction the experience of (non-fatal) system limitations and even errors can support users in making sense of the system and calibrate their trust and eventually their usage decisions.
- Learning about problems and errors of systems can be a meaningful learning instance that helps users to better calibrate their trust.

7. *The strength of the association between dynamic learned trust and reliance behavior is moderated by user characteristics (e.g., traits and states), situational variables, and task characteristics.*

Changes in trust do not always have to result in behavioural changes in terms of reliance on the system or other observable behaviour results. Rather, there can be specific trust changes for certain situations or part of the functionality of systems which fall below the level of actual behavioural changes but which might be relevant in learning about the system, the development of situation- or functionality-specific trust and usage behaviour leading to a long-term functional interaction and usage pattern.

9.5 Implications for Designing Human-Centered Automated Vehicles and AI Systems

Trust plays a key role in the way users interact with intelligent, autonomous systems, such as automated vehicles and AI systems in general. As described above in the Three Stages of Trust framework trust is a complex construct and different layers of trust and stages of trust development have to be distinguished. This means that the formation of calibrated trust has to be supported on these different layers and in these different stages by appropriate measures.

In educating or assisting users how to functionally use AI systems a calibrated level of trust represents a central design goal. While a basic level of trust has to be established for users to first decide to use a system at all, an unconsidered maximisation of trust cannot be desired and in fact is dangerous as it facilitates overtrust and unsafe overreliance to the systems' recommendations or actions.

Calibrated trust can be promoted by providing users with transparent, truthful and interpretable information about the system's functionalities, capabilities and limitations—both prior to and during the interaction with the system. This is in line with the prominent call for explainable AI (e.g., Rai 2020). However, as explanations of AI algorithms have their limitations and humans might want to (and from an ethical viewpoint probably should) stay in control of decisions in the interaction with AI, provided explanations and information needs to be designed in line with the properties of human attitude formation and decision-making processes in order to support humans in the task they are conducting in cooperation with AI systems.

In this, momentary information processing capacities both based on situational and individual variabilities need to be considered. This includes goals, motivation, available cognitive resources, individual preferences and essentially a certain fit of the provided information to the criticality of the task as well as the task distribution between humans and the AI (e.g. level of automation). Importantly, and above this, it also includes the consideration of the users' needs for autonomy and competence experience. In all of the former sources of variability user dispositions like domain expertise and personality attitudes towards technology in general and in AI in specific might play a role (e.g. Kraus et al. 2021). To support human decision-making in an optimal way instead of providing mere recommendations users can follow or not along with respective explanations in line with the idea of evaluative AI (Miller 2023) AI systems might adaptively provide evidence for or against certain alternatives. In this way, users stay in control and are supported instead of forced to take on all-or-nothing recommendations by AI in shared tasks—potentially reducing negative effects of either mistrusting such potentially constraining advice as well as overtrust and complacency in the interaction with AI systems.

Furthermore, it might be meaningful to implement possibilities for "soft" learning of the properties of AI systems in training environments, simulations, or easy tutorial tasks to build up both realistic expectations towards the systems but also towards one's own capabilities to use their advice and support in an adaptive manner (e.g., correctly weight provided information, etc.). Of course, such measures have to be tailored not only to the system and the task but also the dispositions and expertise of the users.

As trust keeps on developing dynamically during the interaction with intelligent systems AI needs to be equipped with interfaces that foster understanding of what the system is doing why at what time by providing real-time information on how its outputs (e.g., recommendations and decisions) have been established. Also, it should be made clear to users in which level of automation a system currently works, which tasks it currently does and which it can potentially handle, and which (sub-)tasks are in the responsibility of the user. As information needs of different users might be very individual, system and interface personalization provide a meaningful approach to enhance trust calibration in an optimised way.

Taken together, the design and implementation of both prior information about an AI system and its user interface should result from an iterative human-centered design process. This process should involve different stakeholders and essentially future users to decide which information should be provided at which point in the familiarisation and system use. These decisions may vary considerably for different user groups, different systems, contexts and tasks and should thus be based on a case-specific design process (e.g., Kraus 2020). This is also in accordance with the IMPACT framework (Montag et al. 2024) that is the common theme between the chapters of this book. It is essential for understanding the effect of AI on human behaviour and well-being to consider the complex interaction between all these aspects.

References

Beggiato M, Krems JF (2013) The evolution of mental model, trust and acceptance of adaptive cruise control in relation to initial information. Transport Res F: Traffic Psychol Behav 18:47–57. https://doi.org/10.1016/j.trf.2012.12.006

Christoffersen K, Woods D (2002) How to make automated systems team players. Adv Hum Perform Cogn Eng Res 2:1–12. https://doi.org/10.1016/S1479-3601(02)02003-9

Debernard S, Chauvin C, Pokam R, Langlois S (2016) Designing human-machine interface for autonomous vehicles. IFAC-PapersOnLine 49(19):609–614. https://doi.org/10.1016/j.ifacol.2016.10.629

Ekman F, Johansson M, Sochor J (2018) Creating appropriate trust for autonomous vehicle systems: a framework for HMI design. IEEE Trans Human-Mach Syst 48(1):95–101. https://doi.org/10.1109/THMS.2017.2776209

Gold C, Körber M, Hohenberger C, Lechner D, Bengler K (2015) Trust in automation—before and after the experience of take-over scenarios in a highly automated vehicle. Procedia Manuf 3(3):3025–3032. https://doi.org/10.1016/j.promfg.2015.07.847

Hoc J-M, Young MS, Blosseville J-M (2009) Cooperation between drivers and automation: implications for safety. Theor Issues Ergon Sci 10(2):135–160. https://doi.org/10.1080/14639220802368856

Hoff KA, Bashir M (2015) Trust in automation: integrating empirical evidence on factors that influence trust. Hum Factors 57(3):407–434. https://doi.org/10.1177/0018720814547570

Kauer-Franz M, Franz B (2022) Usability and user experience design. Rheinwerk Verlag

Kraus JM (2020) Psychological processes in the formation and calibration of trust in automation. Ulm University. https://doi.org/10.18725/OPARU-32583

Kraus JM, Forster Y, Hergeth S, Baumann M (2019) Two routes to trust calibration: effects of reliability and brand information on trust in automation. Int J Mob Human Comput Interact (IJMHCI) 11(3):1–17

Kraus J, Scholz D, Stiegemeier D, Baumann M (2020) The more you know: trust dynamics and calibration in highly automated driving and the effects of take-overs, system malfunction, and system transparency. Hum Factors 62(5):718–736. https://doi.org/10.1177/0018720819853686

Kraus J, Scholz D, Baumann M (2021) What's driving me? Exploration and validation of a hierarchical personality model for trust in automated driving. Hum Factors 63(6):1076–1105. https://doi.org/10.1177/0018720820922653

Lee J, Moray N (1992) Trust, control strategies and allocation of function in human-machine systems. Ergonomics 35(10):1243–1270. https://doi.org/10.1080/00140139208967392
Lee JD, Moray N (1994) Trust, self-confidence, and operators' adaptation to automation. Int J Hum Comput Stud 40(1):153–184. https://doi.org/10.1006/ijhc.1994.1007
Lee JD, See KA (2004) Trust in automation: designing for appropriate reliance. Hum Factors 46(1):50–80. https://doi.org/10.1518/hfes.46.1.50_30392
Manchon J-B, Bueno M, Navarro J (2022) How the initial level of trust in automated driving impacts drivers' behaviour and early trust construction. Transport Res F: Traffic Psychol Behav 86:281–295. https://doi.org/10.1016/j.trf.2022.02.006
Madhavan P, Wiegmann DA (2007) Similarities and differences between human-human and human-automation trust: an integrative review. Theor Issues Ergon Sci 8(4):277–301. https://doi.org/10.1080/14639220500337708
Mayer RC, Davis JH, Schoorman FD (1995) An integrative model of organizational trust. Acad Manag Rev 20(3):709–734. https://doi.org/10.5465/amr.1995.9508080335
Metzger L, Miller L, Baumann M, Kraus J (2024) Empowering calibrated (dis-) trust in conversational agents: a user study on the persuasive power of limitation disclaimers vs. authoritative style. In: Proceedings of the CHI conference on human factors in computing systems, pp 1–19
Miller T (2023) Explainable AI is dead, long live explainable AI!: hypothesis-driven decision support using evaluative AI. In: 2023 ACM conference on fairness, accountability, and transparency, pp 333–342. https://doi.org/10.1145/3593013.3594001
Montag C, Klugah-Brown B, Zhou X, Wernicke J, Liu C, Kou J, Becker B (2023a) Trust toward humans and trust toward artificial intelligence are not associated: initial insights from self-report and neurostructural brain imaging. Person Neurosci 6:e3
Montag C, Kraus J, Baumann M, Rozgonjuk D (2023b) The propensity to trust in automated technology mediates the links between technology self-efficacy and fear and acceptance of artificial intelligence. Comput Human Behav Reports:100315. https://doi.org/10.1016/j.chbr.2023.100315
Montag C, Nakov P, Ali R (2024) Considering the IMPACT framework to understand the AI-well-being-complex from an interdisciplinary perspective. Tele Inf Reports 13:100112
Mühl K, Strauch C, Grabmaier C, Reithinger S, Huckauf A, Baumann M (2020) Get ready for being chauffeured: passenger's preferences and trust while being driven by human and automation. Hum Factors 62(8):1322–1338. https://doi.org/10.1177/0018720819872893
Muir BM (1987) Trust between humans and machines, and the design of decision aids. Int J Man Mach Stud 27(5–6):527–539. https://doi.org/10.1016/S0020-7373(87)80013-5
Muir BM (1994) Trust in automation: Part I. Theoretical issues in the study of trust and human intervention in automated systems. Ergonomics 37(11):1905–1922. https://doi.org/10.1080/00140139408964957
Muir BM, Moray N (1996) Trust in automation. Part II. Experimental studies of trust and human intervention in a process control simulation. Ergonomics 39(3):429–460. https://doi.org/10.1080/00140139608964474
Parasuraman R, Riley V (1997) Humans and automation: Use, misuse, disuse, abuse. Hum Factors 39(2):230–253. https://doi.org/10.1518/001872097778543886
Rai A (2020) Explainable AI: from black box to glass box. J Acad Mark Sci 48(1):137–141. https://doi.org/10.1007/s11747-019-00710-5
SAE International (2018) Taxonomy and definitions for terms related to driving automation systems for on-road motor vehicles (SAE J3016_202104)
Scholz DD, Kraus J, Miller L (2024) Measuring the propensity to trust in automated technology: examining similarities to dispositional trust in other humans and validation of the PTT-A scale. Int J Human–Computer Interact:1–24. https://doi.org/10.1080/10447318.2024.2307691
Shladover SE (2022) Opportunities, challenges, and uncertainties in urban road transport automation. Sustainability 14(3):1853. https://doi.org/10.3390/su14031853

Stanton NA, Eriksson A, Banks VA, Hancock PA (2020) Turing in the driver's seat: can people distinguish between automated and manually driven vehicles? Human Factors Ergon Manuf Service Industries 30(6):418–425. https://doi.org/10.1002/hfm.20864

Sindermann C, Sha P, Zhou M, Wernicke J, Schmitt HS, Li M, Montag C (2021) Assessing the attitude towards artificial intelligence: introduction of a short measure in German, Chinese, and English Language. KI-Kunstliche Intelligenz

Thielmann I, Hilbig BE (2015) Trust: an integrative review from a person-situation perspective. Rev Gen Psychol 19(3):249–277. https://doi.org/10.1037/gpr0000046

Walch M, Mühl K, Kraus J, Stoll T, Baumann M, Weber M (2017) From car-driver-handovers to cooperative interfaces: visions for driver—vehicle interaction in automated driving. In Meixner G, Müller C (eds) Automotive user interfaces: creating interactive experiences in the car. Springer International Publishing, pp 273–294. https://doi.org/10.1007/978-3-319-49448-7_10

Walker GH, Stanton NA, Salmon PM (2015) Human factors in automotive engineering and technology. Ashgate Publishing Ltd., Farnham, UK

Walker F, Boelhouwer A, Alkim T, Verwey WB, Martens MH (2018) Changes in trust after driving level 2 automated cars. J Adv Transp 2018:1–9. https://doi.org/10.1155/2018/1045186

World Health Organization (2023) Global status report on road safety 2023. World Health Organisation

Zhang B, de Winter J, Varotto S, Happee R, Martens M (2019) Determinants of take-over time from automated driving: a meta-analysis of 129 studies. Transport Res F: Traffic Psychol Behav 64:285–307. https://doi.org/10.1016/j.trf.2019.04.020

Chapter 10
On Country and Culture in AI Attitude Research

Christian Montag and Raian Ali

Abstract In this chapter it is discussed how country and culture variables might impact upon AI attitude formation. Country is described as the variable being more linked to the political environment of people—for instance as shaped by AI regulation—and culture is discussed more in terms of psychological and sociological traits such as individualistic or collectivistic world views. The chapter provides a short introduction into this important new research field and provides an outlook on what needs to be done in future research.

Keywords Country · Culture · IMPACT-framework · Artificial intelligence · Regulation · Hofstede

Artificial Intelligence (AI) represents a general-purpose technology, which is in-built in a growing number of products and services. Against the background of the coming AI wave (Suleyman and Bhaskar 2023), where societies transition from pre-AI- to AI-societies, with unforeseen consequences for individuals and their well-being, it is of importance to assess how populations around the world think about AI. Such information might be highly relevant to guide policy makers to find the right balance between allowing the technology to unfold benefits for society, and on the other hand to contain such AI technology bringing harm to societies (Montag et al. 2024b).

In order to better understand AI-attitude-formation and also to provide a framework so that people can build nuanced attitudes towards AI technologies, the IMPACT framework has been proposed (Montag et al. 2024a, c), which also presents the

C. Montag (✉)
Department of Molecular Psychology, Institute of Psychology and Education, Ulm University, Ulm, Germany
e-mail: mail@christianmontag.de

R. Ali
College of Science and Engineering, Hamad Bin Khalifa University, Doha, Qatar

C. Montag and R. Ali (eds.), *The Impact of Artificial Intelligence on Societies*, Studies in Neuroscience, Psychology and Behavioral Economics,
https://doi.org/10.1007/978-3-031-70355-3_10

guiding framework of the present book. The acronym IMPACT stands for the Interplay of Modality, Person, Area, Culture/Country and Transparency categories shedding light on individual differences in AI attitudes, be them positive or negative. The IMPACT model will not be further described here as this has been done already in Chap. 1. Instead, we directly want to focus on the C-variable of the IMPACT framework, which will be the focus of interest of the present chapter. The C-variable of the IMPACT framework stands for Culture and Country, two variables we deem to be of high relevance to understand why people form certain attitudes about AI technology. Culture and Country are variables which overlap but should also be seen as distinct entities. In each country of course certain cultural traditions can prevail, but there are also countries where many different cultures exist (just think of China with its many different ethnicities and cultures—although Han-Chinese culture is dominant).

In this chapter we think of the Country-variable as a more political variable, hence here we try to make the point that countries differ in their approaches to regulate or foster AI-technologies (Novelli et al. 2023; Roberts et al. 2021), which can impact upon how people perceive AI. Additionally, countries exhibit a geo-political environment shaped by history and past experiences, which can impact the adoption of innovation and risk-taking in general. Equally, their infrastructure and currently used technology can determine the general appetite for AI and whether investment in it is worthwhile. Fear of major incidents, attacks, and privacy breaches in critical infrastructure can be influenced by the regulations in each country (Osei-Kyei et al. 2021). AI systems in areas such as smart cities and the health sector require robust critical infrastructure. Hence, with the emerging nature of AI systems and the lack of regulations within most jurisdictions, it is expected that this will affect attitudes towards AI. The job market and political agendas can also be significant drivers; for example, a high unemployment rate can entice fear of AI (McClure 2018). All these factors may influence how AI is portrayed within mass media and by politicians, affecting the general attitude towards it. In contrast, the cultural aspect touches more on psychological and sociological variables, which might well also describe cultural influences on AI-attitudes. For example, using Hofstede's framework of culture (Hofstede 2011), Uncertainty Avoidance is considered a cultural trait, with some cultures being more open to risk and new experiences and others being more risk-averse. This could have a direct impact on attitudes towards AI, especially at the current stage where many new innovations are yet to be trialed and reflected upon. Some facets of AI regulation, such as data management, are still ambiguous and subject to interpretations, which perhaps can be acceptable in cultures scoring low in Uncertainty Avoidance. Against this background, we will present examples for both country and culture variables as being of relevance for AI attitude formation.

Although the field on understanding AI attitude is still young, first empirical evidence exists, showing that study populations from different countries differ in their AI attitudes. Among other two recent papers showed that Chinese study populations were associated with higher positive attitudes towards AI compared to German study populations (Sindermann et al. 2021, 2022). Differences in negative attitudes towards AI interestingly were less pronounced in these works. Of note, recent research suggests that positive and negative attitudes towards AI can be seen as two separate dimensions (Schepman and Rodway 2020). Perhaps this is the case, because in the light of uncertainty how AI will evolve some people might have *both* positive *and* negative feelings about the coming AI revolution (seeing both benefits and dangers alike).[1] Anyhow, the two mentioned studies showed differences in Chinese and German study populations regarding their positive AI attitudes and the question arises how such differences can be explained (Sindermann et al. 2021, 2022). For this, we can use both the country- and/or cultural lens to understand such differences. Considering Country as a political variable it becomes obvious that Germany and China differ in terms of their approaches towards AI. Whereas Germany belongs to the European Union underlying the European Commission EU-AI-Act regulating AI according to its expected risk in different areas (Ulnicane 2022), China formulated already several years ago a highly ambitious strategy with the New Generation Artificial Intelligence Development Plan of China to become world leader in AI technologies by 2030 (Wu et al. 2020). This also mirrors in media coverage in China informing about the plans by the Chinese government. Research on media coverage in China shows that views on AI in the public online sphere on WeChat aligned with what has been presented in the online version of People's Daily—a prominent newspaper in China (Zeng et al. 2022). But further research also suggests that the frequency of use of certain media outlets might play a role in AI attitude formation: Whereas frequency of newspaper use to get informed about AI developments was associated with less AI-benefit perception and AI-policy support, more frequent use of television and WeChat to inform oneself on recent AI developments was associated with more AI-benefit-perception and AI-policy-support (Cui and Wu 2021). In sum, the emerging data from China underlines the idea that government policy—being distributed via media channels— might have an influence on AI attitude formation.

This said, also cultural influences can and should be considered to understand differences in AI attitudes. If we stick with the example of contrasting German and Chinese attitudes towards AI, the German and Chinese cultures[2] are different in terms of cultural dimensions such as individualism vs. collectivism. The Han-Chinese culture is more collectivistic than the German culture which mirrors in more seeing one's own person in relation to others (Moser et al. 2011). Further, the Han-Chinese culture is tremendously influenced by Confucian thought (Montag et al. 2022), which among others stresses upholding harmony in society by obedience towards parents (part of the filial piety) and the ruling class (Confucius in turn expected the emperor to be caring for their citizens; Schuman 2015). Such cultural influences of course could also play a role in attitude formation to general AI (but see a recent interesting work on cultural factors to understand attitudes towards to service robots; Chi et al. 2023), although this needs to be systematically investigated and to our knowledge has not been done until now. Further evidence for the idea that Culture could play a

[1] Please note that a new study presented an attitudes towards AI measure conceptualized with a single general attitude factor (Stein et al., 2024).

[2] We already mentioned that very different cultural influences can be found in China. Here we speak of the prevailing Han-Chinese culture.

role comes from another recent finding observing associations between spirituality and AI-attitudes. In an international English-speaking sample, it could be observed that higher spirituality went along with lower positive and higher negative views of artificial intelligence. Spirituality was operationalized among others as "Feeling a oneness with all of creation" (p. 165; Montag et al. 2021) as an essential part of one's own life. Although this work could not locate participants according to their residence or upbringing, spirituality likely will vary across cultures and might therefore play a role in AI attitude formation around the world. New research showed that a sample from US reported on average higher "AI Hope" levels than a sample from UK, showing that also studies from other countries have been conducted, but here different AI-attitude-constructs as presented above were investigated (Grassini and Ree 2023). In general, we believe that the future will need cross-cultural research directly contrasting many countries with very different cultures and AI-regulations within one study to shed light on the relevance of the C-variable of the IMPACT model.

Culture might also influence how personal differences, such as the Big-5 personality traits, impact attitudes towards AI. In a study involving both Arab and UK participants (Babiker et al. 2024), correlational analysis revealed a significant association between attitudes towards AI and agreeableness, as well as neuroticism, in the UK sample. In the Arab sample, attitudes towards AI were significantly associated with agreeableness, neuroticism, and conscientiousness. Regression analysis further indicated that, in the UK sample, agreeableness positively predicted positive attitudes and negatively predicted negative attitudes towards AI. Similarly, in the Arab sample, conscientiousness positively predicted positive attitudes and negatively predicted negative attitudes towards AI. See for further personality-AI-attitudes associations from a recent study with data from Singapore and Germany (Montag et al. 2024d).

10.1 Limitations and Outlook

The present work is limited by the relatively scarce body of evidence which could be reviewed for this short chapter and also by the way we operationalized the Country and Culture variable. For instance, a recent work claimed to investigate socio-cultural variables in the context of AI attitude formation and understood here variables such as general vs. disadvantaged students (Kim and Lee 2023). The latter group was operationalized as students who are disadvantaged due to "difficulties arising from their social and cultural factors" regarding their "educational opportunities" (p. 9911). Without doubt a myriad of factors in the context of the cultural, but also the political system (here country-variable) play a role to understand AI attitude formation. These variables need to be studied in a systematic way and therefore new taxonomies might be helpful guiding research. Further, in the realm of the IMPACT framework, it will be interesting to investigate how the Country/Culture variables interact with other elements from the IMPACT framework shaping attitudes towards AI.

For instance, it is imaginable that explainable AI to overcome the black box character of AI (belonging to the Transparency-variable) will be perceived as of different importance depending on how AI regulations form trust towards this new technology. Finally, one should also not oversee that some things might be similar across cultures. For instance, a recent work observed that both in samples from Japan and Sweden "worry of less work with AI" showed comparable associations with concrete use of AI (Persson et al. 2021, p. 135). Another work showed that neuroticism links positively to fearing AI in Germany and China (Sindermann et al. 2022). In sum, much work lies ahead to understand how Country and Culture variables shape attitudes towards AI.

References

Babiker A, Alshakhsi S, Supti T, Ali R (2024) Do personality traits impact the attitudes towards artificial intelligence? The 11th International Conference on Behavioural and Social Computing (BESC'24)—IEEE, Harbin, China

Chi OH, Chi CG, Gursoy D, Nunkoo R (2023) Customers' acceptance of artificially intelligent service robots: the influence of trust and culture. Int J Inf Manage 70:102623. https://doi.org/10.1016/j.ijinfomgt.2023.102623

Cui D, Wu F (2021) The influence of media use on public perceptions of artificial intelligence in China: evidence from an online survey. Inf Dev 37:45–57. https://doi.org/10.1177/026666919893411

Grassini S, Ree AS (2023, Sept) Hope or doom AI-ttitude? examining the impact of gender, age, and cultural differences on the envisioned future impact of artificial intelligence on humankind. In Proceedings of the European conference on cognitive ergonomics 2023, pp 1–7. https://doi.org/10.1145/3605655.3605669

Hofstede G (2011) Dimensionalizing cultures: the Hofstede model in context. Online Read Psychol Culture 2(1). https://doi.org/10.9707/2307-0919.1014

Kim SW, Lee Y (2024) Investigation into the influence of socio-cultural factors on attitudes toward artificial intelligence. Educ Inf Technol 29(8):9907–9935. https://doi.org/10.1007/s10639-023-12172-y

McClure P (2018) "You're Fired", says the robot: the rise of automation in the workplace, technophobes, and fears of unemployment. Soc Sci Comput Rev 36:139–156. https://doi.org/10.1177/0894439317698637

Montag C, Elhai JD, Davis KL (2021) A comprehensive review of studies using the affective neuroscience personality scales in the psychological and psychiatric sciences. Neurosci Biobehav Rev 125:160–167. https://doi.org/10.1016/j.neubiorev.2021.02.019

Montag C, Ko H-C, Sindermann C (2022) Individual differences in importance ratings of Chinese values and their associations with the Big Five of personality in Western and Eastern populations. Disc Psychol 2(1):39. https://doi.org/10.1007/s44202-022-00050-6

Montag C, Nakov P, Ali R (2024a) Considering the IMPACT framework to understand the AI-well-being-complex from an interdisciplinary perspective. Tele Inform Reports 13:100112. https://doi.org/10.1016/j.teler.2023.100112

Montag C, Nakov P, Ali R (2024b) On the need to develop nuanced measures assessing attitudes towards AI and AI literacy in representative large-scale samples. AI Soc. https://doi.org/10.1007/s00146-024-01888-1

Montag C, Ali R, Al-Thani D, Hall BJ (2024c) On artificial intelligence and global mental health. Asian J Psychiatr 91:103855. https://doi.org/10.1016/j.ajp.2023.103855

Montag C, Becker B, Li BJ (2024d) On trust in humans and trust in artificial intelligence: A study with samples from Singapore and Germany extending recent research. Comp Human Behav: Artificial Hum:100070. https://doi.org/10.1016/j.chbah.2024.100070
Moser R, Migge T, Lockstroem M, Neumann J (2011) Exploring Chinese cultural standards through the lens of German managers: a case study approach. IIMB Manag Rev 23(2):102–109. https://doi.org/10.1016/j.iimb.2011.02.002
Novelli C, Casolari F, Rotolo A, Taddeo M, Floridi L (2023) Taking AI risks seriously: a new assessment model for the AI Act. AI and SOCIETY. https://doi.org/10.1007/s00146-023-01723-z
Osei-Kyei R, Tam V, Ma M, Mashiri F (2021) Critical review of the threats affecting the building of critical infrastructure resilience. Int J Disaster Risk Reduction 60:102316. https://doi.org/10.1016/j.ijdrr.2021.102316
Persson A, Laaksoharju M, Koga H (2021) We mostly think alike: individual differences in attitude towards AI in Sweden and Japan. Rev Socionetwork Str 15(1):123–142 https://doi.org/10.1007/s12626-021-00071-y
Roberts H, Cowls J, Morley J, Taddeo M, Wang V, Floridi L (2021) The Chinese approach to artificial intelligence: An analysis of policy, ethics, and regulation. AI & Soc 36(1):59–77. https://doi.org/10.1007/s00146-020-00992-2
Schepman A, Rodway P (2020) Initial validation of the general attitudes towards Artificial Intelligence Scale. Comp Human Behav Reports 1:100014. https://doi.org/10.1016/j.chbr.2020.100014
Schuman M (2015) Confucius: and the world he created. Civitas Books
Sindermann C, Sha P, Zhou M, Wernicke J, Schmitt HS, Li M, Sariyska R, Stavrou M, Becker B, Montag C (2021) Assessing the attitude towards artificial intelligence: introduction of a short measure in German, Chinese, and English language. KI—Künstliche Intelligenz 35(1):109–118. https://doi.org/10.1007/s13218-020-00689-0
Sindermann C, Yang H, Elhai JD, Yang S, Quan L, Li M, Montag C (2022) Acceptance and fear of artificial intelligence: associations with personality in a German and a Chinese sample. Discover Psychol 2(1):8. https://doi.org/10.1007/s44202-022-00020-y
Stein JP, Messingschlager T, Gnambs T, Hutmacher F, Appel M (2024) Attitudes towards AI: measurement and associations with personality. Sci Rep 14(1):2909. https://doi.org/10.1038/s41598-024-53335-2
Suleyman M, Bhaskar M (2023) The coming wave: technology, power, and the twenty-first century's greatest dilemma. Crown
Ulnicane I (2022) Artificial intelligence in the European Union. In: Hoerber T, Weber G, Cabras I (eds) The Routledge handbook of European integrations. Taylor and Francis. https://doi.org/10.4324/9780429262081-19
Wu F, Lu C, Zhu M, Chen H, Zhu J, Yu K, Li L, Li M, Chen Q, Li X, Cao X, Wang Z, Zha Z, Zhuang Y, Pan Y (2020) Towards a new generation of artificial intelligence in China. Nat Mach Intell 2(6):312–316. https://doi.org/10.1038/s42256-020-0183-4
Zeng J, Chan C, Schäfer MS (2022) Contested Chinese dreams of AI? Public discourse about Artificial intelligence on WeChat and People's Daily Online. Inf Commun Soc 25(3):319–340. https://doi.org/10.1080/1369118X.2020.1776372

Chapter 11
AI in Finance: Applications for Global Finance Institutions and Adaptations for Islamic Finance

Hassnian Ali, Ahme Faruk Aysan, and Mohamed Mesroua

Abstract This chapter aims to evaluate the applications and significance of Artificial Intelligence (AI) in the context of Muslim societies, most precisely within the Islamic finance sector. Theoretically, Islamic finance, distinct from conventional financial systems, operates on principles of Sharia law which prohibit interest (*riba*), promote risk-sharing and asset-backed financing, and emphasize ethical investments, thereby fostering economic justice and stability. This chapter's purpose is to highlight AI's distinct contributions to Islamic finance beyond its conventional applications in mainstream finance, such as service cost reduction, transparency, and speed in delivery. The chapter concludes that the Islamic finance industry has embraced AI technology. However, the review of the implemented AI technologies within the Islamic finance sector and how this technology is used showed that, overall, Islamic financial institutions use this technology the same way traditional financial institutions use it. This requires more efforts from regulation authorities and industry practitioners simultaneously to adapt the use of AI technology beyond its conventional use. AI technology may fuel the current uptrend of Islamic finance growth if implemented beyond its conventional use.

Keywords Artificial Intelligence · Islamic finance industry · Financial services · Fintech

JEL Classification G20 · G23 · O33 · Z12

H. Ali (✉) · A. F. Aysan · M. Mesroua
College of Islamic Studies, Hamad Bin Khalifa University, Qatar Foundation, Ar-Rayyan, Qatar
e-mail: haal50943@hbku.edu.qa

ICRIE, Minhaj University, Lahore, Pakistan

A. F. Aysan
e-mail: aaysan@hbku.edu.qa

M. Mesroua
e-mail: mome67542@hbku.edu.qa

C. Montag and R. Ali (eds.), *The Impact of Artificial Intelligence on Societies*, Studies in Neuroscience, Psychology and Behavioral Economics,
https://doi.org/10.1007/978-3-031-70355-3_11

11.1 Introduction

The primary objective of Islamic finance is to promote the economic and social welfare of Muslim societies by adhering to Sharia principles, which uniquely emphasize ethical investments, risk-sharing, the prohibition of interest (*riba*) and speculative activities (*gharar*[1]). This approach ensures that financial activities are conducted in a manner that aligns with Islamic values, including principles such as asset-backing for financial transactions, profit and loss sharing, and the avoidance of investments in prohibited (haram) industries, thereby fostering a just and equitable economic environment. The endeavor of implementing AI technology in the Islamic finance sector goes in line with this objective.

The 1970s marked an increased intellectual effort to develop Islamic economics and banking along modern lines. The efforts of the founding fathers of Islamic finance, such as M. Nejatullah Siddiqi on the relevance of Islamic economics to the current global economic system, M. Umer Chapra on Economic Development and Islamic Finance, S. N. H. Naqvi on the economic rationale for Islamic finance, Anas Zarka on the feasibility of eliminating interest from the economy, and Khurshid Ahmad can be seen as a systematic attempt for developing Islamic economics as an applied discipline. These founding fathers were heavily engaged in developing and presenting a human-centered economic system of Islam as a response to the observed economic challenges in the Muslim world (Asutay et al. 2013). The result was the establishment of multiple Islamic financial institutions, starting with the first Islamic development bank, the Islamic Development Bank (IDB), in 1974, which was quickly followed by the first Islamic commercial bank in 1975 in Dubai.

From 1975 to the present day, there has been a notable proliferation of Islamic banks, transforming Islamic finance into a multi-billion-dollar market. A rapid growth not only for small banks offering Islamic financial products and services could be observed. Among the relevant products are *Murabaha*, where the buyer and seller agree on the markup (profit) or "cost-plus" price for the sell transaction. Further, *Ististna* needs to be mentioned, where the commodity is transacted before it comes into existence (this is commonly used in manufacturing). The product of *Salam* is mentioned, where the seller promises to supply specific goods to the buyer at a future date in exchange of an advanced price on the spot. This product is traditionally used in agriculture. *Ijaraha* needs to be mentioned too describing the transfer of the right to use/lend an item from another party for a certain amount of time in exchange of compensation. Also, a substantial number of international banks expanded their offerings using the previously mentioned contracts.

The rapid growth of Islamic finance underscored the necessity for establishing standards and regulations to protect consumers. To address this need, several institutions were established to fulfill this role: the Accounting and Auditing Organization for Islamic Financial Institutions (AAOIFI), the Islamic Financial Services Board

[1] Gharar is the prohibited uncertainty in general, and Maysir is specific to gambling and the hazardous games. So, in Arabic terms, Gharar include Maysir.

(IFSB), the International Islamic Financial Markets Authority (IIFM), the International Islamic Rating Agency (IIRA), the General Council of Islamic Banks and Financial Institutions (CIBAFI), to name a few. Nowadays, despite the multiple challenges presented by the post-COVID-19 pandemic, the total assets of the global Islamic financial system reached $4.0 trillion in 2021, which represents a 17% increase from the previous year. Likewise, the global net return in 2021 tripled compared to 2020, indicating improved performance (IFR 2022).

The rapid growth of the Islamic finance industry indicates that, despite existing criticism of certain industry practices such as *(tawaruq)*, which involves selling something on a deferred payment basis and then repurchasing it for cash, significant social and governmental acceptance has already occurred. In this environment, AI technology was adopted by the Islamic finance industry. Islamic financial institutions such as Dubai Islamic Bank (DIB), Abu Dhabi Islamic Bank (ADIB), and Kuwait Finance House leverage AI and machine learning-driven chatbots to address customer inquiries (Khan and Rabbani 2020). The adoption of such disruptive technology within Islamic finance is contingent upon its adherence to the principles of Sharia law, which necessitates that any technological implementation does not involve interest (*riba*), excessive uncertainty (*gharar*), or investment in prohibited (*haram*) activities. Specifically, technological implementations could involve *riba* if they automate or facilitate interest-bearing transactions, *gharar* if they introduce or exacerbate unpredictability and ambiguity in financial contracts, or *haram* activities if they enable or support investments in industries such as alcohol, gambling, or pork production prohibited in by the Islamic law. Moreover, AI applications must ensure that they uphold the ethical standards and transparency required by Sharia law, thereby ensuring that all financial transactions are conducted in a manner consistent with Islamic legal and moral principles (Rabbani et al. 2020).

An interesting observation is that the adoption of AI technology in Islamic financial institutions is significantly driven by its alignment with Sharia principles, enhancing its acceptance among practitioners and customers. For instance, AI can be employed to ensure compliance with profit-sharing regulations, risk management according to Sharia guidelines, and the prohibition of interest (*riba*). Consequently, initiatives will likely develop expanding the use of AI to address these specific requirements within the Islamic finance industry. Thereby greater integration of Sharia compliance activities with the Islamic finance institution's commercial activities and efficiency will be fostered. However, it needs to be highlighted that little is being done by Islamic finance institutions as an industry to adopt AI beyond its conventional applications in mainstream finance. Even though multiple proposals and initiatives to apply AI in the financial sector are presented in the literature (Khan 2019), they are singular and generally of unique cases or theoretical proposals. This central finding urges Islamic finance institutions to increase awareness and speed up their AI adoption to the specific needs of the industry. Future research is expected to investigate questions regarding the compliance of this technology to industry standards and how it should be regulated in line with Muslim society principles.

The chapter is organized as follows: We already provided an introduction to the topic in Sect. 11.1, which is now followed by an overview of Artificial intelligence and its application for Global financial institutions in Sect. 11.2. In Sect. 11.3 we discuss current innovative use cases and proposals tailored to the Islamic finance industry. Finally, we conclude the chapter by providing possible recommendations and suggestions for further study.

11.2 Artificial Intelligence and Global Financial Institutions

Artificial intelligence, in conjunction with other innovative fintech-based financial services, can potentially transform the delivery of the financial services industry (Baber 2019). In traditional finance, analysts estimated that artificial intelligence will save the banking industry over $1 trillion. For financial institutions, this means in practice a 22% reduction in operating expenses, thanks to AI, with most savings expected to originate from the front office (Joyce 2018).

AI has fundamentally transformed the global financial system by enhancing the accuracy and efficiency of financial data analysis, decision-making processes, and risk management. AI algorithms can process vast amounts of data to detect patterns and anomalies that humans might overlook, leading to more accurate financial forecasting and improved investment strategies. For instance, AI-driven risk management systems can analyze historical data and market trends to predict future market movements and identify potential investment opportunities, thereby reducing financial risks (Zakaria et al. 2023).

In practical applications, AI has revolutionized the banking sector through the deployment of chatbots and virtual assistants that enhance customer experiences by providing personalized services. AI-driven systems are also instrumental in real-time fraud detection and biometric authentication, significantly bolstering security protocols. For example, JP Morgan Chase's AI program, COIN, automates the review of legal documents, saving an estimated 360,000 h of work annually. Similarly, AI is used in high-frequency trading (HFT) to optimize trading strategies and improve liquidity in financial markets, although this raises concerns about market volatility and systemic risks (Mossavar Rahmani 2023).

AI can substitute human resources or enhance the current infrastructure, a prevalent approach aiming at addressing regulatory apprehensions and fostering trust in AI-driven systems. The potential applications of AI can be categorized into the following areas:

11.2.1 Front Office

The task of the front office is to provide customer service. This is highly relevant to foster customer loyalty and trust. The front office can be seen as the backbone of long-term success of any financial institution. In this realm, the staff should possess communication, problem-solving, and conflict-resolution skills to ensure customers receive the appropriate experience. AI is used extensively in this aspect. Some of the use cases in the front office are:

11.2.1.1 Chatbots and Robo Advisors

Estimates suggest that chatbots are generating substantial savings for banks. Juniper's report anticipated that chatbots will contribute to annual cost reductions of more than $8 billion by 2022. Additionally, Gartner predicted that by 2020, chatbots will manage at least 85% of all customer service interactions (Marous 2018). In the realm of investment management, AI-driven robo-advisors have revolutionized how investment portfolios are managed. These platforms use sophisticated algorithms to provide personalized investment advice and manage portfolios automatically based on individual risk preferences and financial goals. For example, the finance institute Wealthfront and Betterment have successfully deployed AI to offer low-cost, automated investment management services to millions of clients, democratizing access to high-quality investment advice that was previously available only to wealthy individuals (Agarwal 2019). These robo-advisors continually analyze market conditions and adjust portfolios in real-time, ensuring optimal investment performance.

11.2.1.2 Credit Scoring

Credit scoring is conducted by financial institutions to evaluate the creditworthiness of individuals or businesses, using statistical analysis or alternative data, to decide on providing loans. AI has paved the way for different methods, and techniques to make more profitable decisions for the bank. This is especially useful for Microfinance Institutions by facilitating the outreach of these institutions, thereby improving financial inclusion to a greater number of low-income beneficiaries (Bumacov et al. 2014). In the UAE, according to the Federal Law No. (6) of 2010 concerning Credit Information and its amendments, Etihad Credit Bureau (AECB) is mandated to collect credit information from financial and non-financial institutions in the UAE. Etihad Credit Bureau aggregates and analyzes this data to calculate Credit Scores and make these available to individuals and companies in the UAE. Islamic banks view AECB services and products as beneficial for credit scoring and risk management, serving as a complement to their internal subjective regulations and guidelines. AECB applies consistent ratings across banks and financial institutions in the UAE (Alhammadi et al. 2024). AI has also made significant strides in credit scoring and loan approval processes. Traditional credit scoring models rely heavily on historical data and often fail to account for nuanced financial behaviors. AI models, on the other hand, use diverse datasets, including social media activity, transaction history, and other non-traditional data sources, to generate more accurate and inclusive credit scores. Companies like ZestFinance utilize AI to offer credit to individuals who might be overlooked by conventional credit scoring systems, thereby promoting financial inclusion (Samsudeen et al. 2020). This application not only enhances risk assessment but also expands access to financial services for underserved populations.

11.2.1.3 Biometrics

Biometrics can boost security measures, ensuring precise identification, and providing convenient solutions across various financial services. Its distinctive characteristics, reliability, and potential for future advancements underscore its importance and value for the financial industry (Marani et al. 2023). Already in 2017, Qatar Islamic Bank (QIB), has implemented facial recognition functionality, known as Face ID, into its iOS and Android Mobile App. This initiative positioned QIB as the first bank in Qatar to enable facial recognition technology across all smartphone devices (QIB 2017). In Pakistan, BankIslami has led the way in Biometric ATMs since its establishment, paving the path for Cardless ATMs. BankIslami introduced One Touch Banking—a comprehensive Biometric banking solution catering to all customer needs. This innovative solution allows conducting transactions effortlessly using just the thumb impression, eliminating the need for an ATM card or checkbook (BankIslami 2014).

11.2.2 Middle Office

Middle-office professionals are responsible for assessing risks, monitoring profit and loss calculations, and ensuring compliance with legal requirements. All activities that are using Artificial intelligence.

11.2.2.1 Fraud Management

Artificial intelligence is employed in fraud management in the context of financial transactions. Through machine learning algorithms, suspicious patterns that might evade human detection can be identified, allowing financial institutions to be promptly alerted before substantial losses occur. Conventional fraud detection systems, primarily rule-based, frequently lack real-time detection capabilities. In contrast, AI can swiftly analyze vast transactional data, identifying anomalies and potentially fraudulent activities as they occur (Hassan et al. 2023). AI's role in fraud detection within the banking sector is another critical practical application. Advanced machine learning algorithms analyze transaction patterns and detect anomalies in real-time, significantly enhancing the ability to identify and prevent fraudulent activities. For instance, HSBC has implemented AI to monitor millions of transactions daily, identifying suspicious activities and reducing false positives, thus improving the overall accuracy of fraud detection systems (Jain 2023). Moreover, AI's predictive analytics help banks to proactively combat fraud by predicting potential fraud before it occurs, thereby safeguarding both the institution and its customers.

11.2.2.2 Compliance with Legal Requirements

In today's complex regulatory environment, financial institutions face significant challenges in fulfilling reporting requirements while maintaining operational efficiency. Artificial intelligence systems equipped with natural language processing capabilities can analyze vast amounts of regulatory documents and financial data, identifying potential violations and evaluating systemic risks (Nembe et al. 2024).

11.2.3 Back Office

While chatbots have traditionally been employed in front-office operations within the banking sector, JP Morgan Chase has innovatively introduced COIN, utilizing chatbots for back-office operations. COIN facilitates the rapid and efficient analysis of complex contracts, surpassing the capabilities of lawyers and saving over 360,000 h of labor (Marous 2018).

The adoption of AI in financial services is not without challenges. Issues such as data privacy, security, and the ethical implications of AI-driven decision-making are critical. The "black box" nature of many AI models, which makes their decision-making processes opaque, can lead to regulatory and compliance issues (Ali and Aysan 2024). Furthermore, AI's impact on employment in the financial sector is significant, as automation could potentially displace jobs that involve routine tasks. To address these challenges, regulatory frameworks that incorporate AI governance, transparency, and human oversight are essential. A balanced approach that leverages AI's benefits while mitigating its risks is crucial for sustainable integration into the global financial system (Buckley et al. 2021).

11.3 Innovative Uses of AI Specific to Islamic Finance

AI can substitute human intervention, enhancing automation with increased efficiency and transparency. Given the stringent Sharia supervision required in Islamic finance, which ensures compliance with Islamic laws prohibiting interest (*riba*), excessive uncertainty (*gharar*), and investments in *haram* (forbidden) industries like alcohol and gambling, AI finds broader applications within the financial sector. This Sharia supervision involves regular audits and certifications by Sharia boards to maintain the integrity of financial products and services. Regulatory technology (RegTech) utilizing AI is employed to monitor and ensure that financial activities adhere to these Sharia principles (Moh'd Ali et al. 2020). AI has Islamic finance tailored applications such as Islamic finance education, automated Sharia compliance, Sukuk development, Zakat calculations, and Waqf Management.

The following are some examples.

11.3.1 Automated Sharia Compliance Audits

AI can enhance the efficiency and accuracy of Sharia compliance audits by automating data analysis, predictive analytics for risk assessment, and real-time monitoring. This approach promotes trust, transparency, and integrity in the Islamic finance industry (John 2024). AI technologies are used to screen potential investment opportunities, ensuring they meet Sharia compliance criteria. By analyzing large datasets, AI can assess the ethical standing of companies and industries, facilitating suitable investment recommendations. Generative AI tools, particularly those using Natural Language Processing (NLP), can analyze and understand Sharia scholar opinions and fatwas, providing real-time insights into the permissibility of financial products and transactions (TechCEOs 2023). One example is the Scharia-compliant robot advisors. This AI powered advisor system, when applied to the investment sector, screens the investment opportunity against the required Islamic law norms. It eliminates those opportunities that involve prohibited activities such as companies selling alcoholic beverages and even excludes companies exceeding the maximum allowed norms in interest use (as put forward by competent internationally recognized Islamic economics norm issuing authorities such as Auditing Organization for Islamic Financial Institutions (AAOIFI)).

11.3.2 Generative AI, Smart Contracts and Sukuk

Generative AI, with its sophisticated capabilities for producing human-like content, is revolutionizing the financial sector, especially in Islamic finance through tools like smart contracts and *Sukuk*. Sukuk, often known as Islamic bonds, are Sharia-compliant financial certificates representing proportional ownership in tangible assets, services, or investments. Unlike conventional interest-bearing bonds, Sukuk emphasizes profit-sharing and asset-backed financing, adhering to the ethical standards of Islamic finance.

When combined with smart contracts—self-executing contracts with terms embedded in code—generative AI enhances the efficiency, transparency, and security of Sukuk issuance and management. AI-driven smart contracts can automate compliance with Sharia principles, ensuring meticulous adherence to contractual agreements in Sukuk without human intervention. This automation reduces the risk of human error and fraud. A potential application is in creating a Sukuk rating system that leverages on AI to evaluate various data points related to the Sukuk project: This could involve analyzing financial information, historical performance data, details about the management team, and other relevant factors. The AI system could identify patterns and trends indicative of the Sukuk project's creditworthiness and risk by processing alternative data points. To achieve optimal performance, accuracy, and compliance with the Islamic law, generative AI such as ChatGPT technology can treat multiple information from different data points and provide a dynamic assessment of the Sukuk project.

Moreover, generative AI can analyze vast amounts of financial data to optimize the structuring and pricing of Sukuk, to predict market trends, and to understand investor behavior. This synergy not only boosts the operational efficiency of Islamic financial instruments but also promotes greater accessibility and inclusivity in global financial markets. By innovatively applying generative AI and smart contracts, the issuance and management of Sukuk can achieve unprecedented precision and reliability, fostering sustainable economic growth within the ethical framework of Islamic finance.

11.3.3 Islamic Chatbot as À Finance Expert

The concept of an artificial intelligence-powered interactive Chatbot known as 'Chatbot as Islamic Finance Expert' (CaIFE) represents one important use case. CaIFE is designed to provide automated assistance in Islamic finance and banking through user interaction with a robot equipped with machine learning-derived knowledge. It offers real-time responses to inquiries related to Islamic finance and banking (Khan and Rabbani 2020). When considering the specific application of AI in Islamic finance, there are special considerations that must be addressed to ensure compliance with Islamic principles. For instance, while training these bots, it is crucial to integrate knowledge that adheres to Shariah law. This involves ensuring that the AI is well-versed in the prohibition of interest (*riba*), together with *gharar*, and investments in prohibited (haram) industries, as described earlier.

Additionally, there is potential to design these AI systems to cater to different schools of thought (*madhabs*) within Islamic finance. By doing so, users can select the madhab that aligns with their personal or organizational preferences, whether it be Hanafi, Maliki, Shafi'i, or Hanbali. This customization ensures that the advice provided by the chatbot aligns with the specific jurisprudential interpretations relevant to the user's context.

Overall, while the use of AI and machine learning in Islamic finance shares similarities with FinTech in general, these special considerations highlight the importance of aligning technology with the ethical and legal standards unique to Islamic finance.

11.3.4 Chatbot for Islamic Finance Education

Islamic Finance Chatbot, a ChatGPT 4 tool trained on an Islamic finance German book, "Islam, Money, and Prosperity," answers questions on the content of Islamic wealth management in over 100 languages (Gassner 2023). Residing and employed in Geneva, the author of the book Michael Gassner holds the position of Head of Islamic Finance at a Swiss private bank and serves as a Sharia Board member at Bosna Bank International in Sarajevo. He made the Islamic Finance Chatbot available free of charge.

11.3.5 AI Application in Zakat Calculations

Zakat al-mal stands as a fundamental tenet of Islam, mandating that Muslims allocate a specific portion of their wealth to support those in need. This obligation encompasses various assets such as cash, gold, silver, property, and investments, with its calculation based on an individual's overall wealth. The minimum threshold, known as *nisab*, determines whether Zakat is due. Should an individual's wealth exceed this threshold, they are obliged to fulfill Zakat al-mal annually. The calculation of nisab and the corresponding Zakat amount is contingent upon the assets held consistently throughout a full lunar year (*haul*). An efficient method for calculating Zakat is to use the AI tool YouChat[2] like ChatGPT. Leveraging its capabilities as an AI language model, YouChat can aid in computing Zakat al-mal by generating calculations derived from the asset values input by the user.

11.3.6 AI Application in Waqf Management

Waqf, an Islamic philanthropic endowment, significantly contributes to supporting social, educational, and economic initiatives within communities. The incorporation of AI in managing Waqf properties offers a wealth of practical applications and transformative potential. AI can significantly enhance the efficiency and transparency of Waqf asset management through sophisticated data analytics and predictive modeling, facilitating optimal resource allocation and strategic planning. By employing machine learning algorithms, historical data can be analyzed to forecast future trends in property values, rental incomes, and maintenance costs, ensuring robust financial management (Mohamed and Ali 2022).

Beyond this, AI-driven platforms can simplify the donation process, providing personalized recommendations to potential donors based on their preferences and past giving patterns. Additionally, AI-powered monitoring systems can deliver real-time surveillance and maintenance alerts for Waqf properties, minimizing the risk

[2] https://you.com/.

of asset deterioration and promoting asset longevity. NLP can further assist by automating legal documentation and compliance processes, ensuring that Waqf administration aligns with Sharia principles and regulatory standards. These AI applications not only boost the operational efficiency of Waqf institutions but also ensure that the social and economic benefits of Waqf are maximized for the community.

11.3.7 AI Robo Islamic Advisor

Wahed Invest,[3] a robo-advisor specializing in Sharia-compliant investing, was introduced in 2015 as the world's first automated Islamic investment platform. With a mission to offer halal portfolio management accessible to the global Muslim community, Wahed Invest aims to target approximately two billion Muslims worldwide. The platform ensures that all investments adhere to Islamic principles by avoiding businesses involved in prohibited activities such as alcohol, gambling, and interest-based financial services. Additionally, Wahed Invest is overseen by a board of Sharia scholars who continuously monitor and certify the compliance of investment portfolios. Initially accessible only within the United States, the platform swiftly expanded its operations to over 100 countries across the globe by 2017 (Friedberg 2019).

11.4 Discussions and Recommendations

Islamic financial institutions could increase their competitive advantage and gain more momentum by adapting AI technologies to the industry specifics. Implementation of AI technology could revolutionize the Sharia decision-making processes and AI could offer a refined approach to evaluating complex Sharia compliance criteria. This could make it possible to rely less on the current Murabaha contract, criticized for its debt nature making it look similar to conventional loan practices, and open the way to long-waited profit and loss-sharing contracts by optimizing the ratios while maintaining adherence to Sharia principles. For that purpose, we have made the following three-dimensional recommendation as illustrated below:

11.4.1 Operational Efficiency and Internal Compliance

Monitoring the Sharia Compliance of its activities constitutes the priority of an Islamic financial institution, whereas AI systems could ease the way Islamic banks ensure compliance with the Sharia law. By leveraging the continuous monitoring

[3] https://www.wahed.com/global.

capabilities of AI, which can identify and address quickly deviations from Sharia principles, the Islamic Finance Institutions will lower the cost of its processes. This could be achieved by an AI powered real-time system, building more transparency and trust for the customers, stakeholders, and the bank Sharia committee. Such a system may also facilitate the implementation of Islamic contracts such as the *Musahraka*[4] and *Mudaraba*[5] contracts and make it easier to validate other risk-sharing operations. The current Sharia audit procedures rely on manual processes. This costs significant time being allocated in repetitive tasks like data collection, sampling, and recording observations. Auditors spend weeks executing identical checklists across numerous files, striving to identify patterns within the extensive documentation. AI-driven audits can review 100% of transactions, employing machine learning models trained on comprehensive datasets.

11.4.2 Regulation and External Compliance

Regulatory compliance involves coordination between several organizations to take full advantage of the AI applications without breaching Sharia and other mandatory compliances. International Islamic finance regulatory organizations, such as the Accounting and Auditing Organization for Islamic Financial Institutions (AAOIFI), the Islamic Financial Services Board (IFSB), the International Islamic Financial Markets Authority (IIFM), the International Islamic Rating Agency (IIRA), are called upon to develop appropriate standards. Governments need to issue policy guidelines to promote the use of AI without being at risk of data privacy issues and other possible challenges. Sharia committees at the bank and central bank levels will analyze the Compatibility aspects between Islamic Law and Artificial intelligence applications. With the appropriate collaboration, an AI system could help the harmonization of Sharia compliance processes, currently different from one jurisdiction to another. Allowing Islamic financial institutions to comply with the different jurisdictions and provide a system that guarantees compliance monitoring to the appropriate authorities.

[4] Musahraka (Partnership) is a form of partnership where two or more parties contribute capital, manage the business jointly, and share profits and losses in proportion to their respective capital contributions. (AAOIFI, Shariah Standard: 12).

[5] Mudaraba (Profit Sharing) is a partnership where one party provides the capital (rab-ul-mal) and the other party provides the expertise and management (mudarib), with profits being shared according to a pre-agreed ratio and losses borne solely by the capital provider, except in cases of misconduct or negligence by the mudarib. (AAOIFI, Shariah Standard: 13).

Fig. 11.1 Overview of a three-dimensional recommendation process for the use of AI in Islamic finance applications

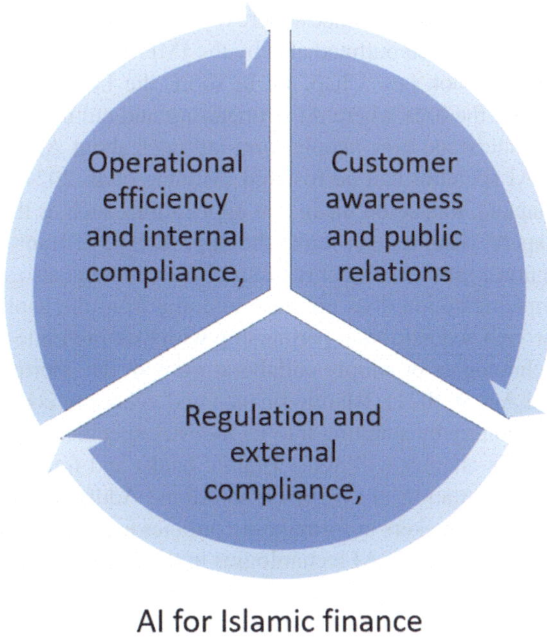

11.4.3 Customer Awareness and Public Relations

This part of the process model as depicted in Fig. 11.1 can be implemented by the Islamic banking industry. We already highlighted that Chatbots are used by Islamic banks, but this needs to be expanded. Next steps represent the integration of Islamic finance education, financial advisory, and zakat calculation alongside the regular customer service chatbot. The adoption of AI-oriented technologies by Islamic finance institutions should be advertised as an important tool for respecting religious authority (Sharia communities). This will augment trust in the industry by using cutting-edge technologies to serve its customers.

11.5 Conclusion

The adoption and implementation of AI technology in business activities of financial institutions can be observed in conventional and the Islamic financial sectors. The present analysis of the implementation and use of AI technologies within the Islamic finance sector showed that at the moment Islamic financial institutions are using this technology in the same way as traditional financial institutions.

To become future-ready and keep growing in a competitive environment, Islamic finance institutions need to leverage AI technologies to propose customized solutions to their customers, hence adhere to cultural specifics in the area of finance, something which has been outlined also by the IMPACT framework providing the basis for the present book (see Chap. 1). In short, the IMPACT framework states that among others, the area where AI is operating and cultural specifics need to be considered to understand how people form attitudes about AI, and in general how well-being in AI societies can be fostered (Montag et al. 2024). In the context of the present chapters, this could mean that applications such as the 'Chatbot as Islamic Finance Expert' (CaIFE) can make the approbation of transactions by the Islamic banks' Sharia committee not only faster and cheaper but also serve needs of customers. This implementation does not have to come from the bank itself; it could also manifest through acquisition or partnership with existing Fintech companies leveraging these technologies or simply collaborating with the appropriate researchers (Abumughli and Aysan 2021). Islamic finance and economy could benefit extensively from AI technology by adapting it to its industry specifics.

This chapter will assist Islamic banks and financial institutions in planning the implementation of AI-driven solutions. Additionally, it will support governments and policymakers in formulating policies and governance frameworks leading to the rapid adoption of AI technologies in the Islamic financial system.

References

Abumughli AA, Aysan AF (2021) The ascent of digital banks in the Gulf region: prospects and challenges. J Digit Bank 6(3):277–286

Agarwal P (2019.) Redefining banking and financial industry through the application of computational intelligence. In: 2019 Advances in science and engineering technology international conferences (ASET). IEEE, pp 1–5. https://doi.org/10.1109/ICASET.2019.8714305

Alhammadi MAA, Fernandez AI, Romero AV (2024) Credit scoring and risk management in Islamic banking: the case of Al Etihad Credit Bureau. Revista Venezolana de Gerencia: RVG 29(105):111–124

Ali H, Aysan AF (2024) Decoding future of generative AI in finance: a machine learning exploration of academic and grey corpus. SSRN Electron J. https://doi.org/10.2139/ssrn.4787211

Asutay M, Aysan AF, Karahan CC (2013) Reflecting on the trajectory of Islamic finance: from Mit Ghamr to the globalisation of Islamic finance. Afro Eurasian Stud 2(1–2):5–14

BankIslami (2014) BankIslami Pakistan Limited. BankIslami. https://bankislami.com.pk/digital-channel/bankislamione-touch-banking/

Baber H (2019). Financial inclusion and FinTech: a comparative study of countries following Islamic finance and conventional finance. Qual Res Fin Mark. https://doi.org/10.1108/QRFM-12-2018-0131

Buckley RP, Zetzsche DA, Arner DW, Tang BW (2021) Regulating artificial intelligence in finance: putting the human in the loop. Syd Law Rev 43:43–82

Bumacov V, Ashta A, Singh P (2014) The use of credit scoring in microfinance institutions and their outreach. Strateg Chang 23(7–8):401–413

Friedberg BA (2019) Wahed invest: a look at the new Islamic robo-advisor. Retrieved 12 Nov 2020 from https://www.investopedia.com/articles/personal-finance/112516/wahed-invest-peek-new-islamic-roboadvisor.asp#:~:text=Both%20access%20and%20investments%20are,risk%E2%80%94than%20their%20traditional%20competitors

Gassner M (2023, June 2) Home—Islamic wealth management. IslamicWealthManagement. https://islamicwealthmanagement.com/

Hassan M, Aziz LAR, Andriansyah Y (2023) The role artificial intelligence in modern banking: an exploration of AI-driven approaches for enhanced fraud prevention, risk management, and regulatory compliance. Rev Contemp Bus Anal 6(1):110–132

Islamic Financial Report (2022) ICD—Refinitiv Islamic finance development report 2022: embracing change. Retrieved from: https://www.zawya.com/en/islamic-economy/islamic-finance-reports/icd-refinitiv-islamic-finance-development-report-2022-embracing-change-qxdi3iat

Jain R (2023) Role of artificial intelligence in banking and finance. J Manag Sci 13:1–4. https://doi.org/10.26524/jms.13.27

John P (2024, March 2) AI use in Shariah audit analytics significantly enhances effectiveness, accuracy of compliance processes—Gulf Times. Gulf Times. https://www.gulf-times.com/article/678237/classified/ai-use-in-shariah-audit-analytics-significantly-enhances-effectiveness-accuracy-of-compliance-processes

Joyce L (2018, May 29) Artificial intelligence and the banking industry's $1 trillion opportunity. Retrieved from The Financial Brand. https://thefinancialbrand.com/72653/artificial-intelligence-trends-banking-industry/

Khan N (2019) AI applications in the Islamic finance industry. In: Global Islamic finance report 2019

Khan S, Rabbani MR (2020, Nov) Chatbot as Islamic finance expert (CaIFE) when finance meets artificial intelligence. In: Proceedings of the 2020 4th international symposium on computer science and intelligent control, pp 1–5

Marani M, Soltani M, Bahadori M, Soleimani M, Moshayedi A (2023) The role of biometrics in banking: a review. EAI Endorsed Trans AI Robot 2(1)

Marous J (2018, March 14) Meet 11 of the most interesting chatbots in banking. Retrieved from The Financial Brand: https://thefinancialbrand.com/71251/chatbots-banking-trends-ai-cx/

Moh'd Ali MA, Basahr A, Rabbani MR, Abdulla Y (2020) Transforming business decision making with Internet of Things (IoT) and machine learning (ML). In: 2020 International conference on decision aid sciences and application (DASA), pp 674–679

Mohamed H, Ali H (2022) Blockchain, fintech, and Islamic finance: building the future in the new Islamic digital economy. Blockchain, Fintech, Islam. Financ Build Futur New Islam Digit Econ:1–278. https://doi.org/10.1515/9783110745016

Montag C, Nakov P, Ali R (2024) Considering the IMPACT framework to understand the AI-well-being-complex from an interdisciplinary perspective. Tele Inform Rep 13:100112

Mossavar Rahmani F (2023) The transformative impact of AI on financial institutions, with a focus on banking. J Eng Appl Sci Technol 5:1–6. https://doi.org/10.47363/jeast/2023(5)192

Nembe JK, Atadoga JO, Mhlongo NZ, Falaiye T, Olubusola O, Daraojimba AI, Oguejiofor BB (2024) The role of artificial intelligence in enhancing tax compliance and financial regulation. Fin Account Res J 6(2):241–251

QIB (2017) QIB is the first bank in Qatar to implement face recognition on its mobile app across all smartphones. QIB. https://www.qib.com.qa/en/news/qib-the-first-bank-in-qatar-to-implement-face-recognition-on-its-mobile-app-across-all-smartphones/

Rabbani MR, Abdulla Y, Basahr A, Khan S, Moh'd Ali MA (2020) Embracing of Fintech in Islamic finance in the post-COVID era. In: 2020 International conference on decision aid sciences and application (DASA), pp 1230–1234

Samsudeen SN, Fathima Sanjeetha MB, Thowfeek MH, Sabraz Nawaz S, Buhary M, Sanjeetha F (2020) Drivers of artificial intelligence in banking service sectors. Solid State Technol 63

TechCEOs (2023, August 4) AI in Islamic finance: sharia-compliant robo-advisors and Fintech solutions. Tech CEOs Magazine. https://tech-ceos.com/ai-in-islamic-finance-sharia-compliant-robo-advisors-and-fintech-solutions/

Zakaria S, Abdul Manaf SM, Amron MT, Mohd Suffian MT (2023) Has the world of finance changed? A review of the influence of artificial intelligence on financial management studies. Inf Manag Bus Rev 15:420–432. https://doi.org/10.22610/imbr.v15i4(si)i.3617

Chapter 12
Introduction to Coarse Ethics: Tradeoff Between the Accuracy and Interpretability of Explainable Artificial Intelligence

Takashi Izumo

Abstract As devices powered by artificial intelligence (AI) become increasingly prevalent, the following question arises: How can these technologies improve human well-being? Transparency, defined as traceability and explainability under the European Union's Artificial Intelligence Act, is vital to human well-being. Given the citizens' varying levels of education and understanding, it is unrealistic to expect a single, uniform eXplainable AI framework to the public; a variety of explanations is necessary. This issue, long known as the tradeoff between AI accuracy and interpretability, remains unresolved. This chapter addresses this topic from a fresh perspective: coarse ethics. The author contends that full traceability is essential for professionals, whereas a coarse explanation of an AI system is sufficient for ordinary citizens and those with comprehension difficulties. Consequently, transparency should encompass not only a narrow concept centered on traceability and accountability but also a basic foundation that non-experts can comprehend. Under this broad definition, an AI must be explainable to the extent that it allows for reasonable informed consent. Adopting this method will alleviate the explanatory burden on developers while avoiding information overload for users and regulators, thereby promoting human well-being.

Keywords AI ethics · Explainable AI · Coarse ethics · EU AI Act · Autonomous driving · medical AI

T. Izumo (✉)
College of Law, Nihon University, Tokyo, Japan
e-mail: izumo.takashi@nihon-u.ac.jp

C. Montag and R. Ali (eds.), *The Impact of Artificial Intelligence on Societies*, Studies in Neuroscience, Psychology and Behavioral Economics,
https://doi.org/10.1007/978-3-031-70355-3_12

12.1 Introduction

Digital devices have become an integral part of our daily lives, a trend heavily influenced by the ubiquity of smartphones in the twenty-first century. As we move forward into the 2020s, we are entering a transformative era characterized by artificial intelligence (AI) and AI-powered digital devices, fueled by advancements in machine learning. Ensuring human well-being during this technological revolution necessitates a thorough physiological, social, and psychological examination (Montag and Diefenbach 2018). However, navigating these complexities poses significant challenges, particularly when assessing the implications of AI technologies for human well-being. In response, scholars have proposed various assessment frameworks, including the Interaction of Modality–Person–Area–Culture–Transparency (IMPACT) categories (Montag et al. 2024a, b). The IMPACT framework "suggests that making predictions regarding AI's impact on well-being will depend on many variables likely interacting with each other" (Montag et al. 2024a, p. 1). This chapter focuses on transparency and its impact on human well-being.

In particular, transparency requires the traceability and interpretability of AI processes from the user's perspective (Hosseini et al. 2018a). Conversely, developers prioritize explainability (Balasubramaniam et al. 2023). Hosseini et al. (2016a, b, 2018b) also emphasize that transparency is not only about software but also about the business model, intention, and quality of information. They argue that transparency can be obfuscated through information overload. Consequently, the advent of eXplainable AI (XAI) has received much attention (Gunning and Aha 2019). Recital 27 of the European Union's Artificial Intelligence Act (AIA) defines transparency as follows: "Transparency means that AI systems are developed and used in a way that allows appropriate traceability, and explainability, while making humans aware that they communicate or interact with an AI system, as well as duly informing deployers of the capabilities and limitations of that AI system and affected persons about their rights." This definition of transparency states that all AI systems should be explainable and that users should be able to trace and interpret the planning, data sets, and algorithms. Recital 131 of the AIA calls for increased transparency toward the public, claiming that increased public understanding of AI content fulfills this requirement.

However, the prevailing dilemma is the tradeoff between accuracy and interpretability: as algorithmic performance improves, interpretability diminishes, and vice versa (Arrieta et al. 2020). Thus, on a practical level, a basic understanding of AI must satisfy some of the transparency requirements. Experts define transparency as the ability to accurately trace the AI's content, whereas non-experts define it as the AI's perceived trustworthiness. This chapter aims to navigate the nuanced terrain of accuracy and interpretability using a novel ethical framework, that is, coarse ethics (CE), to reconcile the tradeoff between algorithmic accuracy and interpretability.

12.2 What is Coarse Ethics?

12.2.1 Definition

Scholars define CE as a branch of meta-ethics that examines the interpretability or applicability of evaluations within large-scale structures (Izumo and Weng 2022). This approach entails identifying a rough norm that is sufficiently similar to the original strict norm. Despite being inspired by today's AI movement and coarse geometry (Roe 2003), the concept of CE originates in the early modern period. Notable philosophers like Thomas Hobbes (1588–1679), an influential figure in English philosophy, expounded in his seminal work *Leviathan* (1651) the idea that social rules could be summarized by the maxim, "Do not do unto others what you would not have them do unto you," thus eliminating excuses based on intellectual inability to understand rules (Hobbes 1651; Singer 1963). Immanuel Kant (1724–1804), one of the most prominent figures in German philosophy, also emphasized in his book *Metaphysics of Morals* (1797) that obsessing over fine ethical distinctions is unfavorable (Kant 2017; Izumo and Weng 2022). These thinkers emphasized the importance of taking a coarse approach to ethics.

The grading of tests in a school setting is an excellent example of this concept (Izumo and Weng 2022). Consider this scenario: A teacher administers a math test with a maximum score of 100. The teacher then assigns grades by categorizing scores as follows: F for 0–59, D for 60–69, C for 70–79, B for 80–89, and A for 90 and above. Is this grading system inaccurate? Under certain conditions, this scoring method may be considered appropriate. However, what conditions warrant its applicability? Often, we can intuitively determine which rough evaluations do not jeopardize the original. For example, if the primary concern is distinguishing between pass and fail, it may be sufficient to classify scores below 60 as failing and 60 or higher as passing. This method reduces the 101-point scale (0–100) to a binary (pass or fail) outcome. In contrast, an evaluation system that alternates between pass and fail in point increments—such as passing from 0 to 59, failing from 60 to 69, and passing from 70 to 79—is considered inappropriate (Table 12.1).

What distinguishes evaluations that are appropriately coarsened versions of the originals from those that are not? CE approaches these issues from a scholarly standpoint.

Table 12.1 Adequacy of evaluation based on human intuition

	0–59	60–69	70–79	80–89	90–100	Adequacy
Method 1	F	D	C	B	A	✔
Method 2	Failure	Pass	Pass	Pass	Pass	✔
Method 3	Pass	Failure	Pass	Failure	Pass	✘

Table 12.2 Comparison of three students by different methods

	Student 1	Student 2	Student 3	Adequacy
Original score	65	68	73	–
Method 4	D	D	C	✔
Method 5	C	D	C	✘

12.2.2 *Two Requirements for Coarsening Norms*

12.2.2.1 Weak Order Preservation of Values

Building on previous research, two fundamental criteria have been established: weak order preservation and sufficiently high coverage (Izumo and Weng 2022). The initial criterion is defined as follows: When comparing two evaluation objects o_i and o_j, if the original assessment ranks $o_i < o_j$, then $o_i \leq o_j$ must also hold in the coarse assessment. For example, compare student s_1 who scored 65 on the previous math test, to student s_2 who scored 68. Based on the original 101-point scale assessment, this means $s_1 < s_2$. Thus, the weak order preservation criterion mandates that $s_1 \leq s_2$ in the ABCDF evaluation. It is possible for both s_1 and s_2 to receive a D grade, or for s_1 to receive a D and s_2 to receive a C. However, it would be inappropriate for s_1 to receive a C while s_2 receives a D, as this violates the order preservation principle (Table 12.2).

Method 5 is intuitively unsuitable in everyday situations. However, in CE, it is evaluated under the clear requirement of the weak order preservation rule. The same request must be satisfied for XAI. For example, a rough description given by an engineer for an algorithm may not be consistent with the original value order. In this case, the engineer must either refine the description so that the two become consistent, or lower the coverage, which will be explained in the next section.

This requirement may seem intuitively self-evident; however, in several instances in daily life, weak order preservation is disregarded. A non-trivial example is the so-called grade point average (GPA). GPA does not preserve a ranking based on the total points that a student has earned in multiple courses. Suppose that student s_1 scored 69 in math and 67 in literature, and student s_2 scored 70 in math and 60 in literature. According to their total score, $s_1(136) > s_2(130)$; however, according to their GPA, $s_1(1) < s_2(1.5)$. In this way, a set of coarse explanations may not preserve weak ordering. Therefore, XAI developers should exercise caution in aggregating multiple parameters into a comprehensive explanation (see Sect. 12.4 of this chapter).

12.2.2.2 Adequately High Coverage

The second criterion is adequately high coverage. This necessitates that the coarse evaluation includes a large enough subset of the original evaluation objects while weakly preserving their value order. For example, if a teacher designates scores from

0 to 59 as failing grades and scores from 61 to 100 as passing grades, this classification does not provide adequate coverage; it is unclear how a student with a score of 60 would be evaluated.

However, full coverage, which encompasses all of the objects evaluated in the first place, is not always required. Full coverage is uncommon in the context of XAI, with exceptions occurring frequently. This prediction is especially persuasive in medical AI contexts. Prior studies have shown that white lies or prosocial lies can be effective in medical practice, such as explaining cancer as a gastric ulcer (Nasrabadi et al. 2020). These lies are also known as benign deception or therapeutic privilege. AI researchers have paid close attention to the ethical permissibility of AI doctors telling prosocial lies (Mao et al. 2024). From the perspective of CE, if a human doctor replaces a highly accurate prediction made by an AI doctor with a white lie, they do not coarsen the AI diagnosis, but rather introduce an exception. Essentially, the human doctor reduces coverage by excluding specific patients from the AI diagnosis (Table 12.3).

In Table 12.3, it is important to distinguish between the inappropriateness of white lie 1 and white lie 2. Although lying to a terminally ill cancer patient may be permissible in some circumstances, for example, a nurse may be permitted to respond to their patient with "It may get better" even if the patient has little chance of recovery from terminal cancer (Nasrabadi et al. 2020). However, such deception will likely violate the patient's order preservation. In the original diagnosis, the severity of the disease follows the order $A < B < C$, but in white lie 1, $A \approx C < B$ (where the symbol $\approx$ denotes that $o_i \neq o_j$ in the original explanation but $o_i = o_j$ in a rough version). To maintain weak order preservation, a human doctor may try to explain to every cancer patient that their disease is an ulcer. However, such an explanation no longer constitutes an adequate diagnosis; simply maintaining order preservation does not support the substantive validity of a rough explanation or assessment (Sect. 12.2.3). In this case, specific patients should be treated as exceptions instead of applying the AI diagnosis to all patients.

Table 12.3 AI diagnosis and prosocial lie

	Patient A	Patient B	Patient C	Adequacy
Original diagnosis by AI	Stomach ulcer	Stomach cancer stage 2	Stomach cancer stage 4	–
White Lie 1	Stomach ulcer	Stomach cancer stage 2	Stomach ulcer	✗ Violation of the order preservation rule
White Lie 2	Stomach ulcer	Stomach ulcer	Stomach ulcer	✗ Not acceptable as a medical diagnosis

12.2.3 Coarse Justification

Some readers may recognize the difficulty that arises when only these two requirements are met: there are countless formally appropriate coarsening methods, and they might indeed be correct. Weak order preservation and adequately high coverage are purely formal requirements. This is evident in school tests. The question of how a teacher should grade a student requires a specific context. As is true in the development of XAI, the best explanation for a variety of users is not singularly defined at the time of conception. For example, heat maps are a common method of visually explaining medical AI predictions, but the risk of not adequately explaining the original black box model has been noted (Jin et al. 2022). The acceptability of using heat maps comes down to how high the coverage of this coarsened explanatory scheme should be in a specific situation. Demonstrating that a coarse norm has practically sufficient coverage while maintaining reasonable order preservation is known as coarse justification (Izumo and Weng 2022).

To determine how far the value order can be weakened, one might consider setting a lower limit based on differences discernible to humans. When $o_i < o_j$ or $o_i > o_j$ for an AI, but the difference Δ (the absolute value of the difference between o_i and o_j) is unrecognizable or impractical for humans, these values are considered equivalent, described as $o_i \approx o_j$ by CE. For example, strictly adhering to a speed limit of 69 km/h may prove difficult; this impracticality justifies broadening the safe zone around the optimal speed p^* (Sect. 12.3). Similarly, CE can provide insights into whether caregiving robots should increase intervention when an older person's cognitive abilities deteriorate (Boch et al. 2023).

When justifying increases or decreases in coverage, we find the case of a white lie as instructive (Sect. 12.2.2.2); exceptions should be addressed accordingly. An exception is defined based on the original evaluation's nature, its coarsening purpose, and other relevant factors. The importance of reliability, understandability, uniformity, and efficiency in handling exceptions during program execution has been well-established since the 1970s (Goodenough 1975). These considerations should also guide in handling exceptions in XAI.

12.2.4 Relationship to Other Fields

The most recent and promising research in this area is the study of the coarsening of human networks and their proximity to CE. In the field of economics, there is a burgeoning interest, distinct from CE, in approaching finance through coarse graining (CG) rather than linear correlation (Balci et al. 2022). CG, first proposed in the study of proteins, is the process of discretizing physical quantities to streamline information processing. Simulating the behavior of all atoms in a protein is extremely complex and requires massive amounts of computation (Kmiecik et al. 2016). Although the relationship between CE and CG requires careful consideration, both agree that understanding the entire process becomes difficult if an object (ethical value in CE and physical momentum in CG) is considered a continuous quantity. Thus, one advantage of CE over traditional ethics is that it reduces information overload. This potential can significantly contribute to studies on AI behavior and transparency assessments, particularly regarding computing power.

12.3 Coarse Ethics and Explainability of AI

The principles of weak order preservation and adequately high coverage provide robust support for XAI. One of the primary challenges in XAI is striking a balance between AI system accuracy and interpretability. This challenge is frequently encapsulated in the notion that as an algorithm's predictive power increases, its comprehensibility for humans diminishes (Arrieta et al. 2020). To address this issue, techniques have been developed that convert a highly accurate predictive algorithm, such as a deep neural network (DNN), into a simpler and more understandable model (Guidotti et al. 2018; Mornal 2023). Local Interpretable Model-agnostic Explanations (LIME) and SHapley Additive exPlanation (SHAP) techniques have gained prominence in this field (Ribeiro et al. 2016; Lundberg and Lee 2017). The relationship between DNNs and XAI tools is analogous to that between a high-precision norm and its derived low-precision counterpart in CE (Izumo and Weng 2022).

Consider the regulation of speed in automated driving. Assume that an automated driving system performs a seamless evaluation of the appropriateness of speed and generates a safety graph for highway driving (Fig. 12.1).

When AI controls the vehicle, human occupants are not required to understand the risk assessment, as it may be beyond most people's comprehension. However, a problem arises when the car owner deactivates the automatic mode and drives manually. If the AI determines that the driver's actions are inappropriate, it may

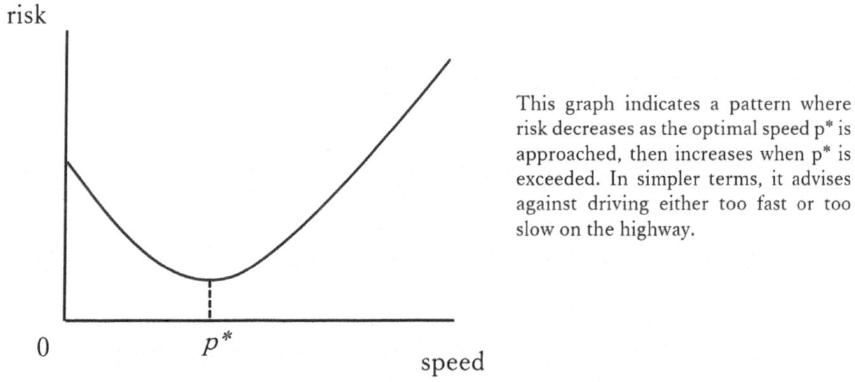

Fig. 12.1 Driving speed and risk evaluation by AI

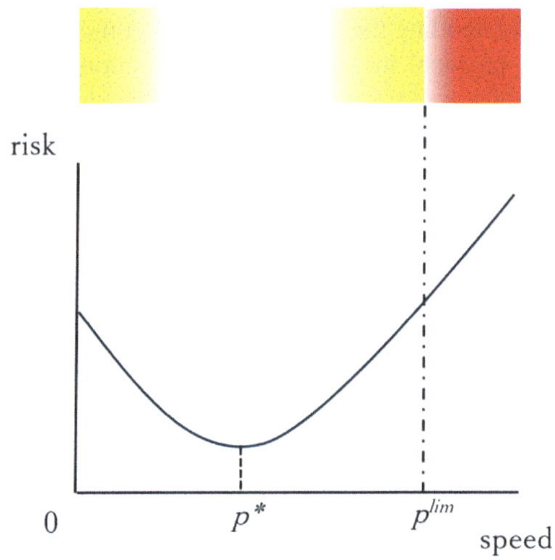

Fig. 12.2 Coarse visualization of Fig. 12.1

forcefully revert to automatic driving mode. However, what constitutes improper driving? It is conceivable that not adjusting to the optimal point on the graph (p^*) is considered inappropriate. However, this is not practical for a human operator. Designers should typically allow for a margin of error of plus or minus 5 km/h when calculating the optimal speed. Essentially, the human driver requires a coarse evaluation, a rough approximation of the AI assessment that can adequately replace the latter.

CE is particularly useful in this context. A regulator could implement a three-step evaluation, as shown in Fig. 12.2, while maintaining weak order preservation and ensuring sufficiently high coverage (Sect. 12.2.2). Ratings could be white (safe), yellow (caution), or red (dangerous). For example, the regulator may enact a rule requiring a switch to automatic driving mode if cautionary warnings are ignored for five minutes or the red area is reached (i.e., if the speed limit p^{lim} is exceeded).

12.4 Applications

This section uses two cases to illustrate the practical applications of CE. The first case involves the rounding of decimal fractions. Rather than using natural language to explain AI systems, certain tools use numerical values. For example, GenEth, a general ethical dilemma analyzer, employs an algorithm to quantify AI's black box, explaining topics such as the safety of automatic versus manual driving based on predefined criteria (Anderson and Anderson 2018). GenEth's output values are presented as integers, but they will likely differ from the original values stored in the black box, as deep learning computations are not typically based solely on integers. As a result, GenEth provides a rough explanation of automatic driving. Therefore,

Table 12.4 Reversal of valuation due to rounding

	Assessment tool	Avoiding a collision	Staying in the lane	Respecting the driver's autonomy	Keeping with the speed limit	Avoiding imminent harm to people	Total
Human	DNN	− 1.01	0.61	0.64	0.67	− 1.38	− 0.47
	GenEth	− 1	1	1	1	− 1	1
AI	DNN	1.18	− 0.66	− 0.49	− 0.85	1.27	0.45
	GenEth	1	− 1	0	− 1	1	0

the two rules required by CE must be followed, and it is critical to understand that weak order preservation may be compromised when rounding the original values to integers. Table 12.4 depicts one possible instance of this violation (Izumo and Weng 2022).

In this table, the DNN suggests that AI takes control of the vehicle, whereas the rounded numerical values indicate that the human driver should maintain control.

Another relevant example is the field of medical diagnosis. In machine learning-based diagnosis, the choice of datasets and algorithms is critical. Researchers frequently focus on prominent features during the training phase when making these decisions (Kumar et al. 2023). For instance, Hosseinzadeh et al. (2023) used CE to create multiple data sets and various combinations thereof, with the goal of covering "the most available features while also studying each feature set separately" (p. 12). This study emphasizes the importance of adequate coverage and demonstrates how CE can help guide the selection of scientific research topics.

12.5 Discussion

The AIA mandates public transparency (see Sect 12.1 of this chapter); hence, the transparency of an AI system should be evaluated incrementally rather than uniformly. Individual intelligence, rather than general smartness or level of education, determines transparency criteria. Everyone has areas of expertise while being a layperson in others. Experts should be able to fully trace AI data sets, algorithms, and outputs, whereas non-experts do not require this traceability. This approach reduces information overload and fosters trust, thereby improving overall well-being.

To ensure traceability, developers must explain AI systems. However, as stated in Sect. 12.3, this explainability involves a tradeoff between accuracy and interpretability. The ideal policy strives for a Pareto optimum, a state in which improving one aspect (e.g., understandability) does not degrade the other (e.g., accuracy). It is unrealistic to expect developers to achieve this optimization independently; AI could help balance this tradeoff for all users. Given AI's finite computational resources, it is practical to classify stakeholders based on their ability to understand AI explanations. At least three categories are required: experts, ordinary citizens, and those who struggle to understand (e.g., individuals with borderline intelligence or intellectual disabilities).

Furthermore, regardless of the categorization, a critical concern about this optimization emerges: How can we ensure that AI does not manipulate us? The average person may be unable to discern whether an explanation is tailored to their understanding or if the AI is intentionally steering them toward a particular decision. Should experts be the ultimate judges of AI's appropriateness? The answer is no, because this simply transfers the trust issue from AI to experts. Unless they lack decision-making capacity, the individual should make the final decision, under the principle of autonomy. CE does not suggest a deus ex machina solution is feasible, but rather emphasizes the importance of each citizen playing an active role to the best of his or her ability. Therefore, informed consent is critical, except when a person cannot consent.

CE facilitates decision-making rather than representing it. Section 12.2.2 of this chapter introduces two requirements—weak order preservation and adequately high coverage—which are minimal guidelines. The extent to which a rough AI can be explained is determined by the specific situation, as discussed in Sect. 12.2.3. This is similar to the various approaches teachers use to evaluate test results. In some cases, teachers may need to use precise one-point increments, whereas in others, they may prefer a broader ABCDF rating system. Similarly, in some cases, an AI developer may need to provide a scientifically accurate explanation, whereas a metaphorical explanation may suffice in others. CE does not advocate for laziness; rather, it emphasizes that individuals have limited abilities and should focus on training and maximizing their potential. Achieving this requires lifelong self-education (Table 12.5).

This study is limited by its focus on theoretical considerations of various transparency forms without addressing practical methods for ensuring it. Establishing transparency based on CE remains challenging due to its reliance on multiple domains, cultures, and individual personalities, variables being covered in the IMPACT model of Montag et al. (2024a, b). Furthermore, the study does not present a mathematically rigorous formulation of these forms. For example, it does not clarify whether the value order constitutes an ordered set. These issues warrant further investigation.

12.6 Conclusion

Given the breadth of human understanding, the term "transparency" must encompass multiple meanings. The criteria for accurate explanation and traceability are primarily applicable to experts, whereas nonspecialists require coarser explanations and traceability that still capture the essence, though less precise. This chapter examines what constitutes an appropriately coarsened explanation within the framework of the new ethics of CE. An appropriately coarse explanation must satisfy

Table 12.5 Three meanings of transparency for different citizens

	Experts	Ordinary citizens	People with comprehension difficulties
Autonomy	Free from outside interference and respectful of the truth	Respect for scientific authority and vigilance against political manipulation	Informed consent should be obtained as much as possible, but paternalistic intervention is allowed to avoid danger to the person
Lifelong learning	Update professional knowledge and use it with integrity	Strive to understand what is comprehensible at the standard level of education	Receive appropriate support in education
Transparency	The subject of the explanation can be accurately traced and interpreted using the scientific method	Their understanding is not confused by information overload, and rough interpretation does not disrupt the value order of an accurate explanation	They are provided with an environment where they can understand the core of the consequences predicted by AI and give informed consent

two requirements. First, it should not disrupt the original explanation's value order, meaning it should not misrepresent good or bad. Second, the coarse explanation must provide enough information relevant to the context in which it is required. For example, the relationship between driving speed and risk in self-driving AI may not be represented as a continuous graph, but rather in three discrete stages: dangerous, cautious, and safe. This trichotomy may constitute adequate coarsening if it meets those conditions. However, identifying appropriate coarsening with fewer formulas is difficult, and external systems cannot guarantee that an explanation is a proper coarsening or malicious manipulation, as coarse explanations facilitate understanding but do not provide full traceability. Consequently, this chapter emphasizes the importance of informed consent and lifelong education in respecting autonomy and increasing knowledge. These findings will promote well-being by reducing information overload and mitigating distrust in AI.

References

Anderson M, Anderson SL (2018) GenEth: a general ethical dilemma analyzer. J Behav Robot 9:337–357. https://doi.org/10.1515/pjbr-2018-0024

Arrieta AB, Díaz-Rodríguez N, Ser JD, Bennetot A, Tabik S, Barbado A, Garcia S, Gil-Lopez S, Molina D, Benjamins R, Chatila R, Herrera F (2020) Explainable Artificial Intelligence (XAI): concepts, taxonomies, opportunities and challenges toward responsible AI. Inform Fus 58:82–115. https://doi.org/10.1016/j.inffus.2019.12.012

Balasubramaniam N, Kauppinen M, Rannisto A, Hiekkanen K, Kajala S (2023) Transparency and explainability of AI systems: from ethical guidelines to requirements. Inf Softw Technol 159:107197. https://doi.org/10.1016/j.infsof.2023.107197

Balci MA, Batrancea LM, Akgüller Ö, Nichita A (2022) Coarse graining on financial correlation networks. Mathematics 10(12):2118. https://doi.org/10.3390/math10122118

Boch A, Ryan S, Kriebitz A, Amugongo LM, Lütge C (2023) Beyond the metal flesh: understanding the intersection between bio- and AI ethics for robotics in healthcare. Robotics 12(4):110. https://doi.org/10.3390/robotics12040110

Goodenough JB (1975) Exception handling design issues. ACM SIGPLAN Not 10(7):41–45. https://doi.org/10.1145/987305.987313

Guidotti R, Monreale A, Ruggieri S, Turini F, Pedreschi D, Giannotti F (2018) A survey of methods for explaining black box models. https://doi.org/10.48550/arXiv.1802.01933

Gunning D, Aha DW (2019) DARPA's explainable artificial intelligence program. AI Mag 40(2):44–58. https://doi.org/10.1609/aimag.v40i2.2850

Hobbes T (1651) Leviathan. Project Gutenberg. https://www.gutenberg.org/files/3207/3207-h/3207-h.htm

Hosseini M, Shahri A, Phalp K, Ali R (2016a) Foundations for transparency requirements engineering. In Daneva M, Pastor O (eds) Requirements engineering: foundation for software quality: 22nd international working conference, REFSQ 2016, Gothenburg, Sweden, March 14–17, 2016, Proceedings. Springer International Publishing, Switzerland, Cham, pp 225–231. https://doi.org/10.1007/978-3-319-30282-9_15

Hosseini M, Shahri A, Phalp K, Ali R (2016b) A modelling language for transparency requirements in business information systems. In Nurcan S, Soffer P, Bajec M, Eder J (eds) Advanced information systems engineering: 28th international conference, CAiSE 2016, Ljubljana, Slovenia, June 13–17, 2016. Proceedings. Springer International Publishing, Switzerland, Cham, pp 239–254. https://doi.org/10.1007/978-3-319-39696-5_15

Hosseini M, Shahri A, Phalp K, Ali R (2018a) Four reference models for transparency requirements in information systems. Requirements Eng 23:251–275. https://doi.org/10.1007/s00766-017-0265-y

Hosseini M, Shahri A, Phalp K, Ali R (2018b) Engineering transparency requirements: a modelling and analysis framework. Inf Syst 74:3–22. https://doi.org/10.1016/j.is.2017.12.008

Hosseinzadeh M, Gorji A, Jouzdani AF, Rezaeijo SM, Rahmim A, Salmanpour MR (2023) Prediction of cognitive decline in Parkinson's disease using clinical and DAT SPECT imaging features, and hybrid machine learning systems. Diagnostics 13(10):1691. https://doi.org/10.3390/diagnostics13101691

Izumo T, Weng YH (2022) Coarse ethics: how to ethically assess explainable artificial intelligence. AI Ethics 2:449–461. https://doi.org/10.1007/s43681-021-00091-y

Jin W, Li X, Hamarneh G (2022) Evaluating explainable AI on a multi-modal medical imaging task: can existing algorithms fulfill clinical requirements? Proc AAAI Conf Artif Intell 36(11):11945–11953. https://doi.org/10.1609/aaai.v36i11.21452

Kant I (2017) The metaphysics of morals. Cambridge University Press, Cambridge, United Kingdom

Kmiecik S, Gront D, Kolinski M, Wieteska L, Dawid AE, Kolinski A (2016) Coarse-grained protein models and their applications. Chem Rev 116(14):7898–7936. https://doi.org/10.1021/acs.chemrev.6b00163

Kumar Y, Koul A, Singla R, Ijaz MF (2023) Artificial intelligence in disease diagnosis: a systematic literature review, synthesizing framework and future research agenda. J Ambient Intell Humaniz Comput 14:8459–8486. https://doi.org/10.1007/s12652-021-03612-z

Lundberg S, Lee SI (2017) A unified approach to interpreting model predictions. https://doi.org/10.48550/arXiv.1705.07874

Mao Y, Hu B, Kim KJ (2024) When AI doctors lie about diagnosis: the effects of varying degrees of prosocial lies in patient–AI interactions. Technol Soc 76:102461. https://doi.org/10.1016/j.techsoc.2024.102461

Montag C, Diefenbach S (2018) Toward homo digitalis: important research issues for psychology and the neurosciences at the dawn of the Internet of Things and the digital society. Sustainability 10:415. https://doi.org/10.3390/su10020415

Montag C, Ali R, Al-Thani D, Hall BJ (2024a) On artificial intelligence and global mental health. Asian J Psychiatr 91:103855. https://doi.org/10.1016/j.ajp.2023.103855
Montag C, Nakov P, Ali R (2024b) Considering the IMPACT framework to understand the AI-well-being-complex from an interdisciplinary perspective. Tele Inf Reports 13:100112. https://doi.org/10.1016/j.teler.2023.100112
Mornal C (2023) Interpretable machine learning: a guide for making black box models explainable. christophm.github.io/interpretable-ml-book/
Nasrabadi AN, Joolaee S, Navab E, Esmaeili M, Shali M (2020) White lie during patient care: a qualitative study of nurses' perspectives. BMC Med Ethics 21:86. https://doi.org/10.1186/s12910-020-00528-9
Ribeiro MT, Singh S, Guestrin C (2016) "Why should I trust you?": explaining the predictions of any classifier. https://doi.org/10.48550/arXiv.1602.04938
Roe J (2003) Lectures on coarse geometry. American Mathematical Society, Providence, Rhode Island, U.S.A
Singer MG (1963) The golden rule. Philosophy 38(146):293–314. https://doi.org/10.1017/S0031819100058290

Chapter 13
Social eXplainable AI (Social XAI): Towards Expanding the Social Benefits of XAI

Mohammad Naiseh

Abstract The eXplainable Artificial Intelligence (XAI) research agenda is constantly expanding. From a mainly technical topic, it has now developed into a multidisciplinary area of research, supporting domain experts, policymakers, and lay users. However, humans working in domains, such as healthcare, media and policing still find themselves questioning the value of XAI and whether it is worth their time and effort. This hampers effective human–machine collaboration and results in various trust-related biases. An emerging field of social XAI introduces the need to operationalise XAI and overcome its potential user issues. For example, XAI has been shown to lead to over-reliance on AI, for some in contrast to algorithmic aversion or is simply ignored as a redundant feature. Based on current work in Human-Centered XAI, I outline a set of design features that could improve human-XAI interaction and ultimately expand the social benefits of XAI. I present a framework of three dimensions that shows how the current work in Human-Centered XAI is increasing the effectiveness of the human-XAI interaction.

Keywords Explainable AI · Social XAI · Human-centered AI

13.1 Introduction

Artificial Intelligence (AI) is becoming an important part of many jobs, supporting decision-making in public services (Davenport and Kalakota 2019), healthcare (Rasch et al. 2003), child welfare services (Dodge et al. 2019), and journalism (Naiseh et al. 2020a). In some cases, AI is intended to automate mundane, repetitive tasks and to allow humans to focus on higher-level and creative tasks (Naiseh et al. 2023). However, humans show resentment toward AI-driven decision-making systems as these systems can be inscrutable and nonintuitive (Sokol and Flach 2020a). Humans

M. Naiseh (✉)
Faculty of Science and Technology, Bournemouth University, Poole, UK
e-mail: mnaiseh1@bournemouth.ac.uk

C. Montag and R. Ali (eds.), *The Impact of Artificial Intelligence on Societies*, Studies in Neuroscience, Psychology and Behavioral Economics,
https://doi.org/10.1007/978-3-031-70355-3_13

report an inability to understand the logic behind AI outputs and have problems establishing meaningful trust in such an AI system (Sokol and Flach 2020b). Without being able to understand and accurately judge AI outputs, decision-makers are prevented from harnessing the benefits algorithmic systems can offer (Bansal et al. 2020).

In recent years, the field of eXplainable Artificial Intelligence (XAI) has seen a surge in research aimed at enhancing AI transparency and interpretability (Sokol and Flach 2020a). Human–Computer Interaction (HCI) research has also looked into various aspects of user-centred explanations (Naiseh et al. 2020a), encompassing presentation, information content, framing, and communication methods. XAI is increasingly recognised as a crucial component of human-AI systems, serving to calibrate user reliance and mitigate potential errors stemming from blind adherence to AI decisions (Naiseh et al. 2023). Despite the emphasis on providing explanations, studies have shown that the performance and reliance of human-AI teams have not necessarily improved (Naiseh et al. 2023; Sokol and Flach 2020b; Bansal et al. 2020). Users have reported that explanations sometimes feel redundant and fail to meet task requirements (Naiseh et al. 2023), leading to misuse or misinterpretation (Naiseh et al. 2021a). This is partly because XAI approaches often offer only short-term solutions, losing relevance over time (Rozenblit and Keil 2002). When explanations are perceived as redundant, they risk being ignored or superficially examined (Naiseh et al. 2021a). Moreover, XAI often lacks the ability to spark curiosity or motivate experts to delve deeper into problem-solving (Lee et al. 2017). There is thus a pressing need to translate XAI into tangible measures and functions within human-AI environments, expanding its social benefits. Additionally, several researchers noted that XAI to be socially effective must address not only technical aspects but also human factors, such as cognitive biases, and raise awareness about XAI (Schneeberger et al. 2019; Sheh 2017; Naiseh et al. 2022).

Several studies already demonstrated how XAI can be used beyond just explaining AI models and expanding its social benefits. In this paper, I refer to social XAI as approaches, tools and design techniques that are to be implemented with XAI systems with the aim that not just explaining AI but also providing benefits to users and the human-AI team. The IMPACT framework structuring this book also makes the point that XAI is highly relevant to foster transparency in the realm of AI likely resulting in more positive views on the AI technology (see Chap. 1 and Montag et al. (2024a, b)). Social XAI has shown promising results to upskill current XAI users. For example, interactive features with XAI helped users discover unknown rules describing certain phenomena and upskilled users in AI terms (Narayanan et al. 1802). Similarly, receiving feedback regarding the reasons for the success or failure of the system has been shown to help users learn how to avoid potential AI mistakes (Naiseh et al. 2020b). Social XAI helped users train for difficult social situations or high-risk tasks in a safe and controlled way (Oinas-Kukkonen et al. 2008) or foster expertise development (Calvaresi et al. 2021), by using techniques such as cognitive forcing (Chromik and Butz 2021). Cognitive forcing functions are HCI interventions that disrupt heuristic reasoning and encourage users to engage in more deliberate and thoughtful decision-making processes by making the process more mentally demanding (Chromik and Butz 2021). In another example, social XAI has helped in teaching new surgeons, by first learning different aspects of expert surgeon performance and then using this information to enhance novices' understanding of medical data (Gao et al. 2022). Further, social XAI has shown its potential to be effective in teaching AI to children. Harjumaa and Oinas-Kukkonen (2007) showed that children can be taught ML concepts when they can experiment with explainable models. The ability to interact with an interpretable model significantly improved 10–14-year-olds' understanding of the concept of bias in terms of gender discrimination (Sokol and Flach 2020b).

Social XAI also allowed domain experts to make data-supported decisions to improve the systems they are using and even make them fairer. Naiseh et al. (2021c) showed that decision-makers have a strong ability to detect and audit potentially harmful algorithmic behaviours when given explanations that allow them to apply their sensemaking strategies. Social explanations are part of user-driven algorithm audits and help leverage users' prior experience of harm and biases (Naiseh et al. 2021c). For example, when XAI enables decision-makers to make holistic risk assessments and adjust for algorithmic limitations, they can reduce the racial disparity in child welfare screening in comparison to if AI was used alone (Te'eni and Sani-Kuperberg 2005). Moreover, social XAI can help users reflect on their own decisions and potentially reduce the potential for biases in the human AI team (Cowan and Lucena 1995). Wijekoon et al. (2024) showed that social XAI can be used to create collective, hybrid intelligence on a complex decision-making task with improved accuracy, and improved consistency of decision-making. These examples illustrate that the importance of XAI extends beyond simply explaining AI decisions to humans. Instead, it is crucial to design XAI that is socially beneficial and minimises biases, enabling more effective and equitable human-AI collaboration.

The significance of this research lies in its ability to bridge the gap between technical advancements in XAI and the human dynamics essential for the successful adoption and utilisation of XAI systems. The author builds upon insights from human-centred XAI research to present a robust framework of design features aimed at expanding the social benefits of XAI within human-AI ecosystems. The framework not only aims to optimise user engagement with XAI interfaces but also to facilitate profound social benefits to XAI users.

13.2 Social XAI Framework

Based on the current literature on Human-Centered eXplainable Artificial Intelligence (XAI), I present a social XAI framework that emerges as a synthesis of research insights and design principles aimed at enhancing the *usability, human-like, and educational* value of XAI.

13.2.1 Usability Enhancement

The concept of usability enhancement within XAI has been discussed by scholars to underscore the role of user interface design in expanding the societal benefits of AI technologies. This dimension embodies approaches to interface design that prioritise accessibility and engagement of AI explanations to ultimately encourage users to interact with AI explanations. It has been shown that encouraging interaction with XAI explanations can expand the social benefits of XAI by fostering greater transparency, trust, and collaboration between users and AI systems (Naiseh et al. 2020a; Bansal et al. 2020; Simkute et al. 2022). When users actively engage with explanations, they develop a deeper understanding of AI outputs, enabling them to make more informed decisions and contribute meaningfully to decision-making processes. Additionally, increased interaction with XAI explanations promotes user empowerment and accountability, facilitating the responsible and ethical deployment of AI technologies in various domains (Narayanan et al. 1802; Oinas-Kukkonen et al. 2008).

One related concept to usability enhancement is *explanation abstraction*. Researchers have used several techniques to break down complex explanations into digestible chunks e.g., (Bansal et al. 2020; Narayanan et al. 1802), as advocated by the reduction principle of the Persuasive Systems Design (PSD) model (Sokol and Flach 2020c). By aligning with human cognitive processing capabilities, this approach ensures that explanations are easily understood and retained by users across different knowledge levels and backgrounds (Naiseh et al. 2021c).

Furthermore, *easy navigation* through XAI interfaces has been identified as a key determinant for usability enhancement (Naiseh et al. 2021c, 2022). Designers in this case aim to make the explanations easy to find and navigate through the design. Therefore, users are more likely to interact and engage with explanations. Similarly, *tunnelling* design has been used in XAI to guide users through the process of reading and interacting with the explanation (Gao et al. 2022; Cowan and Lucena 1995). In one related research, authors have used visual cues to highlight explanations' chunks which are important to read or using navigational cues to switch from one section of the interface to another (Gao et al. 2022). This aligns with the phenomena related to learners' readiness to learn and read. Learners usually tend to follow measures and instructions in which the instructor guides the learning process (Te'eni and Sani-Kuperberg 2005).

Moreover, *interactive XAI* features have been used to allow users to interact with the explanation and ask questions (Sokol and Flach 2020c). Interactive XAI interfaces proved to be an effective way to encourage users to interact with XAI and enable them to construct their own experiences (Chromik and Butz 2021). For instance, in one relevant study, researchers have used interactive Local Interpretable Model-agnostic Explanations (LIME) (Wijekoon et al. 2024) to explain cancer prediction. The interactive XAI allowed users to group and split cancer image segments and experiment with different explainability scenarios. Such interactive and experimental interaction between the XAI system and the users was helpful in improving users' learning experience and serving various learning styles (Walster et al. 1966).

Finally, the literature discussed the role of *personalised presentation* of explanations in increasing engagement with XAI features across diverse contexts and user preferences (Miller 2018). Personalisation in XAI involves tailoring the presentation or the framing of explanations to individual users based on their characteristics, such as demographics, behaviour, and preferences. One related study discussed personalising XAI explanations based on user demographics could involve tailoring the content and presentation of explanations to match the user's age (Naiseh et al. 2020b). For younger or less technically inclined users, the XAI system may provide more visual, simplified explanations using plain language. In contrast, for older or more technically-savvy users, the system may offer more detailed, technical explanations with advanced visualizations and data.

13.2.2 Human-Like Enhancement

In this discussion, I delve into the attributes of explanations that are significant from the perspective of the explainee. These attributes, drawn from research in social science, psychology, and cognitive science, aim to ensure that algorithmic explanations resonate naturally with end users, resembling human-like and everyday social explanations.

One prominent feature of the human-like enhancement of XAI is *novelty*, which has been widely discussed as a means to capture users' attention and encourage interaction with AI explanations (Sokol and Flach 2020a). Novelty involves providing in-depth knowledge and surprising facts while avoiding circularity in the information presented. Repetitive information and obvious assertions can render explanations meaningless and deter users from engaging with them (Naiseh et al. 2021a; Schneeberger et al. 2019). For instance, consider an AI tool generating diet plan recommendations; a circular explanation such as "*This diet plan is effective because it helps lose weight*" may fail to captivate users' interest. *Coherence* is another critical aspect of human-like enhancement, wherein explanation chunks and components must work in harmony to encourage user interaction. Studies have demonstrated that users may disregard explanations that lack coherence or fail to "hang together" (Sokol and Flach 2020a). For example, an AI-based system issuing security device recommendations with an explanation like "*This is the most secure device because it has the cheapest delivery cost*" presents an incoherent rationale, likely to be ignored by users. In other words, the explanations provided must be logical.

Generalisable explanations that encompass a broader range of cases and facts have been found to elicit higher levels of acceptance from users (Naiseh et al. 2021b; Calvaresi et al. 2021). This principle is important, as it suggests that explanations should aim to capture the underlying patterns and principles governing the AI's decision-making, rather than focusing solely on the details of a particular instance. This has been shown to improve human-AI interaction as users are better able to understand the system's reasoning and apply that understanding to new situations (Naiseh et al. 2021c). While this principle may seem contradictory to the novelty feature, general explanations tend to be more engaging in the absence of novelty, as novel explanations are contextually limited. The key is to strike a balance, where the explanations are informative and insightful enough to maintain user engagement, while still being sufficiently generalised to be applicable across a range of scenarios.

Lastly, the concept of *Contractiveness* has emerged as a significant feature in the literature on human-centered XAI (Mirchi et al. 2020; Simkute et al. 2022; Naiseh 2021). Contractive explanations not only elucidate the current AI prediction but also illustrate counterfactual cases, addressing the human tendency to question why a particular action was taken instead of another. By highlighting the alternative actions the AI could have taken and the reasons for the chosen course of action, contractive explanations help users better comprehend the underlying logic and reasoning behind the AI's decisions (Sokol and Flach 2020b).

13.2.3 Learning Enhancement

In this section, I explore how several researchers have endeavoured to develop a *learning-focused XAI* to effectively upskill users and foster enduring mental models of AI operations. The interest in such learning-focused XAI has arisen from empirical evidence indicating that individuals working with AI may lack the algorithmic literacy needed to interpret AI outputs (Schneeberger et al. 2019). Additionally, they may harbour fundamental misconceptions about the workings of algorithmic systems or oversimplify their operations (Chouldechova et al. 2019).

Several studies have developed XAI systems with *guidance features* to help users in the process of interpreting AI explanations (Wijekoon et al. 2024; Cowan and Lucena 1995), e.g., information such as when, how, and why to use explanations was used for a better learning experience. This included video tutorials or FAQ tutorials accessible to users (Bussone et al. 2015). Another approach was to promote *Self-learning* in the XAI interface to enhance the learning experience of XAI (Simkute et al. 2022; Wijekoon et al. 2024). Researchers have argued that people have different learning styles and limited cognitive resources which might require them to follow different learning strategies (Gao et al. 2022). In this context, the XAI developers have designed their interfaces to help users self-learn from the explanation by providing tools that facilitate that process, e.g., taking notes or archiving explanations for future interactions (Naiseh et al. 2022). In this way, users were able to personalise their learning strategies, aims and learning sources without help from the system.

In addition, *suggestion features* have been used to provide users with suggestions for additional reading materials or resources related to AI concepts and explanations (Gao et al. 2022). It has been shown that XAI can deepen user's understanding of AI principles and applications by recommending relevant articles, papers, or educational content. These suggestions can be tailored to users' interests, knowledge levels, and

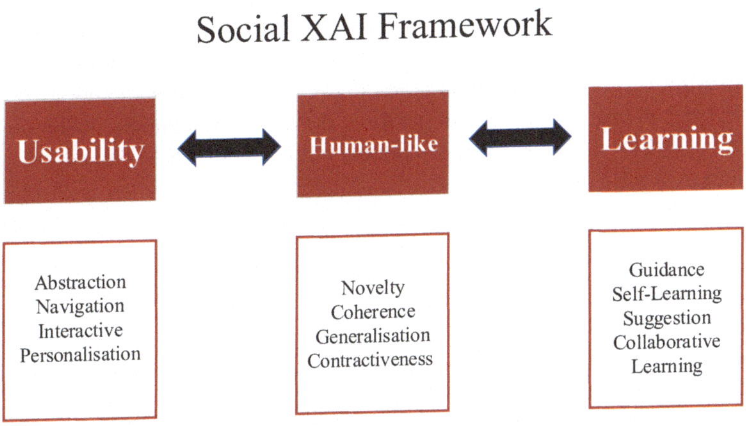

Fig. 13.1 The social XAI framework encompasses three dimensions: usability, human-line, and learning enhancement

learning objectives, enhancing the effectiveness of the learning experience (Chouldechova et al. 2019). Finally, *collaborative learning* functionalities have been shown to enable users to engage in collaborative activities, discussions, and knowledge sharing with peers, experts, or AI systems themselves (Bussone et al. 2015). XAI was designed to leverage collective intelligence, diverse perspectives, and shared experiences to enhance learning outcomes by facilitating collaboration among users (De-Arteaga et al. 2020). For example, in a collaborative learning scenario within an XAI system, users were able to participate in discussion forums or online communities where they could share their experiences, insights, and questions related to AI explanations (De-Arteaga et al. 2020). Users were also able to collaborate with peers to analyse and interpret AI outputs, discuss best practices, and troubleshoot challenges together (Mirchi et al. 2020) (Fig. 13.1).

13.3 Research Gap and Future Directions

The Social XAI framework presented herein synthesises insights from Human-Centered eXplainable Artificial Intelligence (XAI) literature, offering a structured approach to enhance the usability, social, and educational aspects of AI systems. Through an examination of usability, human-like, and learning dimensions, this framework underscores the importance of user interaction, engagement, and empowerment in realising the full potential of XAI. While the framework provides valuable guidelines for designing XAI systems, it is not comprehensive. The main aim of this chapter is to open the discussion for further research and refinement of the framework to encompass a broader range of factors and contexts relevant to social XAI. Future research will focus on validating and expanding the Social XAI framework through empirical studies, user feedback, and real-world applications. Additionally, efforts should be directed towards addressing the ethical, legal, and societal implications of XAI, ensuring responsible and equitable deployment of XAI. Collaborative initiatives involving interdisciplinary collaboration, industry partnerships, and community engagement will be essential in advancing the field of Social XAI and addressing its limitations.

References

Adadi A, Berrada M (2018) Peeking inside the black box: a survey on Explainable Artificial Intelligence (XAI). IEEE Access 6:52138–52160

Bansal G, Wu T, Zhu J, Fok R, Nushi B, Kamar E, Ribeiro MT, Weld DS (2020) Does the whole exceed its parts? The effect of AI explanations on complementary team performance. arXiv preprint arXiv:2006.14779

Bussone A, Stumpf S, O'sullivan D (2015) The role of explanations on trust and reliance in clinical decision support systems. In: 2015 International conference on healthcare informatics. IEEE, pp 160–169

Calvaresi D, Ciatto G, Najjar A, Aydoğan R, Van der Torre L, Omicini A, Schumacher M (2021, May) Expectation: personalized explainable artificial intelligence for decentralized agents with heterogeneous knowledge. In: International workshop on explainable, transparent autonomous agents and multi-agent systems. Springer International Publishing, Cham, pp 331–343

Chouldechova AB, Putnam-Hornstein E, Tobin A, Vaithianathan R (2019) Toward algorithmic accountability in public services: a qualitative study of affected community perspectives on algorithmic decision making in child welfare services. In: Proceedings of the 2019 CHI conference on human factors in computing systems, pp 1–12

Chromik M, Butz A (2021) Human-XAI interaction: a review and design principles for explanation user interfaces. In: Human-computer interaction–INTERACT 2021: 18th IFIP TC 13 international conference, Bari, Italy, August 30–September 3, 2021, Proceedings, Part II 18. Springer International Publishing, pp 619–640

Cowan DD, Lucena CJPD (1995) Abstract data views: an interface specification concept to enhance design for reuse. IEEE Trans Software Eng 21(3):229–243

Davenport T, Kalakota R (2019) The potential for artificial intelligence in healthcare. Future Healthc J 6(2):94

De-Arteaga M, Fogliato R, Chouldechova A (2020) A case for humans-in-the-loop: decisions in the presence of erroneous algorithmic scores. In: Proceedings of the 2020 CHI conference on human factors in computing systems, pp 1–12

Dodge J, Liao QV, Zhang Y, Bellamy RK, Dugan C (2019, March) Explaining models: an empirical study of how explanations impact fairness judgment. In: Proceedings of the 24th international conference on intelligent user interfaces, pp 275–285

Gao Y, Gu S, Jiang J, Hong SR, Yu D, Zhao L (2022) Going beyond XAI: a systematic survey for explanation-guided learning. ACM Comp Surv

Harjumaa M, Oinas-Kukkonen H (2007) An analysis of the persuasiveness of smoking cessation websites. In: Proceedings of the second international symposium on medical information and communication technology. CWC, University of Oulu, Oulu

Lee MK, Kim JT, Lizarondo L (2017) A human-centered approach to algorithmic services: considerations for fair and motivating smart community service management that allocates donations to non-profit organizations. In: Proceedings of the 2017 CHI conference on human factors in computing systems, pp 3365–3376

Miller T (2018) Explanation in artificial intelligence: insights from the social sciences. Artificial Intelligence
Mirchi N, Bissonnette V, Yilmaz R, Ledwos N, Winkler-Schwartz A, Del Maestro RF (2020) The virtual operative assistant: an explainable artificial intelligence tool for simulation-based training in surgery and medicine. PloS One 15(2):e0229596
Montag C, Nakov P, Ali R (2024a) Considering the IMPACT framework to understand the AI-well-being-complex from an interdisciplinary perspective. Tele Inf Reports 13:100112
Montag C, Ali R, Al-Thani D, Hall BJ (2024b) On artificial intelligence and global mental health. Asian J Psychiatr 91:103855
Naiseh M (2021) C-XAI: design method for explainable AI interfaces to enhance trust calibration. Doctoral dissertation, Bournemouth University
Naiseh M, Jiang N, Ma J, Ali R (2020a, Sept) Explainable recommendations in intelligent systems: delivery methods, modalities and risks. In: International conference on research challenges in information science. Springer, Cham, pp 212–228
Naiseh M, Jiang N, Ma J, Ali R (2020b) Personalising explainable recommendations: literature and conceptualisation. In: Trends and innovations in information systems and technologies, vol 2(8). Springer International Publishing, pp 518–533
Naiseh M, Cemiloglu D, Al Thani D, Jiang N, Ali R (2021a) Explainable recommendations and calibrated trust: two systematic user errors. Computer 54(10):28–37
Naiseh M, Al-Mansoori RS, Al-Thani D, Jiang N, Ali R (2021b) Nudging through friction: an approach for calibrating trust in explainable AI. In: 2021 8th International conference on behavioral and social computing (BESC). IEEE, pp 1–5
Naiseh M, Al-Thani D, Jiang N, Ali R (2021c) Explainable recommendation: when design meets trust calibration. World Wide Web 24(5):1857–1884
Naiseh M, Soorati MD, Ramchurn S (2022, Nov) Outlining the design space of eXplainable Swarm (xSwarm): experts' perspective. In: International symposium on distributed autonomous robotic systems. Springer Nature Switzerland, Cham, pp 28–41
Naiseh M, Al-Thani D, Jiang N, Ali R (2023) How the different explanation classes impact trust calibration: the case of clinical decision support systems. Int J Human-Comp Stud 169:102941
Narayanan M, Chen E, He J, Kim B, Gershman S, Doshi-Velez F (2018) How do humans understand explanations from machine learning systems? An evaluation of the human-interpretability of explanation. arXiv preprint arXiv:1802.00682
Oinas-Kukkonen H, Harjumaa M (2008, June) A systematic framework for designing and evaluating persuasive systems. In: International conference on persuasive technology. Springer, Berlin, Heidelberg, pp 164–176
Rasch R, Kott A, Forbus KD (2003) Incorporating AI into military decision making: an experiment. IEEE Intell Syst 18(4):18–26
Rozenblit L, Keil F (2002) The misunderstood limits of folk science: an illusion of explanatory depth. Cogn Sci 26(5):521–562
Schneeberger T, Gebhard P, Baur T et al (2019) PARLEY: a transparent virtual social agent training interface. In: Proceedings of the 24th international conference on intelligent user interfaces, Marina del Ray, CA, 2019, pp 35–36
Sheh RK-M (2017) "Why did you do that?" Explainable intelligent robots. In: Workshops at the thirty-first AAAI conference on artificial intelligence
Simkute A, Surana A, Luger E, Evans M, Jones R (2022) XAI for learning: Narrowing down the digital divide between "new" and "old" experts. In: Adjunct proceedings of the 2022 Nordic human-computer interaction conference, pp 1–6
Sokol K, Flach P (2020a, Jan) Explainability fact sheets: a framework for systematic assessment of explainable approaches. In: Proceedings of the 2020 conference on fairness, accountability, and transparency, pp 56–67
Sokol K, Flach P (2020b) One explanation does not fit all. KI-Künstliche Intelligenz, pp 1–16
Te'eni D, Sani-Kuperberg Z (2005) Levels of abstraction in designs of human–computer interaction: the case of e-mail. Comput Hum Behav 21(5):817–830

Walster E, Aronson E, Abrahams D (1966) On increasing the persuasiveness of a low prestige communicator. J Exp Soc Psychol 2(4):325–342

Wijekoon A, Corsar D, Wiratunga N, Martin K, Salimi P (2024) Tell me more: intent fulfilment framework for enhancing user experiences in conversational XAI. arXiv preprint arXiv:2405.10446

The manufacturer's authorised representative in the EU is Springer Nature Customer Service Centre GmbH, Europaplatz 3, 69115 Heidelberg, Germany. If you have any concerns regarding our products, please contact ProductSafety@springernature.com

Printed and bound by CPI Group (UK) Ltd, Croydon, CR0 4YY
01/10/2026
02225898-0020